MARSHA WEIL and BRUCE JOYCE

INFORMATION PROCESSING

MODELS OF TEACHING

EXPANDING YOUR
TEACHING REPERTOIRE

PRENTICE-HALL, INC., ENGLEWOOD CLIFFS, NEW JERSEY 07632

Library of Congress Cataloging in Publication Data

WEIL, MARSHA.
    Information processing models of teaching.
    (Expanding your teaching repertoire)

    Includes bibliographical references and index.
    1. Teaching.   2. Lesson planning.   I. Joyce,
Bruce R., joint author.   II. Title.
LB1025.2.W444   371.1'02   77-5414
ISBN 0-13-464552-9
IBSN 0-13-464545-6 pbk.

371
.102
W422i

This book is dedicated to our parents

GRACE AND MITCHELL LEWIS
URSULA AND LOUIS JOYCE

PRINTED IN THE UNITED STATES OF AMERICA

10   9   8   7   6   5   4   3   2   1

PRENTICE-HALL INTERNATIONAL, INC., *London*
PRENTICE-HALL OF AUSTRALIA PTY. LIMITED, *Sydney*
PRENTICE-HALL OF CANADA, LTD., *Toronto*
PRENTICE-HALL OF INDIA PRIVATE LIMITED, *New Delhi*
PRENTICE-HALL OF JAPAN, INC., *Tokyo*
PRENTICE-HALL OF SOUTHEAST ASIA PTE. LTD., *Singapore*
WHITEHALL BOOKS LIMITED, *Wellington, New Zealand*

CONTENTS

FOREWORD

The contents of this book are designed to equip classroom teachers with the essential knowledge and skills to use three alternative teaching and learning strategies confidently. These three strategies—Concept Attainment, Inquiry Training, and Advance Organizer—are based on information processing models of teaching that were all developed more than a decade ago. Thus, the ideas for the three models contained in this book are not new. What is new is a common training format that enables a practicing teacher to quickly understand the rudiments of a given teaching and learning model for initial use in the classroom. Coupled with this is an instructional support system that enables teachers to grow in the use of the model over a period of time.

Over the past two years, I have been directly involved with training programs that used field-test versions of the training materials contained in this book with over five hundred participants. The trainees were a mixture of classroom teachers, graduate teacher corps interns, and university faculty. Using the training materials contained in this book, an overwhelming majority of the participants consistently indicated that they felt confident to try out the model with students in their classes. The confidence level for initial classroom use was significantly higher for participants who had actually conducted a lesson with their peers than for those who had not had this experience. After their brief exposure to the field-test version of the training materials in this book, more than 95 percent of the participants indicated that they felt they could use the materials on their own to learn more about the model.

The classroom teachers that we worked with over the past two years have been experienced practitioners. They were honestly searching for new alternative strategies that could be applied in different ways to a variety of teaching and learning situations. Very early in a training effort, we found that these teachers wanted the basic elements of a teaching model, coupled with a demonstration of the model in an actual teaching and learning situation. The training materials in this book provide the basic elements of a model in the syntax, principles of reaction, social systems, support systems, and teaching analysis forms associated with each model. Actual classroom demonstrations of a given model are provided through demonstration transcripts in the text or video tapes that can be purchased to accompany the training materials in this book.

As teachers move through the training sequence toward planning their first lesson for a small group of their peers, they rely heavily on the theory section of the training materials as well as the planning forms and accompanying suggestions. Peer teaching, an integral part of the training format suggested in this book, has been judged by nearly all participants to be the single most helpful experience in preparing them to use a given model in the classroom. Peer teaching is a viable alternative to microteaching. It is not plagued with the logistical problem of finding regular classroom students, yet it provides a nonthreatening atmosphere in which teachers can learn from one another.

After carefully reviewing participant response to the workshops and training programs in which the training materials developed by Bruce Joyce and Marsha Weil have been used, we are convinced that the consistently positive reactions of teachers, interns, and university faculty are due mainly to the unique training format, which enables today's extremely busy teacher to grasp the basic concepts of a teaching model at a brief initial training session and follow that with on-the-job practice and subsequent professional growth in the use of a model.

We hope that you will find the three models presented in this book as exciting and as useful as have those of us who have already been beneficiaries of these training materials.

Roger S. Pankratz

College of Education
Western Kentucky University

ACKNOWLEDGMENTS

We owe an enormous debt to a large number of colleagues and students throughout the United States. At Teachers' College, Columbia University, Rhoada Wald, Michael McKibbin, Michael Feller, Christina Gullion, Kathryn O'Donnell, Clark Brown, Robert Gower, Jill Levine, Kay Vandergrift, Joseph Kelly, Gene Rude, Deane Flood, Daisy Reed, Sam Stewart, Charlie Abate, plus many teachers, school administrators, professors, and researchers helped us develop and test the early versions of what ultimately became these materials. Karl Schmidt, then of Science Research Associates, worked very closely with us and with Drs. Wald and McKibbin to build the first widely disseminated materials. David Hunt, Ed Sullivan, Joann Greenwood, Joyce Noy, Roma Reid and others at the Ontario Institute for Studies in Education helped to structure and conduct some of the most important training research we were able to do and helped us embark on the first research with children.

Roger Pankratz of Western Kentucky University, Carolyn Ellner of the Claremont Graduate School of Education, Pat Murphy of the University of Minnesota, Greta Morine-Dershimer of the Far West Laboratory, Paul and Margaret Collins of the California State University at Hayward worked individually and together with us in developing and testing teacher training ideas relevant to this Models of Teaching series. Christopher Clark, Penelope Peterson, Ronald Marx,

Jane Anton, and Janet Crist-Witzel of the Stanford Center for Research and Development in Teaching helped harden our ideas and conducted a series of investigations with us that advanced our thinking.

National Teacher Corps, especially William Smith, James B. Steffenson, and Paul Collins, helped us greatly. Their colleagues, Art Brill, Jack Ether, Dan Ganeles, Bev Elender, and Jan Hillson provided many interesting ideas and in many ways opened up new areas of research and development before we had perceived them ourselves.

Floyd Waterman of the University of Nebraska, Rupert Trujillo of the University of New Mexico, Bud Meyers of the University of Vermont, Berj Harootunian of Syracuse University, and Chet Hill and Dave Marsh of the University of Southern California also worked with us in a variety of ways. Members of the Allendale School staff in Pasadena, California, including Alma Hill and Elsa Brizzi, advanced our thinking about the adaptation of *Models of Teaching* to multicultural settings, Claudia Ulbrecht, Jennifer Bird-in-Ground, Muata, and Joel Morine contributed imaginative demonstration lessons.

The Bureau of Educational Professions Development supported some of the most difficult early work; we are especially indebted to Allen Schmeider for his counsel and advice during that period. The present materials were piloted in the Corps Member Training Institute of National Teacher Corps. Drs. Smith, Waterman, Pankratz, and McKibbin, Paul Collins, Jim Steffensen, and Beryl Nelson were powerful colleagues during that experience. The National Education Association piloted the training of teachers to operate teacher centers based on *Models of Teaching*. John Leeke of the NEA staff and Ruth Foster of the Omaha Public Schools were especially helpful to us during that experiment.

Finally, we acknowledge with gratitude the contributions of the people who developed the concepts around which the various models are based: Fannie Shaftel, Professor Emeritus of Stanford University, Richard Suchman, Bill Gordon of Synectics Incorporated, Donald Oliver of Harvard University, James P. Shaver of the University of Utah, and other colleagues are gratefully acknowledged.

Marsha Weil
Bruce Joyce

Supplementary audio-visual materials to accompany this text can be ordered from:

Dr. Bruce Joyce
Center for Research and Development in Teaching
Stanford University
Stanford, California 94305

INTRODUCTION

A POINT OF VIEW ABOUT TEACHING

How do we think of ourselves as professional teachers and educators? We are responsible for many types of instruction, for helping our students grow in self-awareness and in their ability to relate to others, for clarifying values, for promoting moral development, and for a host of other objectives. Our responsibilities can conveniently be described in three categories: responsibility for the personal growth of our students, responsibility for their social development and preparation for national and world citizenship, and responsibility for their mastery of academic subjects, including the basic skills of reading and computation that are so essential to contemporary life. In order to accomplish these objectives we work in schools, and within these in classrooms, learning centers, and libraries. Much of our contact with students is formal: they are assembled in classes to take one or more courses from us. But we have much informal contact with them as well. In addition, we teachers work either relatively alone or in teaching teams, perhaps with paid and volunteer aides assisting us.

To carry out these multiple responsibilities, we are required to engage in several professional roles, often simultaneously. We are counselors, facilitators, instructional managers, curriculum designers, academic instructors, evaluators of instruction, and, reluctantly, disciplinarians. To fill these roles, we draw on a variety

1

of models of teaching. There are presently available to us many alternatives for organizing and carrying out learning experiences, some formal and traditional and others casual and emergent.

Our initial preparation for teaching is relatively brief, considering the diverse responsibilities and the complexity of our roles. The preparation we receive prior to entering the classroom takes place in university courses and in the relatively short apprenticeship that we call "student teaching" or "internship."

When we begin our teaching, we perceive only dimly that we must master multiple roles. Gradually, as we get our bearings, we begin to see teaching as a cluster of differing roles and responsibilities. We then seek alternative ways to fulfill our tasks as teachers, and we begin to broaden our perspective on the nature of teaching. Finally, we spend the greater part of our professional lives attempting to improve our competence and to sharpen our skills. As we become more professional, we try to expand the ways we can be meaningful to our students—we master more roles.

The authors see the development of professional competence in teaching as an increased ability to play the various assigned roles more effectively. Our point of view is that a large part of this competence consists in mastering a repertoire of approaches to teaching that can be used to carry out these roles. We believe that competence is expanded in two ways: first, by increasing the *range of teaching strategies* that we are able to employ; second, by *becoming increasingly skillful* in the use of each of these strategies.

Different roles *require* different teaching strategies. In our earlier book, *Models of Teaching* (1972), we described our search for teaching strategies that are based on defendable theories about how people learn, grow, and develop. Some of these theory-based models of teaching are more appropriate to some objectives than to others. For example, some are specially tailored to help students grow in self-awareness and strength of self-concept. Others are more appropriate for improving human relations in the classroom and helping students clarify their social values. Yet others are more appropriate for the mastery of subject matter. Some models of teaching are quite narrow in their focus, and others are useful for a wide variety of purposes.

A model of teaching consists of guidelines for designing educational activities and environments. It specifies ways of teaching and learning that are intended to achieve certain kinds of goals. A model includes a rationale, a theory that justifies it and describes what it is good for and why; the rationale may be accompanied by empirical evidence that it "works." In *Models of Teaching*, we deliberately selected models representing different frames of reference toward educational goals and methods. That book was written for the purpose of helping teachers explore a variety of philosophical and psychological positions, which they could then make come to life in the classroom.

We discovered models of teaching in many sources. Educators, psychologists, sociologists, systems analysts, psychiatrists, and many others have all developed theoretical positions about learning and teaching. Curriculum development projects, schools and school districts, and organizations representing particular curriculum areas or disciplines have also developed a large number of approaches to teaching and learning. The task of selection began with compiling a very long list of sources of models. Included were the works of counselors and therapists such as Erikson

(1950), Maslow (1962), and Rogers (1951), as well as those of learning theorists such as Ausubel (1963), Bruner (1966), and Skinner (1957); developmental psychologists such as Hunt (1971), Kohlberg (1966), and Piaget (1952); and philosophers such as Broudy (1965), Dewey (1916), and James (1899). Curriculum development in the academic subjects provided many examples, as did group dynamics. Patterns of teaching from great experimental schools such as Summerhill made their way onto our list. Altogether, more than eighty theorists, schools, and projects were identified, far more than any teacher would be able to master during a career.

Gradually, we began to group the models on the basis of their chief emphases—the ways they approached educational goals and means. We eventually organized them into four families:

1. *Social Interaction Models*. These emphasize the relationships of the individual to society or to other persons. They focus on the processes by which reality is socially negotiated. Consequently, with respect to goals, models from this orientation give priority to the improvement of the individual's ability to relate to others, the improvement of democratic processes, and the improvement of the society. It must be stressed that the social-relations orientation does not assume that these goals constitute the *only* important dimension of life. While social relations may be emphasized more than other domains, social theorists are also concerned with the development of the mind and the self, and the learning of academic subjects. (It is the rare theorist in education who is not concerned with more than one aspect of the learner's development, or who does not use more than one aspect of the environment to influence the learner's development.)

2. *Information Processing Models*. The second large family of models share an orientation toward the information processing capability of students and toward the systems that can improve their information processing capability. Information processing refers to the ways people handle stimuli from the environment, organize data, sense problems, generate concepts and solutions to problems, and employ verbal and nonverbal symbols. Some information processing models are concerned with the ability of the learner to solve problems, and thus emphasize productive thinking; others are concerned with general intellectual ability. Some emphasize the teaching of strategies derived from the academic disciplines. Again, however, it must be stressed that nearly all models from this family are also concerned with social relationships and the development of an integrated, functioning self.

3. *Personal Models*. The third family share an orientation toward the individual and the development of selfhood. They emphasize the processes by which individuals construct and organize their unique reality. Frequently, they focus on the emotional life of the individual. It is expected that the focus on helping individuals to develop a productive relationship with their environment and to view themselves as capable persons will produce richer interpersonal relations and a more effective information processing capability.

4. *Behavior Modification Models*. This fourth type of model has evolved from attempts to develop efficient systems for sequencing learning tasks and shaping behavior by manipulating reinforcement. Exponents of reinforcement theory, such as Skinner (1957), have developed these models and operant conditioning as their central mechanism. They are frequently referred to as behavior modification theories because they emphasize changing the external behavior of the learners and describe them in terms of visible behavior rather than underlying and unobservable

behavior. Operant conditioning has been applied to a wide variety of goals, in education and other areas, ranging from military training to the improvement of interpersonal behavior and even to therapy. It is represented by a large number of models, some of which are media-oriented (such as programmed stategies) and some of which are oriented to interactive teaching (such as the use of tokens to shape social behavior).

These families of models are by no means antithetical or mutually exclusive. The actual prescriptions for developing the instructional activities and learning environments that emerge from some of them—even those classified in different families—are remarkably similar. Also, within the families, models share many features with respect both to goals and to the kinds of means they recommend. All educational activities evoke different meanings in different people. In this sense, everything we do is personal. Similarly, most of our experiences, especially educational ones, involve some intellectual or information processing activity.

Over the years, we have discussed our original classifications with many of our colleagues, agreeing with many of their objections and rethinking our position. In this text, we have reclassified a few of the models. In general, we feel it is the basic framework of families that has become a powerful intellectual tool for teachers and curriculum planners, rather than the specific classification of individual models. However, we have made an effort to classify models according to the most prominent goal or features that distinguish them from another family.

In this three-volume series, we are concerned only with models from the information processing, social, and personal families. It seemed to us that there are presently available several excellent sources on the adaptation of behavior modification and its variations to the classroom. We therefore decided to concentrate on models that are less available in the literature. Models from these three families are listed in Figures 1A-1C.

To us, growth in teaching is the increasing mastery of a variety of models of teaching and the ability to use them effectively. Some philosophies of teacher education maintain that a teacher should master a single model and utilize it well. We believe that very few teachers are so limited in capacity. Most of us can quite easily develop a repertoire of six or eight models of teaching, which we can use in order to carry out our roles. We should choose our "basic" repertoire to meet the needs generated by our teaching assignment. Certain models are more appropriate for some curriculums than for others; that is, the curriculum helps define our role and the kinds of competencies that we need. For example, a secondary school science teacher of biology who is using Biological Sciences Study Committee materials will want to master the particular kind of inductive approach that fits best with those materials; an elementary school social studies teacher who is helping children study values may want to master one of the models appropriate to clarifying values and analyzing public issues. Once a teacher master the "basic" repertoire of models, he or she can then expand it by learning new models and by combining and transforming the basic ones to create new ones. In the midst of a social studies unit, a teacher may use a highly specific model to help children master map skills, and combine this model with group-dynamic models that help students attack social issues. A highly skilled performance in teaching blends the variety of models appropriately and embellishes them. Master teachers create new models of teaching and test them in the course of their work.

Model	Major Theorist	Mission or Goals for Which Most Applicable
Inductive Thinking Model Inquiry Training Model	Hilda Taba Richard Suchman	Designed primarily for development of inductive mental processes and academic reasoning or theory building, but these capacities are useful for personal and social goals as well.
Science Inquiry Model	Joseph J. Schwab (also much of the Curriculum Reform Movement of the 1960s)	Designed to teach the research system of a discipline, but also expected to have effects in other domains (sociological methods may be taught in order to increase social understanding and social problem-solving).
Concept Attainment Model	Jerome Bruner	Designed primarily to develop inductive reasoning, but also for concept development and analysis.
Developmental Model	Jean Piaget Irving Sigel Edmund Sullivan	Designed to increase general intellectual development, especially logical reasoning, but can be applied to social and moral development as well (see Kohlberg, 1966).
Advance Organizer Model	David Ausubel	Designed to increase the efficiency of information processing capacities to meaningfully absorb and relate bodies of knowledge.

Figure 1A. *The Information Processing Family of Models.*

Making Theories Practical

We did not make up the models of teaching you will learn here, nor did we invent the theories upon which they are based. Most of these ideas have been available to educators for many years. Our contribution has been to develop a way of making these theories operational, and to describe what teachers *do* when they teach according to one theory or another.

To translate a theory into practical teaching form, we employ a set of four concepts: *syntax*, *principles of reaction*, *social system*, and *support system*. The first two concepts are especially important in making a theory practical.

Syntax describes the model as a flow of actions. If teachers were to use the model, how would they begin? What would they do first, second, third? We describe syntax in terms of sequences of events, which we call *phases*. Each model has a distinct *flow* of phases—for example, present material to the learner, develop confronting situation—or, present organizing ideas to students, provide data sources. A comparison of the structural phasing of models reveals the practical differences

Model	Major Theorist	Mission or Goals for Which Most Applicable
Group Investigation Model	Herbert Thelen John Dewey	Development of skills for participation in democratic social process through combined emphasis on interpersonal (group) skills and academic-inquiry skills. Aspects of personal development are important outgrowths of this model.
Classroom Meeting Model (Social Problem-Solving)	William Glasser	Development of self-understanding and responsibility to oneself and one's social group.
Social Inquiry Model	Byron Massialas Benjamin Cox	Social problem-solving, primarily through academic inquiry and logical reasoning.
Laboratory Method Model	National Training Laboratory (NTL), Bethel, Maine	Development of interpersonal and group skills and, through this, personal awareness and flexibility.
Jurisprudential Model	Donald Oliver James P. Shaver	Designed primarily to teach the jurisprudential frame of reference as a way of thinking about and resolving social issues.
Role Playing Model	Fannie Shaftel George Shaftel	Designed to induce students to inquire into personal and social values, with their own behavior and values becoming the source of their inquiry.
Social Simulation Model	Sarene Boocock	Designed to help students experience various social processes and realities and to examine their own reactions to them.

Figure 1B. *The Social Family of Models.*

among them. An inductive strategy has a different phase and a different sequence than a deductive one.

Principles of reaction guide the teacher's responses to the learner; they tell the teacher how to regard the learner and respond to what he or she does. In some models, the teacher overtly tries to shape behavior by rewarding certain student activities and maintaining a neutral stance toward others. In other models, such as those designed to develop creativity, the teacher tries to maintain a nonevaluative, carefully equal stance so that the learners become self-directing. Principles of reaction provide the teacher with rules of thumb by which to "tune in" to the student and select appropriate responses to what the student does.

The social system provides a description of student and teacher roles and relationships and the kinds of norms that are encouraged. The leadership roles of the

Model	Major Theorist	Mission or Goals for Which Most Applicable
Nondirective Model	Carl Rogers	Emphasis on building the capacity for personal development in terms of self-awareness, understanding, autonomy, and self-concept.
Awareness Training Model	Fritz Perls	Increasing one's capacity for self-exploration and self-awareness. Much emphasis on development of inter-personal awareness and understanding, as well as body and sensory awareness.
Synectics Model	William Gordon	Personal development of creativity and creative problem-solving.
Conceptual Systems Model	David Hunt	Designed to increase personal complexity and flexibility.

Figure 1C. *The Personal Family of Models.*

teacher vary greatly from model to model. In some models, the teacher is a reflector or a facilitator of group activity; in others, a counselor of individuals; and in still others, a taskmaster. The concept of hierarchical relationships is explained in terms of the sharing of initiating activity by teacher and learner, the location of authority, and the amount of control over activity that emerges from the process of interaction. In some models, the teacher is the center of activity and the source of input—the organizer and pacer of the situation. Some models provide for relatively equal distribution of activity between teacher and student, whereas others place the student at the center. Finally, different models reward different student behaviors. In some, the students are rewarded for completing a job done or sticking to a prescribed line of inquiry; in others, the students' reward is knowing that they have learned something.

One way to describe a teaching model, then, is in terms of the degree of structure in the learning environment. That is, as roles, relationships, norms, and activities become less externally imposed and more within the student's control, the social system becomes less structured.

The support system refers to additional requirements beyond the usual human skills, capacities, and technical facilities necessary to implement a model. For example, a human relations model may require a trained leader; a nondirective model may require a particular type of personality (exceedingly patient and supportive). If a model postulates that students teach themselves, with the role of the teacher limited to consultation and facilitation, what support is necessary? A classroom supplied only with textbooks would be limiting and prescriptive; additional support in the form of books, films, self-instructional systems, travel arrangements, and the like is necessary. Support requirements are derived from two sources: the role specifications for the teacher and the substantive demands of the experience.

Those of you who have used our *Models of Teaching* text will notice that some descriptions of the model in the present book are slightly different from those in the earlier work. This is because, as we worked with different models, we gained greater ability to describe them and could incorporate more elements of the theory of a model into its basic set of activities. Therefore, we are now more precise about the events that take place within any given phase of activity. Occasionally, we have revised or expanded the phases of activity. In all cases, we are able to identify specific planning and teaching skills that facilitate the implementation of a model. We have learned and changed over the years!

Although we are delighted with our increased ability to describe initial teacher (and student) behaviors for each model, and although we feel this will greatly enhance easy and early mastery of each model, we offer a caution to our supporters, and to our critics. A model of teaching is not a simple fixed formula for completing a job. It provides definite ideas for creating an environment from which students are likely to learn certain kinds of things, but it has to become a flexible, fluid instrument that is modified to fit different types of subject matter and that responds to students who are different from one another.

There is an old saying that fencing coaches preach to their students: Treat the sword like a bird. If you hold it too tightly, you choke it! If you hold it too loosely, it will fly away! So it is with a model of teaching. If one uses it too rigidly, it becomes a blunt instrument. If one holds it too lightly, it dissolves and becomes undistinguishable from any other method of teaching. It fails to do its work!

Experience and Research with Models

Our impression from experience is that in-service teachers learn models of teaching that are new to them somewhat more easily and rapidly than do teachers-in-training or inexperienced teachers. This is probably because experienced teachers have more of the general competencies of teaching in hand and are more comfortable working with children during the first stages of practice with a new teaching approach.

In a series of research studies, we asked the question: How does the "natural" teaching style of teachers affect their ability to learn new models of teaching? The answer to this appears to be that teachers of nearly any style can master any of the models of teaching identified above with relatively little difficulty. Not everyone learns every model equally well or needs to use any given model regularly. However, nearly all teachers are capable of mastering the fundamentals of several models of teaching and of applying them effectively in the classroom.

Teachers very definitely have preferences for different models and use some more than others. We believe, however, that a range of approaches is needed. Once this is accepted, teachers who attempt to widen their repertoire will discover delights in some models of teaching that at first seemed unattractive.

Generally speaking, the time needed to learn new models of teaching shortens with each new acquisition. It takes several, perhaps five or six trials, for a teacher to be able to comfortably handle unfamiliar models in the classroom at first, but fewer trials are needed with each successive model.

Over the years, we have conducted a series of investigations into how people acquire and use models of teaching that are new to them. At this point, we believe that most of us first learn a model in a form appropriate for short lessons or units.

This "short form" is relatively rigid: we "follow the steps" (phases) of the model rather closely during the first practice sessions. With increasing practice, we learn to transform the model and expand it, adapting it to the kinds of things that we teach best, to the children being taught, and to the local conditions. In time, we learn to apply the model more effectively to curriculum materials and to combine it with other models of teaching, thereby incorporating it into the working repertoire. Following that, we gradually learn to teach the model to the children, helping them to make the model their own as part of their quest to "learn how to learn." For example, in science classes we help students learn to carry on inductive inquiry by themselves, our function as teachers becoming one of helping them learn rather than one of leading them through a sequence of learning steps.

To reiterate, the stages of mastering a model are: (1) learning how to apply it in some acceptable form; (2) expanding, embellishing, and transforming it to our own styles and curriculum; (3) applying its elements to the roles we play in our classroom; (4) combining it with other models; and (5) teaching it to the children themselves.

Some people quickly grasp the essential ideas and procedures of a model after reading brief introductory materials and viewing or experiencing a demonstration. We have found that approximating the sequence of activities of a model—its syntax —is not difficult in most cases. However, implementing a model in a way that truly reflects its theoretical underpinnings and fulfills all its potential objectives requires a deeper understanding. Consequently, we have chosen to err on the side of specificity in the explanation in our training systems. Some teachers, maybe most teachers, will not need the extent of explanation, illustration, and step-by-step training that our systems offer. They may be turned off by what is perceived as prescription. However, other teachers we have worked with prefer a highly structured training approach with many illustrations and examples.

We hope you do not take our effort to provide as much detail as we can as a belief that there is only one way to learn new models of teaching (or only one way to teach them). Our primary purpose, rather, is to provide something for everyone, something for an audience representing all grade levels, subject matter, and learning styles! When you feel ready to move on to the next steps in training, by all means do so. (We shall speak more about learning options later in this introduction).

Expanded Uses of a Model

We have mentioned that the goal in the initial stage of training (and throughout our training systems) is for teachers to use a model to develop short lessons, and to try these out several times with colleagues and small groups of students. The ultimate uses of a model extend far beyond the construction of the relatively short, isolated lessons that conveniently serve the training function.

A model can be used to guide learning activities extended over a long period of time, to diagnose and evaluate pupils, and to train students to use the model independently. Teachers can create many variations on each model, or they can take the "essence" of a model, dropping the syntax and phases, and perceptively use the key elements in an impromptu learning situation. Models can be designed into learning materials, and thereby become materials-mediated instead of teacher-mediated. (Programmed instruction, for example, is designed around Skinner's work.)

The models of teaching we present in these three books are applicable to all types of learning settings, both traditional and open. In open environments, self-directed, materials-mediated learning activities can be developed by designing them around the phases of the model. Students can work with one another, using key elements of the model. Bulletin boards can be based on one or more models of teaching. Learning centers can be developed around different models of teaching. For example, there can be an Inquiry Corner—or, alternatively, a Science Corner—that is based on the Inquiry Training Model. There can be a Concept Corner where students acquire concepts for many subject areas through concept attainment activities.

We touch on these expanded uses briefly in the last portion of each instructional system, but we do not train directly for them. We strongly urge small groups of teachers to brainstorm regarding the adaptation of models to different learning settings.

TRAINING TO LEARN A MODEL

The three books in this series are designed to help present and future teachers teach themselves a variety of models of teaching. One book presents teaching models from the information processing family; another presents models from the social family; and another, models from the personal family.

The Training Approach: Four Components

In these books, the materials for each model have been organized into four components: I) Describing and Understanding the Model; II) Viewing the Model; III) Planning and Peer Teaching; and IV) Adapting the Model. This organization reflects our belief about how one goes about training individuals to learn a complex performance behavior such as teaching (or tennis or computer programming or flying).

The notion is quite simple. First, you will read or hear a verbal description of the new model; this will give a general overview of the major operations and an explanation of the rationale, or theory, behind the activities included in the model. You need to become familiar with the goals of the model—that is, what its activities can and cannot accomplish—and with its key ideas. For example, if you were learning tennis, you would need to know at the onset that there are forehand shots, backhand shots, serves, lobs, and net play. You would also have to know something about scoring and about when the objective of the activity is accomplished—that is, about "games," "sets," and "matches." Learning a model of teaching is like learning to play tennis; at first, then, you would need a description of the activity—its objectives and key features. Component I of each model provides this.

Many of us prefer to see a demonstration of the activity. Demonstrations make words come alive, especially if the new activity is unfamiliar to us. So, in training for a model of teaching we move next to a demonstration, the model in action. In these learning systems, demonstration is accomplished through annotated transcripts of actual teaching sessions and/or through the optional use of audio tapes of lessons. In Component II of these models, you will find a transcript of a demonstration of the model, which we refer to as the *demonstration transcript.* In addition, you may have available a demonstration audio tape. In the exercises and activities, we shall be referring primarily to the demonstration transcript, but other forms of demonstration could also be used, or someone skilled in the model could conduct a live demonstration.

Finally, we practice. In tennis, you hit balls against a backboard or return "shots" from a ball-machine, spending hours, first on the forehand and then on the backhand, gradually learning more and more about the discrepancy between what you are doing and a *good* stroke. Similarly, in learning a model of teaching, you study and practice the *major elements* of a model several times before actually playing a game. Aspects of the theory are further explained and opportunity to apply your knowledge of them is provided through written exercises.

In Component III, it is time to move from practice to the "court." In teaching, this means planning and teaching an actual lesson. In tennis, it means playing one or two games at a time—not an entire match! In teaching, we select a topic, shape it according to the model, plan lessons, and teach them to a group of peers. Peer teaching is different from practice with children and has advantages over such practice when we are just trying out a model, namely that adult "learners" can coach us as we practice. Peer teaching gives us a chance to master the elements of the model before we try it with children, so that we are more surefooted when we do work with them.

After peer teaching, we suggest that you try the model with children, preferably small groups, but perhaps classroom-size groups. Again, these trials should be relatively short lessons or sets of lessons. Remember, at this point you are just sharpening your skills. (It is important to master the basics of your own tennis game before figuring out how to defend against such players as Chris Evert, Jimmy Connors, or Arthur Ashe! Or before learning how to play on different types of courts, such as grass, clay, and asphalt.) Mastering the basics comes before working out your own personal style, which surely will develop and be unique to you even though the model remains the same.

Finally, with the basic skills and activities in place, it is time to explore the model in the context of your actual teaching situation, your curriculum, and your students. It's time to think about the long-term goals of the model—for yourself, your subject area, and your students. You ask questions such as: How do I take the materials and curriculums I work with and enhance them with the model? How do I teach students to use a model over a long period of time? How do I develop variations on the basic model or incorporate elements of it into my style? How can I "stretch" a model so that it's not a cookie-cutter, thirty-minute lesson, but instead becomes a paradigm for many days and weeks of learning activities? How do I move from using the model of teaching as a guide for a short lesson to using it as guidelines for larger curricular sequences and, finally, for organizing the classroom as a learning environment? These questions are covered in Component IV, Adapting the Model.

In summary, the written materials (and the audio-visual materials, if available) are designed to help you 1) master the theory and basic elements of a model (describing and understanding the model), 2) provide demonstration (viewing the model), 3) initiate practice (planning and peer teaching), and 4) extend the model to your classroom setting and curricular planning (adapting the model). These components and their parts are listed in Figure 2.

COMPONENT I: DESCRIBING AND UNDERSTANDING THE MODEL

Materials	Activity
1. Theory and Overview	Reading
2. Theory in Practice	Reading
3. Taking Theory Into Action	Reading/Writing
4. Theory Checkup	Writing

COMPONENT II: VIEWING THE MODEL

Materials	Activity
1. Analyzing Teaching	Reading/Writing
2. Viewing the Lesson	Reading/Writing/Discussion

Optional Material	Optional Activity
3. Analyzing the Demonstration	Discussion/Writing

COMPONENT III: PLANNING AND PEER TEACHING

Materials	Activity
1. Selecting the Topic	Reading/Writing
2. Preparing and Organizing Materials	Reading/Writing
3. Determining Educational Objectives	Reading/Writing
4. Completing the Planning Guide	Writing
5. Peer Teaching	Teaching
6. Analyzing the Lesson	Discussion/Analysis

Optional Material	Optional Activity
7. Microteaching and Analysis	Teaching/Analysis

COMPONENT IV: ADAPTING THE MODEL

Materials	Activity
1. Curriculum Transformation	Reading
2. Long-Term Uses	Reading
3. Combining the Model With Other Models of Teaching	Reading

Figure 2. *Components of the Training System.*

Ways to Go Through the Training System: Options

We have provided options for two reasons: teachers differ in their learning styles and preferences, and training situations differ in their organizational possibilities, flexibility, and support systems. The major training options are three. They concern:

1. the sequence and order of components
2. the medium for demonstration of the model: written transcript, live, audio-filmstrip, or photostrip
3. the role of the trainer: self-instructional, group instruction with instructor as facilitator, and instructor-led presentations

Essentially, the material is self-instructional: you can work through it on your own (except for peer teaching), or with a group of colleagues. An instructor is not necessary. On the other hand, a knowledgeable instructor can greatly enhance the learning situation by serving as a facilitator and reactor. Our preference is for teachers to work in groups, selecting the models they wish to concentrate on and helping one another master them. However, the material can form the basis for pre-planned workshops in which all participants study the same models.

Although this series is designed so that one first learns the theory of the model, then analyzes demonstrations of it, then practices it with peers, and finally practices it in the classroom, there are many alternative sequences, all equally viable. Some groups prefer to begin with demonstration. These people would like to see the model before they read about it. This makes perfectly good sense. In other groups, the beginning activity might be to appoint one teacher to demonstrate the model live with children or with those being trained. This requires that the demonstrator master the theory, read the transcript lesson, and practice the model so that he or she can introduce the training with the live demonstration. It is also possible to begin with curriculum materials, analyzing them to find which model of teaching is most appropriate and then concentrating on learning how to adapt the model to the curriculum materials. For example, most approaches to the teaching of reading are built upon a particular model of teaching or the combination of a few of them. Teachers of reading may prefer to begin with the models that underlie the curriculums they are using. For most of us, the "understanding first" sequence is the most comfortable (see Figure 3).

Many of us can handle abstract ideas only after we have experienced the concrete situation. We also do not like to perfect isolated skills without seeing the whole; we find that it's easier to go back to the task of mastering the basics when we have seen an example of the end product! For those who prefer a quick overview and then need to see a model of the activity before going further in training, we suggest another sequence. Figure 4 indicates a way of meeting these needs.

Some people (not the authors) like to go right to the tennis match before learning anything about the game. That is another alternative. It is possible to view a filmstrip and/or read the demonstration transcript before undertaking the Overview and Theory into Practice Steps (see Figure 5).

Flexibility in developing the training sequence will depend, of course, on

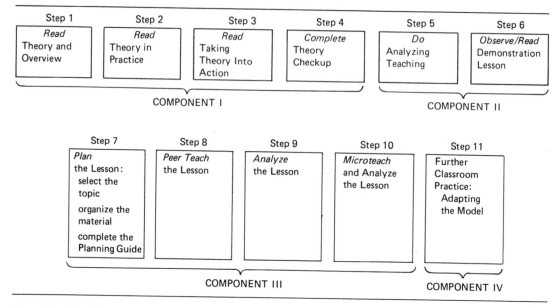

Figure 3. *The "Understanding First" Approach.*

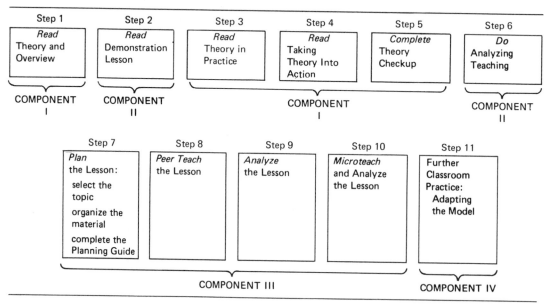

Figure 4. *"A Quick Overview and the Real Thing" Approach.*

whether the materials are used on an individualized or an instructor-directed basis. However, we do want to alert both instructors and trainees that alternatives are possible!

In the early years of our work with models of teaching, we used to spend weeks of instruction on a single model, going deeply into the theory, the issues in the particular field of knowledge, and our own and our students' personal philosophy of education. Besides believing that these considerations were important for our students, we believed they were necessary for performance mastery. What we have learned in recent years is that initial training in a model can take place in a relatively short period of time—perhaps four to five hours from introduction through peer teaching. Teachers are quick to sense their own problems and correct their behavior. In the first planning and peer teaching sessions, they note their points of confusion. For clarification, they go back to the training materials, to their instructor, or to their colleagues. After that, it is *practice* and *more practice*! What teachers need is time to absorb the ideas, to master the skills, and to try out the model with many topics and pupils.

Discussions of the philosophy of learning and teaching underlying particular models, and questions concerning specific difficulties in applying the model in the classroom are more valid and are dealt with more meaningfully following some degree of practice with the model. This is less true with experienced teachers than with preservice students. Even so, we strongly advise *everyone* to get into practice as soon as possible. It has been amazing to us how much a satisfactory learning experience alters initial questions, concerns, and doubts, regardless of previous experience.

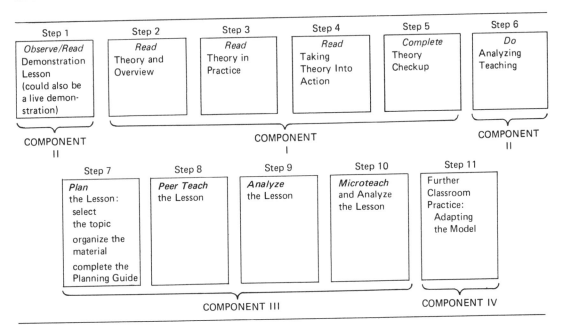

Figure 5. *"See the Real Thing First and Find Out Later" Approach.*

Everyone feels some insecurity in learning a new skill; however, we can almost promise that in four or five hours of earnest work, you will have enough initial competence in a model to, first, feel comfortable about your own strength and skill, and, second, to correct problem areas on your own and polish and shape the model in your own style!

This system is aimed almost exclusively at developing *initial clinical* (or performance) competence in a model. Although the overview materials discuss the philosophical and theoretical rationale for the model, we have not designed these materials to explore very many of the interesting issues surrounding these theories. We can imagine instructors supplementing practice in a model with readings and discussions on the philosophical, theoretical, or even empirical background and issues of a model.

Analysis of Teaching

One of the features of this training is the constant analysis of teaching that is included. We regard the analysis of teaching, not as an evaluation of teacher performance, but as a *feedback* tool, one that enables teachers to obtain reasonably objective information about their performance of the model of teaching and that provides guidelines for modifying teaching activities the next time.

In our training system, teaching analysis is introduced in the demonstration component. We have developed a Teaching Analysis Guide for each model that covers the major activities and principles of reaction for the phases in that model. The Guides usually consist of between fifteen and twenty questions and are first used in conjunction with the demonstration lessons. A more important use comes during peer teaching, when feedback is based on the Guide. A sample portion of a Teaching Guide appears in Figure 6.

The Guide is divided according to the phases of the model with a scale for analyzing important activites in each phase. Because every teaching situation is (and should be) sufficiently unpredictable that different teaching behaviors are necessary, we cannot be exact in measuring just how well any given teaching situation turns out; hence, the scale. We have grown more and more committed to the idea that once teachers have mastered the basics of a model, they should transpose and transform it, so that every model assumes a variety of forms. Thus, measuring competence and providing feedback should be flexible. There are standards of performance, but good performance appears in many forms. The Guide tells where to look for the essential competencies of each model and provides latitude so that different forms of competence can be identified.

Skills in Teaching

Two terms that you will come across in these books are *skill* (teaching skill) and *move*, by which we mean a particular teaching behavior that contributes to the effectiveness and uniqueness of that model. Asking a higher-order question, paraphrasing a student's comment, and summarizing the major points of a discussion are examples of teaching moves or skills. Sometimes a teaching skill is a single teacher comment or question, and sometimes it is a series of comments or questions.

During the course of a model or any thirty- or forty-minute learning activity,

PHASE TWO: Testing Concept Attainment

12. After the concept was agreed upon, did the teacher present additional exemplars and ask whether they contained the concept?	Thoroughly	Partially	Missing	Not Needed
13. Did the teacher ask the students to justify their answers?	Thoroughly	Partially	Missing	Not Needed
14. Were the students able to supply their own exemplars to fit the concept?	Thoroughly	Partially	Missing	Not Needed
15. Did the teacher ask the students to justify their exemplars by identifying the essential attributes?	Thoroughly	Partially	Missing	Not Needed

PHASE THREE: Analyzing Strategies

16. Did the teacher ask the students to describe the thinking processes they used in attaining the concept?	Thoroughly	Partially	Missing	Not Needed
17. Did the teacher ask the students to reflect on the role of attributes and concepts in their thinking strategies?	Thoroughly	Partially	Missing	Not Needed
18. Did the teacher ask the students to evaluate the effectiveness of their strategies?	Thoroughly	Partially	Missing	Not Needed

Figure 6. *Part of a Teaching Analysis Guide.*

the teacher (and students) exhibit hundreds of behaviors and many skills. Some models are dependent on how we master particular teacher skills. We have tried to identify and describe these skills. In addition to *interactive* teaching skills, we have identified critical *planning* skills. Some training approaches separate planning and teaching skills from teaching strategies. We prefer to introduce skills as part of the models and teach them in the context of the model, where the phases of activities provide guidelines as to when and how to use a particular skill.

WHAT IS IN THIS SYSTEM AND HOW TO USE IT

There are three books in this series. They cover description and understanding, demonstration, planning and peer teaching, and adaptation for models in the information processing, social, and personal families. Within each family, the models dealt with are:

Information Processing Family
    Concept Attainment Model(s)
    Inquiry Training Model
    Advance Organizer Model

Social Family
    Jurisprudential Model
    Simulation Model
    Role Playing Model
Personal Family
    Synectics Model
    Nondirective Model

We repeat that these materials are designed to be used on a self-instructional basis, usually in a student-directed group with the instructor serving as a facilitator. We strongly urge that teachers share their learning of a model with one another. It's usually richer, more instructive, and more fun that way.

Component I:
Describing and Understanding the Model

The first of the four components of our training approach is Describing and Understanding the Model. This component consists of two readings and a Theory Checkup. The first reading (Theory and Overview) discusses the goals, assumptions, key ideas, and procedures (syntax) of the model. The second reading (Taking Theory Into Action) provides further discussion and illustration of the model's major concepts. Through short written exercises, you are given opportunities to apply these concepts and to identify any difficulties you may have. We have made a special effort to select the major ideas you will apply when you teach and to develop a strong training sequence for them. It is one thing to read about an idea in the overview and another to practice and apply it. We urge you to concentrate especially on this reading and to do so at the point in the training sequence that is the most appropriate for you.

Finally, the Theory Checkup enables you to check your understanding of the ideas discussed and illustrated in the three previous readings. The checkup is for your use only; it is not a test. If you did not grasp an item, you may want to re-read the relevant pages in the readings. Some people may want to complete the Theory Checkup after the first reading; others may want to wait until they have finished the second reading. One way to view the checkup is as a guide to tell you what to concentrate on. It can also be viewed as a means of checking your understanding before going on to Components II and III. No doubt you will be better prepared for the Theory Checkup after you complete the second reading.

Component II: Viewing the Model

Component II (Viewing the Model) includes two learning activities. The first is reading the Teaching Analysis Guide and identifying any items that you do not understand. The second activity is reading the demonstration transcript. As you read the lesson, your attention is directed to the occurrence of the phases of the model. We suggest that you share your spontaneous reactions and comments with the group.

One thing to keep in mind is that there is no such thing as a "perfect" model.

There are always ways to enrich the lesson, or to improve a particular aspect. Besides, each of us have our preferred styles and expressions, which have nothing to do with the model per se. We have tried to select demonstrations that reveal the phases of the model and the major elements discussed in the text. Sometimes this does not happen, even in demonstration lessons. One of your jobs as an observer is to comment on those places in the lesson that may deviate (either by commission or omission) from your understanding of the model up to that point. Besides being critical, we'd like you to be attuned to the strengths of the lessons, the teacher moves that were particularly strong, the way the topic and material were designed for the model, and the way the lesson was organized for presentation. If there is time, you may want to read the model a second time, using the Teaching Analysis Guide as a format for analysis. Optional activities are included for use with audio tapes, where available, or with live demonstrations.

Component III: Planning and Peer Teaching

The activities in this component will guide you through the steps in planning a model lesson, which you will then peer teach to a small group of colleagues. The planning steps include topic selection, designing and organizing materials, and selecting behavioral objectives. Each step is discussed in terms of its unique features for the particular model you are studying. Special planning skills are taught in this part of the training program. A Planning Guide is provided to assist you in completing the various aspects of planning and to alert you to problem areas. Sample planning forms are provided for some of the models. In some cases, materials are provided from which to develop peer teaching lessons, in the event that you want to teach from them rather than use them as guides or suggestions. (Component IV also includes curriculum materials from which lessons may be planned.) We strongly urge you to select your own topics and prepare your own materials. This is one of the best ways to apply the ideas of the model and test your planning skills.

Peer teaching is just what the name suggests. It means that teachers practice teaching skills or models of teaching in groups, taking turns playing the role of the learners. Peer teaching accomplishes several things. First, it enables you to practice a new teaching strategy before you try it out with students. This gives you a chance to familiarize yourself with the structure of the model, to become more comfortable with it as you work it out in the classroom. It provides practice, not only in the actual teaching, but also in the planning for it. Translating material into new and unfamiliar models of teaching requires you to think differently about your teaching than you may have done before, and you need practice to become comfortable with the new approaches and moves.

A second benefit of peer teaching is that, because you do it with one another, you gain the kinds of feedback that fellow professional teachers can give. If a half-dozen teachers are practicing the same model and take turns teaching it, you can coach one another. Often, when you are in the role of student you see things that you do not see when you are in the role of teacher. Thus, you can avail yourselves of one another's professional opinion and coaching.

Third, peer teaching gets people working together to improve their classroom performance. It increases dialogue about the dynamics of teaching, gives a language for discussing the problems of teaching, and provides a warm and enriching experience in itself. Also, when you teach with others, you add their ideas to your own. When you see four or five people teaching the same model that you are trying to learn, you are exposed to new ideas about variations on that model, and so your learning is richer.

Being a Teacher in Peer Teaching. When you plan a lesson for your peers, you should plan one for their level. That is, you should select material that will be stimulating for your colleagues. This does not mean that you cannot select material that is also appropriate for children. Many concepts in mathematics, science, social science, and literature are fun for adults to learn again, especially when you see them highlighted by a fresh approach. Because of the constraints of time, most peer teaching lessons have to be relatively short—they are simulations of the kind of teaching we do with children. Make sure that there is enough time both to be taught and to provide feedback. Talk through your planning before beginning the model, describe the materials you are going to use, and be certain that everyone is oriented to the lesson.

Being a Learner in Peer Teaching. As learners in peer teaching, you should be yourselves. The best way to kill peer teaching is to "act the role of the child." You should permit yourselves to be engaged by your fellow teachers as you would if they were teaching a course or workshop, or engaging in any other kind of learning activity. However, not only are you learners to the teacher, but you are also learning yourselves, and you need to be in a position to provide feedback and coaching to the one who teaches. Thus, you need to familiarize yourselves thoroughly with the model before you begin, and perhaps to have copies of the Teaching Analysis Guide so that you can analyze the teaching as it goes along, in preparation for the feedback session.

Being an Observer in Peer Teaching. In a group of five or six, it is wise for one person to be the teacher, three or four to be the learners, and one person simply to assume the role of observer. The observer uses the Teaching Guide and should be in charge of the feedback session, helping the teacher analyze the teaching process and drawing from the learners their opinions and insights about what went on. In most cases the observer becomes the leader of the post-mortem.

Organizing the Peer Teaching. It is our experience that the most comfortable size for a peer teaching group is between five and seven. With that size, there are enough people to play the role of learner, someone is available to be observer, and the group is large enough to provide diverse opinions, yet small enough to conduct its business in a relatively short period of time. Optimally, the six or seven people are all studying the same model of teaching, learning the theory, viewing the demonstrations, and then taking turns as teachers in a series of peer teaching activities. If this is the case, then before each individual tries out the teaching with children, she or he will have taught the model at least once and seen it taught a half-dozen times. By the end of that period of time, they should all begin to feel extremely comfortable with the model and well aware of the role of the learner. One of the most artful aspects of learning the new model of teaching is to "feel" what the learners feel when they are introduced to the model. The more we can anticipate how children will react, the more we can prepare ourselves for their reactions and ease their way into the new role required by the model.

Microteaching. The last activity in the planning and peer teaching component is to teach the lesson to a small group of students—what we call microteaching. We recommend that you make an audio tape of your microteaching session, so that alone, or with colleagues, you can review the lesson, using the Teaching Analysis Guide.

Component IV: Adapting the Model

The major purpose of this component is to present ways of adapting the model for long-term use in the classroom. We discuss how to incorporate existing curriculum materials by including samples of elementary and secondary texts and showing how the models can provide new approaches to them. We also discuss long-term goals with respect to the development of pupil skills and teacher skills. In addition, we offer a few ideas we may have for "stretching the model" or distilling its essence. In other words, we share our notions about moving away from sequential phases and toward applying elements of the model in a dynamic, ongoing instructional context. The third section in this component covers suggestions for combining the model with other models of teaching.

The major organizational decisions that trainees and/or instructors will need to anticipate during training are summarized in Figure 7.

Tips to the Instructor:
Some Ways to Simplify the Training System

1. Provide more direct instruction and less self-directed reading. For example, in Component I (Describing and Understanding the Model), assign the first reading (Theory and Overview) for the students to read on their own. Plan to teach the ideas in the second reading (Taking Theory into Action) in a lecture-recitation session, using the materials and exercises from the section.

2. Review the syntax of the models at the different stages of instruction.

3. Augment the demonstration transcript with a live demonstration of your own. This will give the students an opportunity to experience the model directly as a learner before planning and peer teaching.

THE MODELS IN THIS BOOK

The three models in this book belong to the information processing family. Their major goals share an emphasis on *intellectual development*—the means by which students obtain, process, and retain knowledge.

Two of the models, the Concept Attainment Model and the Advance Organizer Model, are concerned with the acquisition and retention of concepts. The former involves an inductive mode of teaching, whereas the latter reflects a more didactic, expository form of instruction.

The authors of the Concept Attainment Model (Jerome Bruner) and the Advance Organizer Model (David Ausubel) share a common view about the nature of concepts and about conceptual learning. In addition, Ausubel's ideas on how knowledge is organized in the mind constitute a very useful framework for anyone

COMPONENT I: DESCRIBING AND UNDERSTANDING THE MODEL

1. The order in which the readings should be covered.
2. How much, if any, discussion to have about the material in Component I.

COMPONENT II: VIEWING THE MODEL

1. Reading the model individually *or* as a group.
2. Whether to observe a live demonstration, read the demonstration transcript, or hear a taped lesson.
3. Whether to analyze the demonstration lesson using the Teaching Analysis Guide, and if so, how to organize groups to do this.
4. Whether to see several live demonstrations in addition to the demonstration transcript.

COMPONENT III: PLANNING AND PEER TEACHING

1. Allow time for planning; provide feedback.
2. Organize and schedule small groups for peer teaching.
3. Arrange for microteaching. If possible, video-tape or audio-tape the lesson. Obtain the equipment.
4. Analyze the microteaching lesson, alone or with someone. Obtain equipment, either video tape or audio tape.

COMPONENT IV: ADAPTING THE MODEL

1. Whether a group discussion and/or learning activity should be developed around this component.

Figure 7. *A Summary of Organizational Decisions for the Trainee and/or Instructor.*

teaching concepts, regardless of the particular concept model. We urge you to think about Ausubel's theory of knowledge even while working with Concept Attainment.

Whereas Ausubel's model is concerned exclusively with the acquisition and retention of information, Bruner's Concept Attainment Model(s) also focuses on the development of the students' capacity for inductive thinking and on their capacity for developing alternative thinking strategies. Thinking processes are emphasized as much as the attainment of particular concepts.

The third model, Inquiry Training, is much like Concept Attainment in that it is an inductive model of thinking and teaching. Inquiry Training is designed to encourage students to inquire on their own into puzzling problem situations and apply the operations and skills of scientific inquiry in their search for an explanation or theory. The major purpose of the Inquiry Training Model is to help students develop the skills of scientific inquiry. Inquiry Training is a very exciting and involving model, which, used imaginatively, will enable students to acquire vast amounts of information along their way to a problem solution.

The Concept Attainment and Inquiry Training Models are also interesting means for carrying out informal evaluation of student learning. In their own ways, both provide opportunities for students to apply previous knowledge. As you work with Concept Attainment and Inquiry Training, remember their potential as informal evaluation activities.

We regard all three of these models as staples of the teacher's repertoire. They are certainly basic models of instruction for the development of the intellect, which is, after all, a primary goal of schooling.

CONCEPT

ATTAINMENT

MODEL

SCENARIO FOR CONCEPT ATTAINMENT

We are at a summer camp in Santa Barbara County, California. A group of boys and girls are beginning a hike through a ravine in the foothills of the Santa Ynez Mountains. The leader says, "Among other things, I am going to try to teach you how to identify a particular plant today. It is a plant that we all need to recognize, and in order to identify it we need to know what it is; that is, we need to know the *concept*, or principle, that distinguishes it from other objects."

A short way down the ravine, the leader pauses at a vine that has crawled up the trunk of an oak tree. He points at the vine, at the leaves, at the place where it enters the ground and where the beginning of the divisions of the roots can be seen, and says, "This is an example of the concept. This is the plant we are looking for. Please don't touch it. Just look at it carefully, closely." The leader gives the campers a few clues, "You want to notice particularly the shape of the leaves, the trunk and its branches, the way it holds on to its host tree, and what it looks like as it enters the ground."

A little further along, he pauses at a plant that is standing in the shade of a large tree and that has small pink flowers. "This is not what we are looking for," he says. "Notice again its leaves, its branches and trunk, and what it looks like as it enters the ground."

So it goes. He points to a good-sized tree and says, "This is not what we are looking for." He points to a small vine crawling across the ground in a sunny place at the base of some pampas grass and says, "This is another example of the plant we are looking for." He points to another vine; this one has tiny spade-shaped leaves and a very slender trunk and is crawling up a shady tree. "This is not what we are looking for," he says.

After a while, the students begin to anticipate. "This isn't one," says one of the children. "Here is one," says another. "You're wrong," the leader says, "but not by much." The students gather around and examine the various plants. Finally, the leader is able to ask, "Is this one?" "Is that one?" and the students are able to say "Yes" or "No" for that plant. The leader then gathers them all around. "How would you describe the plant I have in mind?"

"Well," says one, "its leaves always come in groups of three; no matter how many little branches there are, there are always three leaves close together."

"Yes," says another, "and they are shiny, at least on one side."

Another adds, "They look almost like they have oil on them."

"It likes to climb up," says another, "but it doesn't always do that."

"It likes the sun," says another, "but it can grow in the shade."

"That's it," says the leader, "you have put together the attributes of my plant—its leaves, its trunk, and the beginnings of its roots. You can discriminate these attributes from those of other plants. Now I'll tell you something else about it and see if you can guess its name. Notice that I have asked you not to touch it, although you could have learned more about it by touching it. One of the things you would have learned is that most of you would have developed an angry red rash on your skin and it would have itched and hurt for several days before it went away. Some of you might even have gotten quite sick and had to go to the hospital. Others would just have had a little bit of reddening of the skin. Do you know what the name of my plant is?"

"Poison oak," says one.

"No, you're almost right," says the leader, "but poison oak has five leaves in cluster."

"Poison ivy," chorus the others, and the leader smiles.

The leader has taught the students by pointing out positive and negative examples of the concept of poison ivy until they have learned the concept itself. Most of them will not forget the concept. They can tell you its characteristics and name, and they will be able to recognize poison ivy for the rest of their lives. Just as important, they will have learned a way of attaining concepts about other plants and animals.

When the children return to camp, they go to the cages where varieties of snakes are housed. "Teach us how to identify some kind of snake," says one of the children. The leader laughs. He looks into one of the cages where a snake about two feet long is coiled up. The patterns on its back form diamonds. "This is it," he says, pointing to the diamonds on its back. "This is one of the ways that this snake looks."

AN OUTLINE OF ACTIVITIES FOR THE CONCEPT ATTAINMENT MODEL

Objective	Materials	Activity
COMPONENT I: DESCRIBING AND UNDERSTANDING THE MODEL		
1. To recognize the goals, assumptions, and procedures of the Concept Attainment Model and to understand the nature of concepts.	Theory and Overview	Reading
2. To gain a sense of the model in action.	Theory in Practice	Reading
3. To recognize and generate the elements of a concept; to identify different types of concepts.	Taking Theory Into Action	Reading/Writing
4. To evaluate your understanding of the Concept Attainment theory.	Theory Checkup	Writing
COMPONENT II: VIEWING THE MODEL		
1. To become familiar with the Teaching Analysis Guide and identify items you do not understand.	Teaching Analysis Guide	Reading
2. To identify phases of the model and comment on the lesson.	Demonstration Transcript	Reading/Writing/ Discussion
3. **Option:** To analyze an alternative demonstration using the Teaching Analysis Guide.	Video tape or live demonstration/Teaching Analysis Guide	Viewing/Group discussion or individual analysis
COMPONENT III: PLANNING AND PEER TEACHING		
1. To select an appropriate concept for teaching.	Selecting the Concept	Reading/Writing
2. To analyze the concept you have selected for its attributes and type.	Analyzing the Concept	Reading/Writing
3. To determine the behavioral objectives for the microteaching lesson.	Determining Objectives and Model	Reading/Writing
4. To select and organize the exemplars for the microteaching lesson.	Preparing Exemplars	Reading/Writing
5. To complete the Planning Guide for the Reception Concept Attainment Model	The Planning Guide	Reading/Writing
6. To peer teach the Reception Concept Attainment Model.	3 or 4 peers, exemplars	Teaching
7. To analyze the Concept Attainment lesson using the Teaching Analysis Guide.	Teaching Analysis Guide	Writing/Group discussion or individual analysis

AN OUTLINE OF ACTIVITIES FOR THE CONCEPT ATTAINMENT MODEL

Objective	Materials	Activity
8. **Option:** To teach the Concept Attainment Model to a small group of students.	Small group of students, problem statement, teacher fact sheet (audio-cassette recorder, audio-cassette, video tape)	Teaching/Taping
9. To analyze the microteaching lesson.	Teaching Analysis Guide	Self or group listening to audio tape/writing

COMPONENT IV: ADAPTING THE MODEL

Objective	Materials	Activity
1. To recognize possible Concept Attainment lessons in existing curricular materials and make any necessary changes.	Curriculum Possibilities and Transformations	Reading
2. To plan the use of Concept Attainment for long-term development of pupil and teacher skills.	A Long-Term Plan	Reading
3. To be aware of the possibilities of combining Concept Attainment with other models of teaching.	Combining Concept Attainment with Other Models of Teaching	Reading

Component I

DESCRIBING
AND UNDERSTANDING
THE MODEL

THEORY AND OVERVIEW

Helping children learn concepts and teaching them how to learn concepts is a fundamental purpose of schooling. Until recently, however, most educators did not consciously distinguish the learning of concepts from other types of learning, even though many otherwise useful models of teaching are not efficient for concept learning.

In the 1960s, the Academic Reform Movement, led by scholars from the traditional academic disciplines, raised our consciousness about the importance of concepts. These academicians emphasized the importance of teaching the conceptual "structure of discipline" and its "mode of inquiry." All over the country, elementary and secondary school curriculum in each of the subject areas was redesigned around a core of concepts. The so-called New Math, Physical Science Study Committee physics, New Social Studies, and Biological Science Study Committee biology are some of the results of this effort, as are linguistic approaches to reading and structural approaches to art, music, and physical education. Textbook publishers revised their series, shifting to a "conceptual approach." Games, films, and concrete aids were invented to accompany the textbooks. Although these curriculum projects varied in their designs and to some extent their instructional formats, all of them stressed the learning of the major concepts from their respective disciplines.

Unfortunately, much of these curriculum changes took place without a simultaneous effort to expose educators to the vast research literature on the nature of concepts and the process of concept learning. In fact, this area is one of the most well-developed in educational psychology. What concepts are, how people acquire new concepts, and the conditions that impede or facilitate concept learning are all questions that researchers have explored. From these sources, a number of instructional models for teaching concepts have been generated. Our text, *Models of Teaching*, discusses three of these: Hilda Taba's Inductive Thinking Model, David Ausubel's Advance Organizer Model, and Jerome Bruner's Concept Attainment Model.

In this unit, we shall focus on the Concept Attainment Model developed from the work of Jerome Bruner, Jacqueline Goodnow, and George Austin. Their work, *The Study of Thinking*, culminated many years of research into the processes by which people acquire concepts. To examine this question, Bruner and his associates had to answer a prior question, "What is a concept, and what is meant by knowing a concept?" Their discussion concerning the nature of concepts forms the basis for understanding all types of concept learning, whatever teaching strategy is used. We refer to Bruner's description of the basic elements of concept as the theory of concepts and recommend his discussion. In this first reading you are introduced to the theory of concepts and to the Concept Attainment Model of teaching, and in the second reading (Taking Theory Into Action), you are given practice using the theory.

There are actually three variations, or models, of Concept Attainment that have been built from Bruner and his colleagues' basic study. Each has a slightly different set of activities (syntax), but all are developed from a common conceptual base. We describe the three variations but concentrate primarily on the Reception Model of Concept Attainment.

Goals and Assumptions

Bruner, Goodnow, and Austin begin with the assertion that the environment is so tremendously diverse and we humans are able to discriminate so many different objects that "were we to utilize fully our capacity for registering the differences in things and respond to each event encountered as unique, we would soon be overwhelmed by the complexity of our environment."[1] It is in order to cope with the environment that we engage in the process of categorizing, which means that we "render discriminately different things equivalent . . . respond to them in terms of their class membership rather than their uniqueness.[2] In other words, we invent categories and form concepts. These categories enable us to mentally group together objects that have real differences but that classify together on the basis of what they have in common. Categorizing enables us to "reduce the complexity of the environment"[3] because we do not have to respond to each stimulus as if it were entirely different and had its own label. Every car

---

[1]Jerome Bruner, Jacqueline Goodnow, and George Austin, *The Study of Thinking* (New York: Science Editions Inc., 1967), p. 2.
[2]Ibid., p. 12.
[3]Ibid., p. 12.

does not require a different name! Similarly, categorizing helps us reduce the necessity for constant learning. As long as an object or event displays the defining characteristics of a class, we do not have to relearn at each encounter. Finally, knowing a concept in advance, we can anticipate or plan future activities. For example, if we understand the concepts "dishonesty" or "loyalty" and we know the person we are meeting next week is loyal or dishonest, we can direct our behaviors and expectations accordingly.

Bruner and his colleagues set out to study the cognitive activity or thinking process called *categorizing*. They see categorizing as the "principal means by which a growing member of a society is socialized, for the categories that one is taught and comes to use habitually reflect the culture in which they arise."[4] They assume that although the content of categories may differ among cultures (Eskimos have many classes of snow, and Americans have several types of automobiles), all sets of concepts are the product of the same thought processes. This is because all concepts, regardless of their simplicity or complexity, are composed of the same basic elements. Thus, the means of acquiring any concept is essentially the same.

Another of Bruner's assumptions is that there are more and less effective strategies for forming concepts or categorizing. A second contribution of Bruner's research, then, in addition to the basic description of concepts, is the description of strategies people use to learn concepts (concept attainment).

Bruner's work has important and immediate application to teaching. First of all, by understanding the nature of a concept and of conceptual activity, teachers can better determine when students have attained a concept and when they are only using words without full conceptual understanding. Second, teachers can recognize the categorizing strategies their students are using and help them use more effective ones. Third, they can improve the quality of instructions for concept learning by using models of teaching that capitalize on the nature of the concept attainment process.

Categorizing, Concept Formation, and Concept Attainment

All categorizing activity involves identifying and placing events into classes on the basis of using certain cues (criteria) and ignoring others. Suppose that a female college senior is trying to describe to someone who is trying to get her a blind date the kind of man that she would like to be matched up with. In order to do this she tries to *communicate* her concept, and her friend tries to *attain* the concept. Our senior communicates by identifying to her friend several men who do not fit her concept. Finally, in the middle of her description her friend interrupts:

"Ah, I see, Aha!" she says. "You like short men who laugh a lot and you tend to avoid men who are very good students and are very intelligent."

"You've got it, but how did you know?"

"All the time you were talking, I kept thinking about why you put each man on the preferred and not-preferred lists. Gradually, I began to get the idea that those were the reasons why you did it. For example, most of the preferred men laugh a lot and are short, and only one is a good student and he gets his grades by working hard and selecting his courses carefully."

The process used by the matchmaker was one of concept attainment, "the

[4]Ibid., p. 12.

search for and listing of attributes that can be used to distinguish exemplars from nonexemplars of various categories."[5] In other words, in *concept attainment* the concept is determined in advance, as in the case of the preferred and not-preferred men, and the task is to determine the basis of the yes and no examples. The distinguishing features of the concept in this case were "laughing a lot" and "short." *Concept formation*, in contrast, is the act by which *new* categories are formed; it is an act of invention. If the two seniors had listed the names of all the men and then grouped them according to similarities, they would have been involved in concept *formation*. This would have been a useful thing to do if a third friend from another college had written asking, "What are the men like at your place?" Trying to come up with a few common descriptions, the women would try to determine how the men were alike. The task of identifying a suitable blind date, however, called for concept attainment, a second person trying to determine the category that was already formed in another person's mind.

According to Bruner, categorizing activity actually has two components: the act of *category formation* and the act of *concept attainment*. He maintains that concept formation is the first step toward concept attainment. The distinction between concept formation and concept attainment, though subtle, is relevant for three reasons: First, the purpose and emphasis of these two forms of categorizing behavior are different. Second, the steps of the two thinking processes are not the same. Third, the two mental processes require different teaching processes. Hilda Taba's Inductive Thinking Model is an example of a concept formation strategy. Bruner and his associates are concerned with the process of concept attainment. What is common to both processes is their reliance on the same interpretation of the nature of concepts.

The requirements for concept attainment games are relatively simple: an array of instances or examples that are alike in some ways and different in others. A person encounters these examples and must find out or be told whether each instance does or does not exemplify the concept. At each encounter with an instance, the person formulates and reformulates a hypothesis about the concept. Each instance or example provides potential information about the characteristics and attribute-values of the concept.

The process of sorting "yes" and "no" instances is a concept attainment game and is the core of the Concept Attainment Model of teaching. Exercise 1 is an example of a concept attainment game that uses a simple concept.

EXERCISE 1

Step 1:   Assume you are teaching this concept to a young child. Present her with the following list of words labeled "yes" or "no." Say each word as you present it. Ask the student to try to guess the idea you have in mind. Explain that the words with a "yes" contain your idea and the words with a "no" do not contain your idea.

FAT	Yes
FATE	No
MAT	Yes
MATE	No
RAT	Yes
RATE	No

What is the concept?

[5]Ibid., p. 233.

Step 2: "Let's see if the idea you guessed as my concept is correct by testing it. I'll give you some examples and you tell me if they are a "yes" or "no" based on your idea."

KITE	_____	(No)
CAT	_____	(Yes)
HAT	_____	(Yes)

Step 3: "Now you add examples of your own. These words should show my idea. Make another test that does not show my idea."

What is the concept? What was the pattern of the child's decisions? If she identified the concept as the "ât" vowel-consonant blend and correctly recognized "cat" and "hat" as a "yes," she has attained the concept on a simple level. Now, can the child verbalize the distinguishing features (essential attributes) of the "ât" sound? That's harder. Bruner makes the point that there are different *levels* of attainment; correctly distinguishing examples and nonexamples is easier than verbalizing the attributes. In other words, the student will be able to distinguish examples correctly before she will be able to make a verbal statement of the concept.

The Concept Attainment Model of teaching includes an analysis of the thinking processes and a discussion of the attributes of concept attainment. In addition, there are variations on the basic model that involve greater student participation and control and more complex material. The commonality among these variations, however, is the application of the theory of concepts. This is what distinguishes genuine Concept Attainment from a guessing game.

Thus far, several terms have been used repeatedly to define or describe categorizing activity and concept attainment—terms such as *example*, *criterial* or *essential feature*, and *attribute*. These are derived from Bruner's conception of the nature of concepts. Each has a special meaning and function in all forms of conceptual learning, especially Concept Attainment.

Theory of Concepts

Bruner sees any concept as having three elements:

1. examples (also, exemplars or instances)
2. attributes
3. attribute-values

Examples are instances of the concept. In Exercise 1, each word (kite, cat, hat, etc.) was an exemplar of the concept. Some were *positive* exemplars and some were *negative* exemplars. In concept formation, examples of a concept are grouped together; in concept attainment, the negative and positive examples are tested and searched for their features.

Every example, both positive and negative, can be described in terms of its *attributes* and in terms of its *attribute-values*. Suppose there is an array of fruit in front of you, mostly apples but one or two oranges and a pear. Each fruit is an example or instance. If my concept is "apple," the pears and oranges are negative instances and the apples are positive instances.

Each example can be described in terms of its basic characteristics. In the case of fruit, these are color, size, weight, shape, and costs. These basic characteristics are called *attributes*, and each attribute has an *attribute-value*. The term attribute refers to the basic category, such as color, whereas the attribute-value is the specific content of that category (yellow or red). Most attributes have a range of acceptable values. The attribute-value for an apple is a range from red to yellow. Purple is out of the acceptable value range for the concept "apple." If we see a roundish, purple object, we know it is not an apple. The shape of every apple is not exactly the same: there are degrees of roundness. On the other hand, in the case of the concept "record-disk" the attribute of shape does not have a range; records are exact circles.

What makes one concept different from another is the combination of attributes. Oranges and peaches have roughly the same shape but differ in other attributes, such as color and taste. Thus far, we have discussed oranges, apples, and peaches in terms of the attribute-values that distinguish them from other objects with the same attributes. The distinguishing attributes and their value-range are called *criterial attributes*. If any one criterial attribute is missing from an object, that object is an example of a different concept.

Usually, the attributes in the examples we come across every day are not so clear. For instance, in the grocery store, fruit is often packaged in boxes or surrounded by tissue paper. Imagine for a moment that you are a young child accompanying your father to the grocery store. You do not yet have the concepts of these different fruits. How would you know that neither the tissue paper nor the box is an essential feature of the concept of apple or orange? Packaging, like shape, color, and taste, is an attribute of the examples you see, but it is not an *essential attribute* of the concept. We refer to such nonessential features in our examples as *noisy attributes*. Noisy attributes make it more difficult to find the common essential features of our concept.

It is relatively easy to eliminate the noisy attributes when the media of our examples are objects or short words (as in Exercise 1). In real life, the data are much more complex—books, films, newspaper articles. High school teachers especially work with abstract concepts—such as "culture," "protagonist," and "tragic figure"—whose attributes and attribute-values are not so clear and whose examples are filled with noisy attributes.

These terms—examples, exemplars, positive and negative instances, attributes, essential features, criterial attributes, noisy attributes, attribute-values—are all part of the language that Bruner and his colleagues used to describe the nature of concepts and the process of concept attainment. If, as teachers, we want to know whether students have formed or attained concepts, we must determine whether they describe their categories or concepts in terms of the essential attributes and whether they distinguish examples from nonexamples. All conceptual learning, according to Bruner, rests on knowing which features are nonessential.

Much of our language is acquired by association rather than conceptually. Consequently, we are hard-pressed to recognize new examples or readily identify their essential features. "Democracy," "leadership," even "transportation" are a few concepts. Try quickly to list the essential features of one of these—it's not so easy! The difference between association (or rote) learning and conceptual learning has significant implications for the power of our thinking in new situations, especially our ability to sort and make sense of the multitude of data, events, and behaviors we encounter daily.

By now you should have perceived how Bruner's description of the elements of a concept fits in with the teaching process for concept learning and with the diagnosis of students' acquisition of concepts. It requires that the teacher, prior to instruction, analyze the concept in terms of its elements. Using the "ât" concept from Exercise 1, see if you can "diagram" that concept for its essential elements. For each term from concept theory shown in Figure 1, some answers are given. Supply additional answers on the blank lines. Check your responses with the commentary that follows.

Positive Exemplars	Negative Exemplars	Nonessential Attributes	Defining Attributes	Defining Attribute-values
fat	mate	length of word	sound	ât
fate	_____	_____	letter(s)	a, t
_____	_____	_____	_____	_____
_____	_____	_____	_____	_____

Figure 1. *Diagraming the "Ât" Concept.*

Commentary. The "ât" sound is a multi-attributed concept, and because of this, it is a less simple concept than it seems. Some of its essential or defining characteristics are sound (at), location (not before a silent e), and letters (a, t). Word meaning and length of word are some of its nonessential attributes. In Exercise 1, letters such as *f* (fat) and *r* (rat) and the word kite are somewhat "noisy" attributes in that they are not essential to the concept, although they help us distinguish its essential attributes. However, the data would be even "noisier" if we used sentences as instances of the concept, for they would contain more extraneous information.

Notice that every positive example contains all the essential features (attributes) of the concept. As you develop concept attainment exercises with different types of instructional materials (such as objects, pictures, paragraphs, books, movies, and stories) make sure that every instance is an example of the concept. That is, make sure that every instance has *all* the essential attributes of the concept.

The next concept attainment game involves more complex data: there are more characteristics to focus on and the concept itself is more abstract. However, the instructions should give you a clue to the concept. A subsequent section of this reading discusses the thinking strategies involved in concept attainment. As you work through Exercise 2, hypothesizing about the concept, be aware of your thought processes: Do you focus on the attributes of each example, checking subsequent examples for those attributes, or do you hold a concept in mind from the beginning? Do you hold more than one concept in mind, or do you wait until the one you are testing is eliminated and then return to the first example and try a new concept? The annotations at the end of each example should help you focus on the attributes in the example and on possible hypotheses.

EXERCISE 2

Each of the following passages is labeled "yes" or "no," depending on whether it represents a concept that I have in mind. As you read the passages, think of the concepts that the "yes" passages might represent—the principle by which they were designated "yes"—and the concepts that were designated "no." The attributes that are relevant to the concept are actions by which people communicate emotions to one another. Note the attributes of each instance in the margins.

Example One

A group of children are playing on the playground. One child makes an error that lets the other side win a point. The other children crowd around him, shouting at him. Some take his side. Gradually, the hubbub subsides, and they all return to the game.   YES

The previous passage does provide an example of the concept. What is the concept? Is it argument, or shouting, or punishment, or game playing? What are the other possibilities? Let us turn to another passage, one in which the concept is not contained.

Example Two

Four children are sitting on the floor of a room. The floor is covered with a rug, on which they are shooting marbles. At one point, there is a dispute over a shot. However, the problem is soon settled, and the game resumes.   NO

This passage contained a game, so we have to eliminate game playing as an expression of mutuality. There was an argument, so we have to eliminate that possibility. What are some of the other concepts that are and are not exemplified in this passage and the previous one? Let us turn now to another example in which our concept is represented.

Example Three

It is bedtime. A harried mother is putting her children to bed. She discovers that one of the children has not scrubbed his teeth. The mother berates the child, sending him back to the bathroom and his toothbrush. When he returns, the mother smiles, the children crawl into bed, and the lights are put out.   YES

What is our concept? Is it punishment? Is it possibly the resolution of conflict? Let us look at one more passage in which the concept is present.

Example Four

In a track meet, one boy crosses the finish line in the one-mile race far ahead of his competition. The next two runners approach the line, straining all the way as they vie for second place. As they slow down after the race, their parents and friends crowd around them, praising them for their effort.   YES

We must rule out punishment, for there is none in this sample. If we develop a more general concept, such as "things people do to influence one another's behavior," or a concept that includes "approval and disapproval," then we have identified the principle on which the selections were made. The concept is: *expressions of approval and disapproval*. The attributes were specific rewarding and punishing behaviors. The "no" sample did not contain any attributes relevant to approval or disapproval, but all the others (the "yes" samples) did.

This game could continue through several more passages. However, we have included enough examples to illustrate the purpose of this activity, which is to focus attention on the basis on which we make a categorization. Because that basis is not revealed clearly with the first "yes" or "no" samples, we have to keep several possibilities in mind. Gradually, we receive more information, which enables us to eliminate some possibilities and think of some new ones. How would more examples affect the possibility of attaining the concept? Did your strategy change in the second exercise because the concept was more abstract and the nature of the data was different?

Analyzing Thinking Strategies for Attaining Concepts

In addition to attaining a particular concept, a second purpose of the Concept Attainment Model is to enable students to become aware of the conceptualizing process itself. This includes understanding the relationships among data (examples), attributes, and concepts and the thinking patterns that are being used to attain the concept. Consequently, analysis of thinking is included as one of the phases (Phase Three) of the Reception and Selection Models of Concept Attainment.

Bruner uses the term *strategy* to refer to the sequence of decisions people make as they encounter each instance of a concept. As anticipated, the researchers found regularities in people's decision-making processes (or thinking strategies). Strategies of thinking are not always perceived consciously by the person using them, and they do not remain fixed. We use different strategies for different types of concepts and different kinds of learning material, or data. Bruner defines a strategy and its function as follows:

> Obviously strategies employed by people are not fixed things. They alter with the nature of the concept being sought, with the kinds of pressures that exist in the situation, with the consequences of behavior, etc. . . . What is most creative about concept attainment behavior is that the patterning of decisions does indeed reflect the demands of the situation in which the person finds himself. We do not know how strategies are learned. . . .[6]

An ideal strategy is one that is most efficient in attaining the concept but has the least amount of cognitive strain due to memory overload, ambiguity, and so on.

> For any given concept attainment task, for example, there is an ideal strategy that can be constructed having the property that by following it one can attain the concept with a minimum number of encounters—but without regard to the cognitive strain involved. There are other ideal strategies having the property of minimizing cognitive strain, that one must encounter en route

[6]Ibid., p. 55.

to a solution. And indeed, there are also ideal compromise strategies that serve both the purpose of cognitive economy and rapid solution.[7]

In identifying the strategies people use to attain concepts, Bruner and his associates distinguish between the two learning conditions of *selection* and *reception*. In selection conditions, the examples are not marked "yes" or "no." An individual, looking over the array of unmarked examples, *selects* one and *inquires* whether it is a "yes" or a "no." In reception conditions, the teacher presents the examples in a prearranged order, labeling them "yes" or "no." Exercises 1 and 2 are examples of reception conditions.

Selection conditions permit the student to control his hypothesis and testing because he controls the order of presentations, whereas in reception conditions the student's "major area of freedom is in the hypothesis he chooses to adopt, not in the manner in which he can choose instances to test."[8]

In schools, the most common instructional method, expository learning, represents reception conditions. However, in real life the flow of events and data from which we build concepts is not organized and labeled neatly, as in Concept Attainment games. If we want to process information conceptually, we must initiate selection conditions on our own. In our training system, the Concept Attainment Model of teaching is based on reception conditions. Variations on the model—which are based on selection conditions and on the analysis of concepts in unorganized data, respectively—move toward greater student control and more unstructured data situations.

The type of instructional condition (reception or selection) influences the particular thinking strategy that the student will employ. Bruner and his associates have identified six strategies—four selection strategies and two reception strategies. The four selection strategies are:

1. simultaneous scanning
2. successive scanning
3. conservative focusing
4. focus gambling

The major differences among them are (1) in the use of either attributes or concept-hypotheses as a basis of searching, and (2) in the number of attributes or hypotheses held at one time. The two scanning strategies are based on the use of a concept-hypothesis, whereas focusing strategies utilize attributes (see Figure 2). Simultaneous scanning uses each example to determine which hypotheses to hold and which to eliminate. Many hypotheses are held at one time.

	Attribute(s)	Concept(s)
Many	Conservative focusing	Simultaneous scanning
One-at-a-Time	Focus gambling	Successive scanning

Figure 2. *Strategies of Searching.*

[7]Ibid., p. 55.
[8]Ibid., p. 126.

EXERCISE 3

FAT	(Yes)	(Remember: In selection
FATE	(No)	conditions the examples are
MAT	(Yes)	not marked "yes" or "no."
MATE	(Yes)	The student picks one and
RAT	(No)	*inquires* whether it is a
RATE	(No)	"yes" or a "no.")

The searcher using a simultaneous-scanning strategy in Exercise 3 above, might see the first example and think, "The concept might be the 'at' sound, three-letter words, 'FA' words, or adjectives." If the searcher used a successive-scanning strategy in the present exercise, he or she would try *one* of these concepts, "FA" words. She would inquire whether FAT was a "yes" and whether FATE was a "yes." Finding that FATE was a "no," the searcher would drop "FA" words as a hypothesis and go on to test the next concept, three-letter words, by inquiring whether RAT is a "yes." Since RAT is a "no," three-letter words had to be dropped as a hypothesis. The successive-scanning searcher tests one concept at a time and selects an example that provides a direct test for the hypothesis. The fact that FATE was a "no" did not tell the searcher anything about "three-letter words," so she would not have selected that example to test the concept "three-letter words." Focus gambling and conservative focusing are similar, except that instead of testing a concept the searcher tests individual attributes of a concept, such as the letter "f" or "a" and then the letter "t." Focus gamblers use a positive instance as a focus and change more than one attribute at a time; conservative focusers find a positive instance and choose instances that alter one attribute at a time.

The two reception strategies are wholist (akin to focusing) and partist (akin to scanning). The wholist's strategy is to take the first positive instance of the concept and use it in toto as a guide, comparing all the attributes of the first instance to those of subsequent instances and modifying the hypotheses accordingly. The first instance then becomes the concept-hypothesis, and subsequent decisions depend on the attribute similarity and difference between the first instance and subsequent ones. The wholist strategy is similar to focusing. In the partist (or part-scanning) strategy, the choice of a hypothesis is based on only part of the initial example. In Exercise 1, the initial hypothesis might have been the letter "a." If the initial hypothesis is not confirmed, the partist refers back to all previous instances and changes the hypothesis. (Think back now on Exercises 1 and 2: were you using a wholist or partist strategy?)

Bruner and his colleagues found that most people, under reception conditions, are wholists in their initial approach to the problem. Wholists tend to follow up with focusing (the use of attributes), whereas partists follow up with scanning (the use of hypotheses), a more cognitively demanding procedure. Because scanners have to keep track of more information, the wholist strategy is regarded as the "ideal" selection strategy—one that minimizes strain and maximizes performance.

Concept Attainment as a Model of Teaching

As we mentioned earlier, several models of teaching have been developed from the work of Bruner and his colleagues. The purposes of these strategies include (1) to understand the nature of concepts—to help students see that objects, ideas, and events are distinguished by attributes and placed into categories; (2) to be more effective in attaining concepts, by understanding the thinking strategies being employed and by finding out the basis of the categories other people use to organize their environment; (3) to teach specific concepts; and (4) to become more aware of conceptualizing activity and to employ it at will, especially with unorganized data.

The first Concept Attainment Model is a concept attainment game under reception conditions. A second variation of the model is the concept attainment game under selection conditions, and the third variation is the analysis of concepts in unorganized data. The first two models incorporate analysis of thinking as a phase of the model. Together, the three variations form a sequence in conceptual activity. The Reception Model is more direct in teaching students the elements of a concept and their use in Concept Attainment. The Selection Model permits students to apply this awareness of conceptual activity in a more active context, one that permits their own initiation and control. Variation 3, the analysis of concepts in unorganized data, transfers concept theory and attainment activity to a real-life setting.

The Reception-Oriented Concept Attainment Model

The phases and activities of the Reception Model of Concept Attainment are outlined in Figure 3.

Phase One: Presentation of Data and Identification of the Concept	Phase Two: Testing Attainment of the Concept	Phase Three: Analysis of Thinking Strategies
Present labeled examples. Compare attributes in positive and negative examples. Generate and test hypotheses. Name the concept. State a definition according to the essential attributes.	Identify additional unlabeled examples as "yes" or "no." Generate examples.	Describe thoughts. Discuss role of hypothesis and attribute. Discuss type and number of hypotheses. Evaluate the strategies.

Figure 3. *Syntax of the Reception Model of Concept Attainment.*

Syntax of the Reception Model
of Concept Attainment

Phase One: Presentation of Data and Identification of Concept. This phase involves presenting data to the learner. Each unit of data is a separate example or nonexample of the concept. The data may be events, people, objects, stories, pictures, or any other discriminable unit. The learners are informed that there is one idea that all the positive examples have in common; their task is to develop a hypothesis about the concept. The instances are presented in a prearranged order and are labeled "yes" or "no." Learners are asked to compare and justify the attributes of the different examples. (The teacher or students may want to maintain a record of the attributes.) Finally, they are asked to name the concept and state the rule or definition of the concept according to its essential attributes.

Phase Two: Testing Concept Attainment. In this phase, the students test their attainment of the concept, first by correctly identifying additional unlabeled examples of the concept and then by generating their own examples.

Phase Three: Analysis of Thinking. In this phase, students begin to analyze the strategies by which they attain concepts. As we have indicated, some learners initially try broad constructs and gradually narrow the field; others begin with more discrete constructs. The learners can describe their patterns as to whether they focused on attributes or concepts, whether they did so one at a time or several at once, and what happened when their hypothesis was not confirmed. Did they change strategies? Gradually, they can begin to compare and contrast the effectiveness of different strategies.

Principles of Reaction

During the flow of the lesson the teacher wants to be supportive of the students' hypotheses, emphasizing, however, that they are hypothetical in nature and creating a dialogue in which the major content is a balancing of one person's hypothesis against another's. In the later phases of the model, the teacher wishes to turn the students' attention toward analysis of their concepts and strategies, again being very supportive. The teacher should encourage analysis of the merits of various strategies rather than attempt to seek the one best strategy for all people in all situations.

The Teacher's Role

Prior to teaching with the Reception Model of Concept Attainment, the teacher selects the concept, selects and organizes the material into positive and negative examples, and sequences the examples. Most instructional materials, especially textbooks, are not designed in a way that corresponds to the nature of concept learning as described by educational psychologists. In most cases teachers will have to prepare examples, extracting ideas and materials from texts and other sources, but designing them in such a way that the attributes are clear and that there are, indeed, both positive and negative examples of the concept. In using the Reception Model of Concept Attainment, the teacher acts as a recorder, keeping track of the hypotheses (concepts) as they are mentioned and of the attributes. In the initial uses of Concept Attainment, it is helpful to be very structured. The teacher also supplies additional examples as they are needed. The three major functions of the teacher during Reception-oriented Concept Attainment activity are to record, prompt (cue), and present additional data.

The Support System

Concept Attainment lessons require material that has been designed so that concepts are embedded in the material. The material must be organized so that positive and negative exemplars are pointed out to the student. It should be stressed that the student's job in a Concept Attainment strategy is not to invent new concepts, but to attain the ones that have previously been selected by the teacher agent. Hence, the data sources need to be known beforehand and the aspects of Concept Attainment activity made visible. Thus, as students are presented with an example, they are asked to describe its characteristics (attributes). These can then be recorded in a column depending upon whether the example is a "yes" or "no." A blackboard or tagboard for a Reception Model of Concept Attainment might look something like Figure 4. The four columns clearly reveal the basic elements of a concept. The teacher can work from the record to help students attain the concept. As hypotheses are generated, they can be compared to the characteristics of the "yeses." After the concept is attained, new examples can be contrasted with the "yes" characteristics.

| Examples | Characteristics of the | | Possible Concepts (Hypotheses) |
	"Yeses"	"Nos"	
HATE Yes AT No ATE Yes TEA No PLAN No	long a four letters three letters silent e	two letters four letters short a	

Figure 4. *An Example of Attribute Analysis.*

The Selection-Oriented Concept Attainment Model

The major difference between the Reception and Selection Models of Concept Attainment is in the labeling and sequencing of the examples. In the Selection Model, an example is not labeled until the student asks whether it is a "yes" or a "no." Another difference is that students may do this with their own examples in order to attain the concept. The students also control the sequence of the examples, by choosing from among them the ones they want to inquire about. The tracking and analysis of attributes is not as formal in the Selection Model as in the Reception Model. Students may be encouraged to make notes about their hypothesis and attributes. In general, the Selection Model places responsibility for concept attainment and attribute tracking in the hands of the students. Its syntax is similar to that of the Reception Model, but its activities and roles within Phases One and Two are slightly different (see Figure 5).

The students can work as individuals, each person inquiring about examples—even though the person will necessarily be influenced by the findings from someone else's inquiry—or they can work as a group, making a joint decision about the examples to inquire into. Working as individuals is probably desirable at first.

Phase One: Presentation of Data and Identification of the Concept	Phase Two: Testing Attainment of the Concept	Phase Three: Analysis of Thinking Strategies
Present *un*labeled examples.	Identify additional unlabeled examples.	Describe thoughts.
Students inquire which examples, including their own, are positive ones.	Students generate examples.	Discuss role of hypothesis and attributes.
Generate and test hypotheses.		Discuss type and number of hypotheses.
Name the concept.		Evaluate strategies.
State its essential attribute.		

Figure 5. *Syntax of the Selection Model of Concept Attainment.*

Unorganized Materials Model

Not all concepts have defining attributes that everyone would agree on. This is particularly true of "ideal-type" concepts such as "democracy," "capitalism," and "socialism," as well as other abstractions, such as "racism," "conservative," and "liberal." One of the purposes of understanding that objects or ideas are distinguished by attributes is to identify the defining features people associate with them. If we view some of our ideological differences as definitional problems, using Concept Attainment theory to do so, we can gain a better grasp of both the meaning of the concept and the underlying value conflicts.

The real payoff of the "Concept Attainment Game" occurs when we begin to apply it to unarranged material in order to help ourselves become aware of the attributes that are being employed. The analysis of concepts and attributes in written material is essential to any kind of meaningful and critical reading, for verbal assertions of concepts appear throughout written material—the attributes on which they are based being made explicit considerably less often. For example, consider the following passages from a secondary social studies textbook. These passages were constructed to teach students the attributes of one concept of United States military policy, the policy of containment.

As the word itself indicates, containment is a defensive policy; we react to Communist moves. . . .

Our defensive military policy rests on the idea that the United States must be strong enough to endure any attack and still have the power to crush the aggressor. If the Communists are aware that we can destroy them even if they strike the first blow, they are unlikely to follow an aggressive course.

In recent years the United States has taken the following steps to insure that we will be able to strike back after an atomic attack: the development of the Polaris submarine, which, because of its mobility, cannot be easily destroyed; the concealment of intercontinental missiles . . . ; the development of a worldwide warning system against impending attack; and keeping nuclear bombers on around-the-clock alert.

The defensive nature of the United States military policy creates certain difficulties. Not only can an enemy choose the time of attack, he can also choose the place and the manner. Therefore, the United States not only must maintain troops in many parts of the world, but it must maintain highly mobile forces which can be dispatched to any trouble spot on short notice. The most serious problems, in some way, grow out of the fact that the Communists are free to choose their manner of aggression. Because they prefer to attack from within, using subversion and guerrilla forces, we, too, must adopt new tactics. To that end, the United States has undertaken the training of some of its forces in guerrilla warfare. Our government has sent such specially trained groups to allied countries that have needed help in fighting Communist rebels. In South Vietnam, for example, American special forces have taken an important part in the struggle against Communist guerrilla fighters.[9]

The concept of defensive military policy (containment) is explicated with several attributes. In addition, several other concepts are taught. What attributes are attached to them? Can you identify other concepts and related attributes in these passages?

For another instance, let us look at two concepts of criminality contained in the professional literature. Attributes are italicized.

It has been traditional to impute to the criminal certain distinctive and peculiar motivations and physical, mental, and social traits and characteristics. Historically, crime has been ascribed to *innate depravity, instigation of the devil, constitutional abnormalities, mental deficiency, psychopathology* and many other conditions inherent in the individual. Criminals have been thus set off as a distinctive class, qualitatively different from the rest of the population.[10]

From this frame of reference, the dominant attributes of criminality are personal—the criminal is a kind of person different from the noncriminal. Compare this with the concept in the following passage about five delinquent brothers:

The delinquent careers of the brothers had their origins in the *practices of the play groups and gangs* with which they became associated as children. The initial *acts of theft were part of the undifferentiated play life of the street.* From these simple beginnings, the brothers *progressed, by social means, to more complicated,* more serious, and more specialized forms of theft. *The situation in the home community not only failed to offer organized resistance to this development,* but *there were elements which encouraged it* and *made any other course of action difficult.*[11]

[9]Robert P. Ludlum et al., *American Government* (Boston: Houghton-Mifflin, 1969), p. 333. By permission of the publisher.
[10]Ernest W. Burgess and Donald J. Bogue, "The Delinquency Research of Clifford R. Shaw and Henry D. McKay and Associates," in Burgess and Bogue (eds.), *Urban Sociology* (Chicago: University of Chicago Press, 1962), p. 308.
[11]Ibid., p. 11.

The concept attached to the word "criminal" now has social attributes rather than personal ones. The passages, in fact, succeed in helping us contrast two concepts of criminality.

The procedure for analyzing concepts in unorganized materials involves (1) locating the concept (for instance, the policy of containment); (2) identifying the attributes being used; (3) discussing the adequacy and appropriateness of the attributes; and (4) comparing the examples to other passages using the same concept (see Figure 6). We see the progression to the analysis of concepts in unorganized materials as part of a sequence of instruction in concept attainment activity.

Phase One: Description of Concept As It Is Used	Phase Two: Evaluation of Concept
	Discuss adequacy and appropriateness of concepts being used.
Locate and label concept.	
Identify attributes being used.	Compare exemplars to other data using same concept.

Figure 6. *Analyzing Concepts in Unorganized Materials.*

By now, the students should be thoroughly familiar with concept-theory terminology. This third version of Concept Attainment is much more a group discussion than an instructional game, like the reception and selection strategies. The teacher's role is to facilitate discussion and insure that it focuses on the development of a concept in the material.

Summary

Concept Attainment Models facilitate the type of learning referred to as conceptual learning, in contrast with the rote learning of factual information or of vocabulary. Knowing a concept means distinguishing examples from nonexamples, generating new examples of the concept, and articulating the attributes of the concept.

Three Concept Attainment Models of teaching have been presented here: the Reception Model, the Selection Model, and the Model for Unorganized Material. These three models constitute a continuum from direct instruction in concept theory under teacher-structured conditions to student control and application in naturalistic data situations.

The Concept Attainment Models are appropriate for several educational objectives. They can be used to:

1. help students acquire a new concept

2. enrich and clarify their thinking on previously acquired concepts

3. teach them the "concept of a concept," including the terminology and meaning of a concept theory and conceptual activity

4. help them become aware of their own thinking processes and strategies.

THEORY IN PRACTICE

No amount of description can convey a sense of a model of teaching as well as an example of the model in practice. In fact, reading too much theory before gaining a rough "image" of the practice can be confusing and, for some people, frustrating and discouraging. So we encourage you, at this point of your study of the Concept Attainment Model, to read the following abbreviated transcript of an actual classroom session. We suggest that you first read only the teacher-student dialogue and then go back to note the annotations. Remember, the goal at this point in your training is to gain a sense of the model—its flow and feeling—not to master the techniques of implementation.

This transcript presents excerpts of a dialogue from Phase One of a Selection Model of Concept Attainment. The concept is a complex, abstract one concerning the feudal system of power relationship. The data is drawn from previous readings about life in a medieval castle and pictures of daily life in the castle. Notice the student inquiry procedures involved in the Selection strategy and note the curriculum possibilities.

T: TODAY WE ARE GOING TO WORK ON A NUMBER OF WAYS TO FORM IDEAS OUT OF INFORMATION. LAST NIGHT YOU READ SOME INFORMATION ABOUT AN ENGLISH CASTLE. UP HERE JUST BEHIND ME IS A PICTURE OF CASTLE LUDLOW, AND WE ARE GOING TO WORK WITH INFORMATION FROM THESE PICTURES. OUR CONCENTRATION IS GOING TO BE ON WAYS THAT YOU CAN THINK ABOUT INFORMATION. WE ARE GOING TO CONCENTRATE ON TEACHING YOU, IF WE CAN, SOME STRATEGY FOR THINKING ABOUT INFORMATION AND TRYING TO FORM IDEAS ABOUT IT. I AM GOING TO GIVE YOU THE FIRST ONE AND THEN IT'S YOUR GAME. THESE CARDS GIVE YOU AN IDEA ABOUT LIFE IN THAT PLACE. FIRST ONE IS A "YES." WRITE DOWN THE IDEA THAT YOU THINK I'M THINKING ABOUT WITH RESPECT TO LIFE IN THAT MEDIEVAL TOWN. NOW TELL ME ANOTHER CARD THAT YOU WOULD LIKE. MAYBE I BETTER NUMBER THESE BECAUSE THERE ARE A LOT OF THEM. OK? PICK A CARD. JUANITA?

Phase One: Presentation of Data and Identification.
The teacher is cuing the students about the nature of the concept—life in that place.

S: 10.

T: 10. OK, NUMBER 10 IS A "NO." IF YOU CAN'T THINK OF ANOTHER IDEA, JUST LEAVE IT BLANK FOR A LITTLE BIT AND JUST REMEMBER THAT THAT WAS A "NO." OK. WHAT'S ANOTHER PICTURE THAT YOU WOULD LIKE TO KNOW? SARA?

Student inquires which are positive examples.

S: 5.

T: OK. NUMBER 5 IS A "NO."

S: NUMBER 2.

T: NUMBER 2 IS A "NO." OK. SARA?

S: NUMBER 4.

T: NUMBER 4 IS A "YES." NOW YOU HAVE TWO "YESES" AT THIS POINT AND SEVERAL "NOS." NOW THINK TO YOUR SELVES, WHAT DO THE

The teacher cues the students on the structure of the Concept Attainment process.

"YESES" HAVE IN COMMON THAT THE "NOS" DO
NOT SHARE WITH THEM?

S: NUMBER 11.

T: NUMBER 11. WHO THINKS THAT'S A "YES?" WHO   Creating dialogue among students.
THINKS ITS A "NO?" JUANITA, WHAT DO YOU
THINK?

S: I THINK IT IS JUST PEOPLE THAT WORK FOR HIM.   Student generates concept hypothesis.

T: PEOPLE THAT WORK FOR HIM. NOW LETS SEE,   Teacher tests hypothesis, showing students how
ARE THERE PEOPLE IN ANY OF THE "NOS?"   to test the concept.
HERE IS A "YES." HERE IS A "NO." PEOPLE
THERE, AND ARE THERE PEOPLE IN THIS ONE?

S: YES.

T: ALL RIGHT, SO IT ISN'T PEOPLE, IS IT?   The hypothesis is eliminated.

S: PEOPLE HELPING PEOPLE.

S: LEADERSHIP.

T: POWER. WHICH IDEA COMES OFF THE BEST?

S: OWNERSHIP.

T: LORDS, POWER, OWNERSHIP, RELIGION. WHERE IS   The teacher states some of the attributes.
RELIGION, SARA? LORDS, POWER, OWNERSHIP.
ALL RIGHT, YOU ARE CLOSE. I HAD IN MIND THE
SYSTEM BY WHICH POWER IS USED IN THE PLACE.
THERE ARE WAYS THAT THE LORDS AND
PEASANTS AND OTHERS HAVE RELATIONSHIPS
TO EACH OTHER.

TAKING THEORY INTO ACTION

This reading provides additional discussion, illustrations, and training exercises on the theory of concepts, particularly on the elements of a concept. In addition, three types of concepts are identified and their relevance for planning Concept Attainment lessons is described. Successful planning and implementation of Concept Attainment lessons requires careful definition of the concept and selection of appropriate examples.

Throughout the reading are short training exercises designed to help you locate any difficulty you may have in applying the ideas in this reading. Please complete the training exercises, noting any difficulty you encounter. Discuss these problems with your instructor or colleagues.

Distinguishing Conceptual Activity
from Symbol Transmission and Factual Learning

In many classrooms (and textbooks), much of what passes for conceptual understanding is more than likely either symbolic transmission or situational meaning. Peter Martorella, in his book on concept learning, speaks to this point:

A shrewd student confronted with a question from his teacher such as, "What do you like best about our country?" may discover that he can ease his conceptual burden by replying, "Our democratic process." By doing so, he reflects his grasp of the situational meaning of the terms "democratic process," indicating he recognizes these symbols can be positively related to characteristics of the United States. . . . Students may use terms such as, for example, "universe," "black power," "democracy," or "justice," either verbally or in writing, and still be conceptually ignorant of their basic meanings. The transmission of symbols, a student quickly learns, will often pass for "learning" in the conceptual sense in the classroom or in society at large. Both examinations and casual conversation with elders, he finds, frequently place emphasis upon symbol transmission and recognition rather than conceptualizing.[12]

The use of contextual clues is an important staple in the process of learning to read, the purpose of which is to link the written symbol with the sound. Conceptual meaning, on the other hand, involves knowing the elements of the concept—that is, being able to identify the essential attributes, to recognize positive examples of the concept, and to distinguish them from negative examples. Even when we can correctly state the definition (or rule) of a concept, we cannot always recognize new instances of it. The capacity to recognize examples of the concept in new situations distinguishes conceptualizing from symbol transmission. The alternative to learning conceptually is to memorize examples or facts.

In the Theory and Overview section of this model, we presented the case of the young woman, her roommate, and the blind date. If the roommate had not tried to attain the concept of the young woman's preferred type of man, the roommate would have tried to remember each man that she mentioned and whether he was a "yes" or a "no." By treating the problem as a concept attainment task, she need only remember the attributes of the concept, "short" and "laugh a lot," the next time she arranges a blind date for her friend. Conceptual learning is much more economical than factual learning.

Most of us spent many hours as elementary and secondary students learning new vocabulary words and memorizing their definitions. However, the proportion of these words, particularly the more abstract terms, that we retained at a conceptual level is very small. We simply do not apply these concepts actively in our thoughts and descriptions as information containing examples of them passes before us.

In short, the learning of concepts primarily involves knowing the criterial attributes of the concepts, distinguishing them from the nonessential attributes, and recognizing exemplars. Simply being able to state the name of a concept or a partial definition does not entail conceptual understanding. It is unlikely that one would be able to recognize an example of the concept with this level of knowledge.

EXERCISE 4. CONCEPTUAL VERSUS SYMBOLIC ACTIVITY

To illustrate the difference between learning *symbols* and learning *concepts*, see if you can identify the essential attributes of the following concepts, which should be familiar to you. This will indicate whether you learned these terms as vocabulary (or symbols), or as concepts.

[12]Peter Martorella, *Concept Learning: Designs for Instruction* (New York: Intext Educational Publishers, 1972), pp. 8-10.

Concept	Essential Attributes
Family	
Food	
Transportation	
City	
Religion	

Elements of a Concept

In the Theory and Overview section above, we identified six aspects of a concept:

1. name
2. essential attributes
3. nonessential attributes
4. positive examples (exemplars)
5. negative examples (exemplars)
6. rule

The first step in planning to teach using the Concept Attainment Models is to *analyze the concept you are teaching for its essential elements*. Only by doing this can you select the most appropriate learning material and guide students' thinking toward these elements. The six elements also form the basis for evaluating student learning, each one indicating progressively deeper levels of conceptual understanding.

The first element, the *name*, is the term or label given to a category. "Fruit," "government," "dogs," "ghettos" are all names given to a range of experience, objects, configurations, or processes. Although the items or data (the term *data* is used synonomously with *example* or *information*) in each category differ slightly from the other items, common features cause these different phenomena to be referred to by the same general term.

The common features or characteristics that cause us to place dissimilar items in the same category are called *essential attributes* (also, *criterial* or *critical attributes*). If an animal does not have four legs, it would not be placed in the category of dog. On the other hand, all four-legged animals are not dogs, so the concept of dog must have other essential attributes besides "four legs." Some of the slight differences among items in a category reflect *nonessential attributes*. Clothing, a collar, and a leash are nonessential attributes of the concept "dog." On the other hand, size and color are essential attributes. There can be a *range* of difference in each essential attribute, but at some point the variation would have to exclude the four-legged animal from the category of dog. A five-foot-high four-legged animal cannot be a dog.

Variations in the examples in any category have two sources—the range of permissible values in the essential attributes (for instance, the range of sizes and colors of dogs) and characteristics that are nonessential (for example, dog clothing, leashes, and collars). The task of learning a new concept is made more difficult by the presence of many nonessential attributes. For example, if we want to teach students the concept of "dog" and we present examples in which there are many other stimuli (such as a picture of a house, trees, and a person with a dog) it is harder for the students to focus on the essential features of a dog.

A common misunderstanding about attributes is for people to refer to a particular feature of a concept as an attribute when it is actually an attribute-value. Black, for example, is a *value* of the attribute *color*. Usually, attributes have an acceptable range of values, for instance, the color of dogs encompasses red, brown, gray, and some other colors; purple, however, is not within this acceptable range. When you analyze a concept for its attributes, think of the basic idea first. Is *color* an essential attribute? Then ask yourself, "What is the acceptable range of values for this attribute?"

At this point, try identifying the attributes and their value range for two simple concepts. Also, list some nonessential attributes. Next, select a concept from your subject area. See if you can list its essential attributes and their value range.

EXERCISE 5. ATTRIBUTES AND ATTRIBUTE-VALUES

Concept	Essential Attributes	Nonessential Attributes	Value Range for Essential Attributes
apple	1. color 2. 3.		
television			

The function of attributes is to help us distinguish between examples of the concept and nonexamples. As we said earlier, the distinction between symbol transmission and conceptual activity is the ability to recognize new instances of the concept. Bruner uses the term "exemplar" to refer to instances of the concept. Those instances that contain all the criterial attributes are called *positive exemplars*. The absence of one or more criterial attributes makes an instance a *negative exemplar* of the concept. A circle is not a record-disk, even though these two concepts share one common attribute—round shape. A house shares no common attributes with a circle or a record-disk.

In the following example, the figures on the left are positive exemplars of the concept *rectangle* and the ones on the right are negative exemplars. Each negative exemplar is missing one criterial attribute.

Positive Exemplars   Negative Exemplars

An important consideration in selecting material for Concept Attainment activities is the *modality* of the exemplars. Modality refers to two features—the *medium* and the *size* of the exemplars. There are three basic types of media—objects (realia), pictures (still or motion), and words or symbols (letters, words, paragraphs, and books). Sound is another possible medium, as in the case of records or songs. The choice of media can facilitate or hinder the Concept Attainment process. For example, if we want to teach the concept of shape of triangle or square, it is preferable to have actual objects or pictures rather than verbal descriptions of shapes. Can you imagine trying to visualize a triangle from a verbal description of it? Similarly, it's hard to visualize a painting when it is described in words. On the other hand, some attributes, such as motion and relationship, do not appear clearly in pictures. If it is important to know that a man and a woman are married (an essential attribute), you might have to add a caption such as "Mr. and Mrs. John Smith" under a picture of them. The use of media and exemplars is important. *Select the medium that most accurately conveys the attributes of your concept.*

Size refers to the complexity of the unit of the exemplar. With the medium of symbols, for example, individual letters or words are "smaller" than sentences, paragraphs, or books. The latter are larger in the sense that they contain many more attributes, especially many more noisy attributes. The size of the exemplar, like that of the medium, can increase or reduce the difficulty of concept attainment. If you want to teach students the sound of "ât," you should not use paragraphs or books as individual exemplars. These contain too many extraneous attributes! On the other hand, many teachers make the mistake of not selecting "large" enough exemplars for their concept.

Some concepts are difficult to teach without using large-scale exemplars. Concepts in literature such as "romantic novel" or "antihero" may require the whole book. If "plot" is an essential attribute of "romantic novel," it cannot be fully conveyed through excerpted sentences or phrases. However, the teacher could include a short plot summary in the information relative to each exemplar. One thing to remember in collecting or devising your exemplars is the unit-size of the exemplar; *does it fit the attributes of the concept? Remember, every positive exemplar has to contain all the essential attributes of the concept.* (Examples of relational concepts do not have to contain all the attributes, as will be discussed later.)

EXERCISE 6: EXEMPLARS

For each of the following concepts, describe at least two positive and two negative exemplars. Identify at least one missing essential attribute in each of your negative exemplars.

Concept	Positive Exemplar	Negative Exemplar
hat	1. 2.	1. 2.
poverty	1. 2.	1. 2.

Questions: Is a newspaper a positive or negative example of "hat"?

Is a scarf a positive or negative example of "hat"?

Is the woman walking down the street during a rainstorm with a newspaper held over her head a positive or negative example of "hat"?

The Role of Definitions

The last element of a concept is the *rule*. A rule is a definition or statement specifying the attributes of a concept. Martorella cites the following example of a rule:

Thus, "a natural elevation of the earth's surface rising to a summit" is a *rule* stating essential or criterial *attributes* with the *name* "mountain," of which "Fuji" is a positive *exemplar* or illustration.[13]

A rule statement should evolve at the end of the Concept Attainment process. The teacher often uses it as a device for having students summarize the findings of their search for attributes. A "correct" rule statement merely reflects successful utilization of the other elements of a concept—negative and positive exemplars and nonessential and essential attributes—in the Concept Attainment Models.

Usually, when you teach a concept with the aid of Concept Attainment Models your students will have a symbolic understanding of the concept; that is, they will be able to apply a verbal label or *name* to it. Sometimes you may teach an entirely new concept and have to supply the new label to the rule statement once the students have identified the criterial attributes in the positive exemplars.

Exercise 7 checks your understanding of all six elements of a concept. If you have any difficulty, reread the sections concerning the element in question.

EXERCISE 7: ELEMENTS OF A CONCEPT

1. name
2. essential attributes
3. nonessential attributes
4. positive examples (exemplars)
5. negative examples (exemplars)
6. rule

[13]Ibid., p. 7.

Instructions: For each concept in the following table, supply the missing element(s).

Concept Name	Positive Exemplar	Negative Exemplar	Essential Attribute	Nonessential Attribute
1. Triangle	△ △	○ □ L		
2. Automobile			mobility engine function: transporation	color size shape
3. Brother				
4.			one or more support flat surface function: work area	size shape drawers

Now, write a rule for each concept.

1.

2.

3.

4.

Types of Concepts

In this section we describe several types of concepts and some of the purposes and problems involved in each, and we distinguish concepts from generalizations.

Bruner identified three types of concepts: conjunctive, disjunctive, and relational. It is important to recognize and distinguish among them because the type of concept affects the nature of the exemplars you choose to present and, in some cases, the objectives of the Concept Attainment activity.

Conjunctive concepts are defined by the joint presence of several attributes. For example, the conjunctive concept "apple" has four attributes—shape: round; color: red-green; taste: sweetish-sour; function: food.

Disjunctive concepts require the presence of some attributes and the absence of others. An example is "red-haired boys who are not thin." Disjunctive concepts are often defined by either-or characteristics. For example, "citizen" is a disjunctive concept—a person who either is born in the United States or whose parents are citizens.

Relational concepts, like conjunctive concepts, have several attributes, but these bear some kind of relationship to one another. "Mother," "brother," "cost-of-living," "garbage," and "inflation" are all relational concepts. The mere presence of the attributes does not make them relational concepts; they must also stand in a particular kind of "relationship" to one another. Think for a minute of the relationship involved in each of these concepts.

Each exemplar of a conjunctive and relational concept has to contain all the essential attributes; an exemplar of a disjunctive concept may contain only one. In the following examples of the disjunctive concept "citizen," the "yeses" each contain a different attribute:

Mrs. Smith was born in Seattle, Washington.	YES
Jean Arendt grew up in New York; his family was originally from France and came to the United States after Jean was born in England.	NO
Ellen Santini is the daughter of the former U.S. ambassador to Peru. She was born in Peru while her father was on a tour of duty.	YES

The concept of citizen is defined as "being born in the United States or having parents who are U.S. citizens." Since the two positive examples of the concept are different, the student seeking to attain the concept would have to say to herself, "Hmm. It must be this and/or that." Bruner and his colleagues make the point that Western cultures are not oriented toward disjunctive concepts.

Try identifying the following concepts as either conjunctive (C), disjunctive (D), or relational (R):

_____ 1. Pen
_____ 2. Religion
_____ 3. Strike (in baseball)
_____ 4. Pair of scissors
_____ 5. Leftovers

Relational concepts are interesting because it is difficult to generate examples of them that clearly show the relationship in question. For example, a picture of a small boy with an adult woman does not clearly indicate the child-parent relationship, an essential attribute of the concept of mother. Be careful, then, when you are selecting your exemplars to utilize a medium that can convey the essential attributes. For example, you might want to add words to the picture that would represent typical parent-child communication. Remember, concepts and characteristics that are not concrete—that can't be seen, touched, heard, or smelled—usually cannot be shown adequately in pictures. A picture of a church, for example, is not a positive instance of the concept of religion because it does not contain all the essential attributes of "religion." In fact, for some religions a place of worship may not even be one of the essential attributes.

Most of the concepts we use are *concrete*: their attributes—objects, physical actions, verbal statements, and so on—can be apprehended by the senses. However, some concepts contain attributes that must be *inferred* by observation. Unless a marital relationship is stated explicitly, we can only infer it from a picture of a man and a woman. The existence of an emotion or value must be inferred from a person's actions or words. Similarly, political or religious stances, such as "radical," "orthodox," and "conservative," must be inferred from observed data. Concepts whose attributes must be inferred are more difficult to plan for and attain than observed concepts such as "table," "triangle," and "building."

Still other concepts are not only inferred but are *idealized*. Ideal concepts

> refer to such complex or large-scale, perfect phenomena that they have no representatives in reality. . . . Ideal-type concepts enable us to classify large masses of information. We classify nation-states, for example, into *technologically developed* and *technologically underdeveloped*. We refer to socialism, nationalism and free enterprise to describe large-scale events, social movements and trends that have something in common but are only loosely related.[14]

Abstractions such as "ghetto," "resort city," "radical," and "conservative" are ideal-type concepts. Ideal types are some of the most powerful and useful concepts we have. They are often the ones that are understood the most superficially and that are the most capable of clarification through Concept Attainment procedures. The selection and construction of exemplars for ideal-type concepts is tricky, and the purpose of Concept Attainment lessons built around ideal-type concepts can easily merge into value analysis and clarification, because the attributes or attribute-values of ideal-type concepts are not fixed and finite. The characteristics of justice, or of democracy, could be debated endlessly, and they have been by many philosophers. Some students would disagree with the teacher's classification of the United States as a positive example of democracy. The Concept Attainment Model for Unorganized Data is very suitable, if not essential, for ideal-type concepts, but the subtle shift in educational objective and expectation that is embodied in this model should be noted.

When you are planning Concept Attainment activity, you should note whether the concept is conjunctive, disjunctive, or relational, and whether it is concrete, inferred, or ideal-type. After determining these characteristics, alert yourself to the special features of the exemplars required for each, as well as the objective of the activity and the most appropriate Concept Attainment Model.

EXERCISE 8: TYPES OF CONCEPTS

List four concepts that you teach during the school year. Check whether the concept is conjunctive, disjunctive, or relational, and whether it is an ideal-type concept.

[14]Bruce Joyce, *New Strategies for Social Education* (Chicago: Science Research Associates, 1972), pp. 80-81. Reprinted by permission.

Concept

1. _____	___ Conjunctive	___ Disjunctive	___ Relational	___ Ideal-Type
2. _____	___ Conjunctive	___ Disjunctive	___ Relational	___ Ideal-Type
3. _____	___ Conjunctive	___ Disjunctive	___ Relational	___ Ideal-Type
4. _____	___ Conjunctive	___ Disjunctive	___ Relational	___ Ideal-Type

Distinguishing Concepts From Other Types of Content

Concepts are just one of several types of content. Others that are commonly referred to in educational literature are *facts*, *generalizations* (abstract relationships among several concepts), and *theories* (sets of related concepts and facts). Most educators believe that each of these types of content requires its own instructional approach. In recent years, educational critics have pointed out that educators and teachers have tended to treat all types of content in a similar fashion, usually memorizing theories, generalizations, and concepts as well as facts. Forming concepts, testing generalizations, and developing theories are very complex, active, intellectual processes that scientists and scholars often spend many years putting together.

A common source of confusion in the early stages of learning the Concept Attainment Model is the distinction between a generalization and a concept. A generalization "states some abstract relationship among several concepts, and . . . as such, it is more complex than any single component."[15]

The statement, "Intelligence is a product of heredity and environment," is a generalization made up of the concepts "heredity" and "environment" and the relationship "product." It is possible to teach the concept of intelligence without referring to this generalization about the origins of intelligence.

Concept Attainment Models are not optimal instructional processes for teaching generalizations. With respect to teaching generalizations, it is important to note that students should understand the concepts that make up a generalization if they are expected to work productively with it. If a student does not know the concept "status," do not teach the generalization that "different roles carry a different status." Concept Attainment Models are useful for teaching the concepts that are prerequisite to learning a generalization. Similarly, do not teach a concept if the student has not already acquired the criterial attributes. Don't teach the concept "ball" if the student does not know the concept "round," which is an essential attribute of "ball." Generalizations should not be confused with relational concepts, such as "strike" or "citizen," whose attributes bear a relationship to one another.

After you have selected the topic or concept you wish to teach, check to

---

[15]W. A. Brownell and G. Hendrickson, "How Children Learn Information Concepts and Generalizations," *Learning and Instruction: Part I: Forty-ninth Yearbook, National Society for the Study of Education* (Chicago: University of Chicago Press, 1950); quoted in Martorella, *Concept Learning*, pp. 121-22.

see that it is not a generalization and identify the type of concept it is. This procedure will prevent many problems later in the lesson and optimize learning for your students.

Summary

This section has discussed several essential ideas to consider in planning a Concept Attainment activity. These include the elements of a concept, which influence the selection of exemplars; the type of concept, which influences the modality of the exemplars; and the identification of a concept, in contrast with other kinds of content. We can see the influence and applicability of these ideas in the following example:

Ms. Herron is a behavioral science teacher at the high school level. She has planned a unit to help students understand some of the social forces underlying human behavior. To do this, she wants to draw on and teach such sociological concepts as "value," "norm," "folkway," "attitude," and "role." At first, Ms. Herron planned to use the Concept Attainment Model to help students learn that (1) for every role there are sets of expected behaviors and attitudes, and (2) a role is determined by the expectations of others. However, she quickly realized that these statements are generalizations, not concepts; that is, they state *relationships* among concepts. She also realized that the students were not yet familiar with the concepts "role" and "expectation." So she revised her plans, deciding to use the concept "sanction" in her initial Concept Attainment lesson.

Ms. Herron defined sanction as a punishment for violation of a rule (a norm, or perhaps a value). She quickly realized after jotting down the definition that "sanction" is a relational concept; that is, the punishment is given in relation to the violation. A behavior may be a sanction in one context and not a sanction in another context. For example, taking away the car keys from your son may be a punishment if there has been a violation, but it is not a punishment if you simply want to use the car. The realization that "sanction" is a relational concept was important in constructing the exemplars, because it meant that each of Ms. Herron's exemplars had to portray both the violation and the punishment.

Once she realized this, Ms. Herron began to think of the optimal medium for the exemplars. Still pictures would not do, because they do not clearly show a sequence of behaviors. The best medium was short film clips. Since these were not easily available, Ms. Herron wrote her own short vignettes, using description and dialogue. For one exemplar she chose a Peanuts cartoon that provided an illustration of a sanction. For another she wrote a description of an event that had occurred in the classroom a few weeks before. For a third she cut out a newspaper article reporting the outcome of a recent trial in which the defendant was judged guilty. Ms. Herron wanted her exemplars to illustrate a range of violations and sanctions, both formal and informal.

When you move into the Planning and Peer Teaching component, you will probably think through your lesson in much the same way that Ms. Herron did.

Although concept theory may seem complicated at first, it all falls into place when you plan a Concept Attainment lesson. The planning steps and their relationship to the issues discussed in this reading are summarized as follows:

Planning Step	Issue
Selecting the concept	Concepts versus generalizations
Analyzing the concepts	Distinguishing essential attributes from nonessential attributes Identifying the range of attribute-values
Determining objectives	Determining which model of Concept Attainment is best suited for the objectives
Selecting and preparing exemplars	Making sure positive exemplars contain all the essential attributes Establishing a range of positive exemplars Selecting positive *and* negative exemplars

THEORY CHECKUP FOR THE CONCEPT ATTAINMENT MODEL

Instructions: Circle the response that best answers the question or completes the statement. Check your answers with the key that follows the exercise.

1. The process of Concept Attainment is best described as
   a. putting data in new categories
   b. learning a new concept
   c. distinguishing the relevant attributes for placing data into defined classes
   d. naming a new concept

2. Concepts have six elements. Which of the following is *not* an element of concepts?
   a. name
   b. positive exemplar
   c. criterial attribute
   d. theory

3. Which of the following is an essential attribute of the concept of "flower"?
   a. yellow
   b. tail
   c. color
   d. decorative

4. As young children learn to speak, they acquire a vocabulary very quickly, putting names with objects and events. Would you use the Concept Attainment Model with a two-year old to teach these symbols?
   a. Yes
   b. No

5. What is the relationship between a rule and an attribute?
   a. Rules give examples of the concept.
   b. Rules are definitions that specify the essential and nonessential attributes of the concept.
   c. Rules specify the name of a concept.
   d. Rules state the essential attributes of the concept.

6. Shape is an essential attribute of a basketball. Is it an essential attribute of the concept of transportation?
   a. Yes
   b. No

7. Size is an essential attribute of the concept of adult. Five feet, six inches is a(n) _____ of the attribute "size."
   a. positive exemplar
   b. negative exemplar
   c. value
   d. attribute

8. If you walked into a classroom and saw the teacher presenting objects and asking students to say whether they were "yeses" or "nos," you would be observing what phase of the Concept Attainment Model?
   a. Phase Two: testing concept attainment
   b. Phase One: presentation of data and identification of concept

59

THEORY CHECKUP FOR THE CONCEPT ATTAINMENT MODEL

    c. Phase Four: analysis of concepts in unorganized data

    d. Phase Three: analysis of thinking (Concept Attainment strategies)

9. "Small" is what kind of concept?
    a. conjunctive
    b. disjunctive
    c. not a concept at all
    d. relational

10. Ms. Smith wanted to teach students the concept "public policy issue," so she developed a curriculum in which the students studied four current public policy issues during a period of six weeks. Criticize Ms. Smith's curriculum plans from the point of view of Bruner's theory of concepts.
    a. Sixth graders are too young to understand conjunctive concepts.
    b. Ms. Smith did not identify the essential attributes.
    c. There are no negative exemplars.
    d. Ms. Smith did not state the rule ahead of time.

11. What is the major difference between conjunctive and disjunctive concepts?
    a. Disjunctive concepts have a relationship to other concepts.
    b. Disjunctive concepts don't have all the attributes.
    c. Disjunctive concepts are not as powerful as conjunctive ones.
    d. Disjunctive concepts require the presence of some attributes and the absence of others.

12. Bob Jones was teaching a Concept Attainment lesson to his students. The concept was "capitalism." Bob showed his students several pictures. Some were of government buildings in the Soviet Union, others were of India and Cuba, and the rest, which consisted of scenes such as a steel mill and the Stock Exchange, were of the United States. The students could not grasp the attributes of the concept. What was the problem?
    a. The students did not understand English very well; their native language was Spanish.
    b. Bob did not have enough exemplars.
    c. The positive exemplars did not contain all the attributes of the concept.
    d. The students did not have an experimental base for the concept.

13. The following statement, "Intelligence is a product of heredity and environment," is a
    a. concept
    b. fact
    c. skill
    d. generalization

14. "Japanese students scored higher on math than other national groups, whereas Swedish students did better in English composition." This statement is a
    a. theory
    b. generalization
    c. concept
    d. datum

15. If you want to present the rule first, you would use which concept learning model?
    a. Taba's Inductive Thinking Model

THEORY CHECKUP FOR THE CONCEPT ATTAINMENT MODEL

    b. Ausubel's Advance Organizer Model
    c. Suchman's Inquiry Training Model
    d. Bruner's Concept Attainment Model

16. Which characteristic is *not* related to the difficulty of a concept?
    a. scope
    b. number of generalizations in which the concept is used
    c. type of concept
    d. concreteness

Theory Checkup Key

1. c	5. d	9. d	13. d
2. d	6. b	10. c	14. d
3. c	7. c	11. d	15. b
4. b	8. a	12. c	16. b

Component II

VIEWING
THE MODEL

One of the purposes of Component II is to provide examples of actual sessions in which the Concept Attainment Model is the strategy being used. Reading the demonstration transcript that follows, hearing a tape of a teacher and students, or viewing a live demonstration are alternative means of illustrating the "model in action."

As you study any of these alternatives, you will be introduced to the Teaching Analysis Guide for analyzing the model. This same Guide will also be used in Component III to analyze the peer teaching and microteaching lessons. We want you to become familiar with the Guide now, however, as it will sharpen your perception of the demonstration lesson.

The two activities in this component are (1) reading the Teaching Analysis Guide and (2) viewing (reading) the lesson. Before going on to them, you may wish to reread the material in the Introduction to this book that discusses the purposes and philosophy of the Teaching Analysis Guide.

Analyzing Teaching: Activity 1

The Teaching Analysis Guide involves much more than simply checking for the occurrence of the phases. The eighteen questions in this Guide cover all the basic activities of the model—the implementation and organization of the lesson, the selection of material, and the focusing moves that prompt students to examine the attributes of the concept.

The first Concept Attainment lessons for both teacher and student probably will not reflect all the items in the Guide, nor should they. For example, it is unlikely that the beginning stages of Concept Attainment will include any in-depth exploration of thinking strategies (Phase Three). It may not be possible to attend to this phase at all, as there are too many other new skills for students to use. It is best to view the items in the Guide as heuristic, in the sense that they suggest the kinds of moves or processes that the teacher and students should work toward as both acquire proficiency with the model. On the other hand, the items are diagnostic in that they pinpoint areas of difficulty you may have observed in the lesson.

The major problem areas in this model, as reflected in the eighteen items, are:

1. implementation of basic model activities (presentation and identification of concept-testing Concept Attainment)
2. exploration of the elements of the concept
3. planning (selection and design of materials)
4. organization of the lesson

Read through the items in the Teaching Analysis Guide that follows. Identify the items you do not understand. Try to determine which of the four areas listed above the items refer to. Discuss any difficulties you may have with your instructor or with a peer.

TEACHING ANALYSIS GUIDE FOR THE
RECEPTION MODEL OF CONCEPT ATTAINMENT

This Guide is designed to help you analyze the process of teaching as you practice the Reception Model of Concept Attainment. The analysis focuses on aspects of teaching that are important to the syntax of the model, the teacher's role, and specific teaching skills.

The Guide consists of a series of questions and phrases. As you observe a practice session (whether peer teaching or microteaching), analyze the teaching using the rating scale that appears opposite each question and statement. This scale uses the following items:

Thoroughly. This item signifies that the teacher engaged in the behavior to the point where students were responding comfortably and fluently. Appropriateness varies from situation to situation. For example, young children may need more assistance in describing the exemplars than older ones.

Partially. This item signifies that the teacher engaged in appropriate behavior, but not as thoroughly as possible. There is some doubt about whether the students are responding fully.

Missing. The teacher did not engage in the behavior; there appears to be a loss in student response or probably will be one.

Not Needed. The teacher did not explicitly manifest the behavior, but there is no loss. Either the behavior was included in others or the students began to respond appropriately without being led to.

For each question or statement in the Guide, circle the term that best describes the teacher's behavior.

PHASE ONE: Presentation of Data and Identification of the Concept

1. Did the teacher state the purpose of the game?   Thoroughly   Partially   Missing   Not Needed

2. Did the teacher explain the procedures of the game (how the "yeses" and "nos" function)?   Thoroughly   Partially   Missing   Not Needed

3. Did the initial "yes" clearly contain the essential attributes?   Thoroughly   Partially   Missing   Not Needed

4. If teaching a conjunctive concept, did the teacher begin with a "yes" exemplar?   Thoroughly   Partially   Missing   Not Needed

   or

   If teaching a disjunctive concept, did the teacher begin with a "no" exemplar followed by a "yes"?   Thoroughly   Partially   Missing   Not Needed

5. Did the teacher ask questions that focused students' thinking on the essential attributes?   Thoroughly   Partially   Missing   Not Needed

6. Did the teacher ask the students to compare the "yes" exemplars?   Thoroughly   Partially   Missing   Not Needed

7. Did the teacher ask the students to contrast the attributes of the "yes" exemplars with those of the "no" exemplars?   Thoroughly   Partially   Missing   Not Needed

TEACHING ANALYSIS GUIDE FOR THE
RECEPTION MODEL OF CONCEPT ATTAINMENT

8. Did the teacher present labeled exemplars?	Thoroughly	Partially	Missing	Not Needed
9. Did the teacher ask the students to generate and test hypotheses about the identity of the concept?	Thoroughly	Partially	Missing	Not Needed
10. Did the teacher ask the students to name the concept?	Thoroughly	Partially	Missing	Not Needed
11. Did the teacher ask the students to state the essential attributes of the concept?	Thoroughly	Partially	Missing	Not Needed

PHASE TWO: Testing Attainment of the Concept

12. After the concept was agreed upon, did the teacher present additional exemplars and ask whether they contained the concept?	Thoroughly	Partially	Missing	Not Needed
13. Did the teacher ask the students to justify their answers?	Thoroughly	Partially	Missing	Not Needed
14. Were the students able to supply their own exemplars to fit the concept?	Thoroughly	Partially	Missing	Not Needed
15. Did the teacher ask the students to justify their exemplars by identifying the essential attributes?	Thoroughly	Partially	Missing	Not Needed

PHASE THREE: Analysis of Thinking Strategies

16. Did the teacher ask the students to describe the thinking processes they used in attaining the concept?	Thoroughly	Partially	Missing	Not Needed
17. Did the teacher ask the students to reflect on the roles of attributes and concepts in their thinking strategies?	Thoroughly	Partially	Missing	Not Needed
18. Did the teacher ask the students to evaluate the effectiveness of their strategies?	Thoroughly	Partially	Missing	Not Needed

Viewing the Lesson: Activity 2

In this section you are asked to read the demonstration transcript that follows, identifying the phases of the model and commenting on the lesson as an illustration of the model. On your own or with a group of your peers, record the phases and comment on the model as it is presented here. You may want to focus on the adequacy of each phase, the quality of the examplars, the nature of the concept, and the skillful moves that the teacher made (or did not make).

Phase One	Adequate	Minimal	Not at All
Phase Two	Adequate	Minimal	Not at All
Phase Three	Adequate	Minimal	Not at All

65

Analyzing the Lesson: Activity 3 (optional)

View a live or taped demonstration and analyze it by completing the Teaching Analysis Guide. This can be done in two ways: either complete the form as the lesson is being viewed, or complete it afterwards. If you are viewing the lesson in a group, you may want to divide the task of analysis with one or more of the others, each person taking a particular phase or aspect of the analysis. Duplicate as many copies of the Guide as are needed.

DEMONSTRATION TRANSCRIPT: CONCEPT ATTAINMENT

The transcript you will read was taught by Muata to a group of upper elementary students at Rogers School, Alum Rock, California. The concept is topography. Notice how Muata skillfully guides the students in the attainment process, getting them away from random guessing to a careful testing of hypotheses against the negative and positive examples.

T: NOW, WE'RE GOING TO PLAY A GAME, ONLY NOW WE'RE GOING TO USE SOME PICTURES. I HAVE PURPOSELY TURNED THEM SO THAT YOU CAN'T SEE THEM, 'CAUSE I DON'T WANT YOU TO SEE THEM AHEAD OF TIME. THERE'S OUR FIRST "YES." YOU WANT TO TELL WHAT IT IS?

Phase I: Presentation of Data and Concept

Teacher presents labeled examples.

S: A DOUGHNUT.

T: IT'S A DOUGHNUT. NO, YOU DON'T HAVE TO WRITE DOUGHNUT. YOU MIGHT WRITE A GUESS AS TO WHAT IT IS. ANYBODY HAVE A GUESS AS TO WHAT THE "YESES" ARE?

S: PASTRIES.

First hypothesis

T: PASTRIES, OK, THAT'S ONE GUESS. SO YOU MIGHT WRITE PASTRY DOWN FOR "YES." IT'S WRONG, OF COURSE, BUT YOU MIGHT WRITE IT DOWN. LET'S TAKE A LOOK AT ANOTHER ONE. SO FAR PASTRY MIGHT BE A GOOD GUESS. WHAT IS THAT? ANYBODY RECOGNIZE 'EM?

S: CUP.

T: A BOWL, I'D CALL IT. IT DEPENDS ON HOW BIG IT IS AS TO WHETHER IT'S A CUP OR A BOWL. LET'S JUST CALL IT A BOWL. OK. SO FAR THE PASTRY IS HOLDING OUT. OOOPS, THERE'S A "YES." WHAT IS THAT?

S: IS IT A CUP?

T: IT'S A CUP. OK. LET'S PUT ANOTHER ONE UP. CHAIR, I THINK THAT WAS CLEAR WHAT THAT IS. ALL RIGHT. NOW, DO YOU HAVE ANY GUESSES? PASTRY WE'RE GOING TO HAVE TO RULE OUT. OK? ANY OTHER GUESSES WHAT IT MIGHT BE?

S: FOR BREAKFAST.

T: THINGS YOU HAVE FOR BREAKFAST, OR THAT YOU MIGHT BE SETTING ON THE BREAKFAST TABLE. A BOWL MIGHT BE ON THE BREAKFAST TABLE FULL OF CEREAL, WOULDN'T IT?

S: AND YOU'D BE SITTING ON A CHAIR.

T: AND YOU MIGHT BE SITTING ON A CHAIR. OK. LET'S SEE. LET'S PULL SOMETHING THAT DOESN'T HAVE A LABEL ON IT. ANYBODY KNOW WHAT THAT IS?

S: A HAT.

T: IT'S A HAT. WHERE SHOULD IT GO? "YES" OR "NO"?

S: "YES."

S: "NO."

T: TAKE A LOOK HERE. TAKE A LOOK HERE. WHERE SHOULD IT GO? DOES IT BELONG OVER HERE, OR DOES IT BELONG OVER HERE?

S: IT BELONGS OVER HERE.

T: YOU SAY IT BELONGS OVER HERE. HOW MANY PEOPLE SAY IT BELONGS ON THE "YES"? OK, EVERYBODY EXCEPT, OOP, NO, KENT. NOW EVERYBODY IS WRONG. OK?

S: WRONG?

T: IT BELONGS ON THE "NOS."

S: OOOOH.

T: OOOOH, ISN'T THAT TERRIBLE? HERE WE HAVE SOMETHING THAT LOOKS LIKE A TENNIS RACKET WITHOUT ANY STRINGS ON IT.

S: A MAGNIFYING GLASS.

T: NO, IT'S NOT A MAGNIFYING GLASS, BECAUSE IT DOESN'T HAVE ANYTHING IN HERE. IT COULD BE THE FRAME FOR A MAGNIFYING GLASS, OK, BUT THIS HAS NOTHING IN IT.

S: THE FRAME OF A MIRROR.

T: THERE'S NOTHING IN THAT PART OF IT. OK, IT'S LIKE A TENNIS RACKET WITHOUT ANY STRINGS. OK. CAN EVERYONE SEE IT? "YES" OR "NO"? BRETT?

S: "NO"?

T: YOU WANT TO PUT IT ON THE "NO"? EVERYBODY WANT TO BE WITH BRETT THIS TIME? HE STEERED YOU WRONG LAST TIME. HOW MANY PEOPLE WILL SAY IT BELONGS ON THE "NO" SIDE? OK. HOW MANY PEOPLE SAY "YES"? OK. ONE BRAVE PERSON SAYS "YES," AND THE BRAVE PERSON IS RIGHT.

S: HEH.

T: OK, NOW TAKE A LOOK. HERE WE HAVE A DOUGH-NUT, A CUP, AND A RACKET. YOU DON'T HAVE TO WRITE DOWN THE NAMES. WHAT YOU SHOULD BE WRITING DOWN ARE SOME GUESSES AS TO WHAT MAKES SOMETHING "YES" AND WHAT MAKES IT "NO." WHAT DO YOU WANT TO SEE NEXT? A "YES" OR "NO"? I'LL LET YOU DECIDE.

S: A "YES."

S: "YES."

T: "YES." ANYBODY WANT TO SEE ANOTHER "YES"?

S: PICNIC, AH, PICNIC. . .

Testing hypothesis

T: YEAH, IT'S A BASKET, A PICNIC BASKET IS RIGHT. A BASKET. OK. NOW LET'S BOUNCE THAT OFF WITH A "NO." WHAT IS THAT?

S: A FLOWER VASE?

T: FLOWER VASE. NOW, LET'S TAKE A LOOK AT THEM. WHAT'S "YES" AND WHAT'S "NO"? WHAT MAKES OBJECTS "YES" AND WHAT MAKES OBJECTS "NO"? ANYBODY HAVE ANY OTHER GUESSES? LET'S SEE, WHAT DID WE RULE OUT SO FAR? WE RULED OUT PASTRY. ANYBODY ELSE HAVE ANY OTHER GUESSES?

S: SOMETHING YOU MIGHT TAKE ON A PICNIC.

T: SOMETHING YOU MIGHT TAKE ON A PICNIC. ANYBODY HAVE ANY FEEL FOR WHETHER THAT'S RIGHT OR NOT? BRETT, LET'S DEAL WITH THAT RIGHT NOW. SOMETHING WE MIGHT TAKE ON A PICNIC. DOES THAT FIT ALL THE "YESES," SOMETHING WE MIGHT TAKE ON A PICNIC?

S: YEAH.

T: OK, ARE ALL THE "NOS" SOMETHING WE WOULDN'T TAKE ON A PICNIC?

S: WOULDN'T TAKE A CHAIR.

S: YOU MIGHT TAKE A CHAIR ON A PICNIC.

T: YEAH, YOU MIGHT TAKE, MAYBE NOT THAT KIND OF CHAIR.

S: A VASE.

T: YOU MIGHT TAKE A VASE, MAYBE NOT A FLOWER VASE, BUT YOU MIGHT TAKE A BOWL. IF WE'RE GOING TO DO SOME BARBEQUEING WE MIGHT TAKE A CHEF'S HAT. OK, SO IT'S NOT SOMETHING WE MIGHT TAKE ON A PICNIC. ANY OTHER?

S: LOOKS LIKE ALL THE "NOS" GO ON A TABLE, AND THERE'S A COOK, AND THERE'S A FLOWER VASE ON THE TABLE, AND ALL THE "YESES," THERE'S LIKE A TENNIS RACKET, AND A...

T: (laughter) DON'T STRETCH IT, DON'T STRETCH IT. YOU SAY YOU MIGHT PUT A CUP AND A DOUGHNUT ON A TABLE. OK, LET'S PICK OUT SOME MORE AND SEE IF WE CAN TELL WHERE IT GOES. THERE'S A GARDEN HOSE. "YES" OR "NO"?

S: "NO."

T: "YES." I THINK I'M GOING TO STOP AFTER THIS ONE. YOU GOING TO LET ME STOP HERE?

S: NO.

T: NO? OK. WHOOPS. THAT'S SUPPOSED TO BE... CAN YOU TELL WHAT IT IS?

S: A CASE.

S: IT MIGHT BE A BOX.

T: IT'S A BOX OR A BLOCK. LET'S CALL IT A WOODEN BLOCK. IS THAT A "YES" OR A "NO"?

S: "NO."

T: IT'S A "NO." RIGHT! IS THAT A GUESS OR DID YOU HAVE SOMETHING IN MIND?

S: GUESS.

T: THAT WAS A GUESS. OK. WELL, TAKE A LOOK HERE. WHAT ABOUT THIS ONE? WHAT'S IT?

S: A BOTTLE.

T: IT'S A BOTTLE. IS IT MORE LIKE THE "YESES" OR IS IT MORE LIKE THE "NOS"?

S: THE "YESES."

S: NO.

T: OK, IT'S A "NO." AH-HAH! ALL RIGHT, COME ON YOU GUYS, WATCH IT! HERE'S ANOTHER "YES." WHAT'S THAT?

S: THAT'S A TIRE.

T: A TIRE, IT'S AN AUTOMOBILE TIRE. JUST THE RUBBER PART OF IT. NOT THE WHEEL, JUST A TIRE. TAKE A LOOK AT THE "YESES" NOW. GARDEN HOSE, AN AUTOMOBILE TIRE, A DOUGHNUT, CUP, TENNIS RACKET WITHOUT THE STRINGS, PICNIC BASKET. WHAT DO THEY HAVE IN COMMON?

S: YOU COULD BUY THEM ALL AT A STORE.

T: YOU COULD BUY ALL AT A STORE. YES, YOU COULD BUY A BOTTLE AT THE STORE, AND A BOWL AT THE STORE, AND A VASE, AND A CUP, I MEAN A CAP. OH, YOU HAVE ANOTHER GUESS?

S: THEY'RE ALL ROUND.

T: THEY'RE ROUND. WHERE ARE THEY ROUND?

S: THE TENNIS RACKET, ON THE TOP, THE BASKET IS ON THE HANDLE, THE CUP'S ON THE TOP, THE DOUGHNUT'S ON THE. . .THE WHOLE DOUGHNUT, THE HOSE IS THE WHOLE HOSE.

T: THAT'S GOOD, THEY ALL HAVE SOMETHING ROUND ABOUT THEM, BUT. . .

S: THE BOTTLE IS ROUND.

S: THE BOWL IS ROUND.

S: AND THE BOTTLE.

S: THE BOTTLE.

S: IT'S NOT ROUND.

T: THAT'S A GOOD THING TO LOOK FOR, THOUGH. THEY DO HAVE. . .NOW CONCENTRATE ON WHAT HE WAS LOOKING AT, THOUGH. THERE'S THE HANDLE ON THE PICNIC BASKET, THE FRAME FOR THE MAGNIFYING GLASS OR TENNIS RACKET, I THINK YOU'RE AFTER THE RIGHT THING. YOU'RE AT THE RIGHT PART, BUT IT'S NOT BECAUSE IT'S ROUND. THERE'S SOMETHING ELSE ABOUT IT. SOMETHING ELSE ABOUT IT. NOT ROUND, BUT THAT'S A GOOD WAY TO LOOK. HERE'S ANOTHER "NO." IT'S A SHOE; IT'S ACTUALLY A SLIPPER. WE'LL CALL IT A SLIPPER. NOW, BRETT, YOU'RE ON THE RIGHT TRACK; YOU'RE LOOKING AT THE RIGHT THING. DO THESE HAVE THOSE KINDS OF THINGS?

S: NOT ALL OF THEM.

T: NOT ALL OF THEM. WHICH ONES DO HAVE?

S: THE BOTTLE, THE BOWL, THE HAT, AND THE VASE.

T: SO MAYBE IT'S NOT THAT ROUND PART OF IT THAT'S IMPORTANT. MAYBE IT'S SOMETHING ELSE. MAYBE IT'S NOT THIS PART OF THE CUP, OR JUST THIS PART.

S: OR THE BOTTOM.

T: OR THE BOTTOM, YEAH. THE BOTTOM WOULD BE KINDA LIKE THIS BOTTOM, WOULDN'T IT? I THINK WE'RE LOOKING AT THE RIGHT THING NOW. THERE'S SOMETHING ABOUT EACH OBJECT THAT THESE HAVE IN COMMON THAT THESE DON'T. LET ME PULL OUT SOME MORE WITHOUT ANY NAMES ON THEM.

S: ON THE "NOS."

T: ON THE "NOS," RIGHT! WHY DON'T YOU PUT IT OVER THERE ON THE "NOS."

S: THAT'S A BOX.

T: THAT'S A BOX.

S: A JUG.

T: THAT'S A JUG.

S: IT WOULD GO ON THE "YESES."

T: OK, HOW MANY PEOPLE SAY YES? YOU GUYS ARE RIGHT AGAIN. HOW DO THESE BOTTLES DIFFER, THOUGH?

S: THAT ONE HAS A HANDLE LIKE A CUP.

T: WHY DID YOU STOP, BRETT?

S: I THOUGHT THAT ALL THESE HAD A HANDLE AND ALL THESE DIDN'T.

T: AND?

S: THE DOUGHNUT DOESN'T, THE HOSE DOESN'T AND THE TIRE DOESN'T.

T: THEY DON'T? WELL, OK.

S: THE VASE DOES HAVE A HANDLE.

T: DOES IT?

S: RIGHT HERE. TWO OF 'EM.

T: IT HAS TWO OF 'EM, OK. THESE HAVE HOLES. LET'S SEE. THERE'S A HOLE, THERE'S A HOLE HERE, THERE'S A HOLE IN THE TIRE, THERE'S A HOLE HERE, THERE'S A HOLE THERE, THERE'S A HOLE THERE, AND A HOLE THERE. WOW, THAT LOOKS PRETTY GOOD. ALL OF THEM HAVE HOLES. JEANNETTE JUST POINTED OUT THAT THEY ALL HAVE HOLES.

S: THERE'S A HOLE HERE.

T: THESE DON'T HAVE HOLES. THE BOTTLE HAS A HOLE? WHERE'S THE HOLE IN THE BOTTLE?

S: THE TOP.

S: THE TOP.

Definition according to essential attributes.

T: IS THAT A HOLE?

S: THAT DON'T GO THROUGH.

T: SEE, IT DOESN'T GO THROUGH.

S: THIS DOES.

T: AH, THAT DOES. LET'S PULL THAT ASIDE FOR A SECOND. PULL THAT CLOSER TO YOU. AND WHAT ABOUT THE REST OF THEM? DO THEY HAVE HOLES?

S: THIS ONE.

T: AH, LET'S PUT THAT ONE DOWN WITH THAT ONE. PUT THAT ONE DOWN. NOW, HOW ABOUT THESE? DO THESE HAVE HOLES?

S: NO.

T: NOPE. NOW LET'S LOOK AT THOSE. WHAT'S DIFFERENT ABOUT THOSE AS OPPOSED TO THE HOLES OVER HERE?

S: THEY DON'T HAVE CIRCLES.

T: LET'S LOOK AT SOME MORE. I THINK YOU'RE ON THE RIGHT TRACK, THOUGH, JEANNETTE.

S: A VISOR.

T: IT'S A VISOR. IT'S A "YES." WHAT ABOUT THE HOLE ATTRIBUTE? DOES THAT SCORE FOR THAT ONE?

S: YEAH.

S: YEAH.

T: GOOD, DOES HAVE A HOLE. HOW ABOUT THIS ONE?

S: "NO."

T: IT'S A BALL, AND IT'S A "NO."

S: I THINK IT'S A "YES."

T: NO, IT'S A "NO." WHAT ABOUT THIS ONE?

S: THAT'S A "YES."

S: "YES."

T: AH, IT'S A "YES."

S: WHAT IS IT, ANYHOW?

T: WHAT IS IT? YEAH, THAT'S A GOOD QUESTION. IT'S LIKE A KINDA DOUGHNUT YOU WOULDN'T EAT. A PLASTIC DOUGHNUT. A TOY FOR A LITTLE BABY, TEETHING RING, SOMETHING LIKE THAT. WHAT ABOUT THIS ONE?

S: "YES."

T: OH, IT HAS TO BE. (laughter) WHY DON'T YOU PUT IT DOWN THERE BY THE OTHER THINGS? KEEP IT ON THIS TABLE.

S: THIS HAS TWO HANDLES, AND THE PHONE HAS ONE.

T: HAS ONE, OK. NOW, WHAT ABOUT THIS ONE THAT ALSO HAD HOLES ON IT? IS THAT MORE LIKE THAT ONE OR IS IT MORE LIKE THESE?

S: WHICH ONE?

Phase II: Testing Attainment of Concept

Identifying additional unlabeled examples.

T: THE CHAIR. WELL, WE SEE IT'S A "NO," BUT WHY IS THAT MORE LIKE THAT VASE THAN IT IS LIKE THE OTHER THINGS?

T: I THINK JEANNETTE GOT IT AGAIN. WHAT'D YOU SAY, JEANNETTE?

S: IT HAS TWO HOLES?

T: IT HAS AT LEAST TWO HOLES; IT HAS REALLY MORE THAN TWO, DOESN'T IT? THESE ARE ALL HOLES HERE, AREN'T THEY, BETWEEN?

S: THE BOTTOM.

T: IT HAS HOLES ON THE BOTTOM. SO IT HAS REALLY MORE THAN ONE. OK, HERE'S THE LAST "NO." NOW, DOES THIS FIT THE OTHER "NOS," IN TERMS OF THE HOLES?

S: YES.

T: OK, NOW I THINK YOU'VE GO IT. SO WHAT IS THE CONCEPT? WHO CAN DESCRIBE WHAT MAKES SOMETHING A "YES" AND WHAT MAKES SOME-THING A "NO," IN THEIR OWN WORDS?

S: THIS IS LIKE THE SAME AS THIS, BECAUSE YOU CAN GO THROUGH THIS, AND THIS TOO.

T: OKAY, THERE'S A HOLE.

S: YOU CAN DO THE SAME WITH THIS ONE TOO.

T: THEY ALL HAVE HOLES, HUH?

S: YEAH.

T: HOW DO HOLES ON THESE OBJECTS DIFFER FROM THE "NO" OBJECTS THAT DO HAVE HOLES?

S: THAT'S ONLY GOT ONE HOLE AND THAT HAS TWO.

T: OK. THE "YES" ONES HAVE...DO ALL THE "YESES" JUST HAVE ONE HOLE?

S: YEAH.

T: MY!

S: AND THE OTHER ONES HAVE MORE THAN TWO.

T: TWO OR MORE.

S: TWO OR MORE.

T: OK, SO THAT'S THE SECRET. ALL THE OBJECTS THAT ARE "YES" ARE SOLID OBJECTS THAT HAVE ONE HOLE; ALL THE OBJECTS THAT ARE "NO" ARE SOLID OBJECTS THAT EITHER HAVE NO HOLES OR MORE THAN ONE HOLE. SO "YES" OBJECTS ARE THE ONES THAT HAVE ONE HOLE. OK. WE HAVE A NICE, BIG WORD FOR THAT, IF YOU'RE INTERESTED. HAVE YOU EVER HEARD OF TOPOLOGY?

S: NO.

S: NO.

T: NO? TOPOLOGY. EVER HEARD OF GEOMETRY?

S: YES.

T: WELL, GEOMETRY IS, WELL, LET ME PUT IT THE OTHER WAY AROUND. TOPOLOGY IS A TYPE OF

GEOMETRY. IT'S A GENERALIZATION OF GEOM-
ETRY. AND IN TOPOLOGY WE LOOK AT OBJECTS,
AND WE CLASSIFY THEM IN SEVERAL WAYS, AND
ONE OF THE WAYS IN WHICH WE CLASSIFY THEM
IS WHETHER THEY HAVE HOLES OR NOT, AND IF
THEY DO HAVE HOLES, HOW MANY THEY HAVE
IN THEM. AND THE IDEA IS THAT, IF THESE
THINGS WERE ALL MADE OUT OF, SAY, SILLY
PUTTY OR SOMETHING, YOU COULD TAKE ONE
AND MAKE THE OTHER ONE OUT OF IT WITHOUT
CHANGING THE HOLE, OR WITHOUT TEARING IT
OR PUTTING A NEW HOLE IN IT. AND IF ALL
THESE OBJECTS, EXCEPT THE ONES THAT DON'T
HAVE HOLES IN THEM, WERE MADE OUT OF SILLY
PUTTY, YOU COULD REMOLD THEM AND MAKE
THEM INTO ANY OF THE OTHER OBJECTS WITH-
OUT TEARING IT. AND THE SAME THING WITH
THE WATER ONE. YOU COULD TAKE SOMETHING
WITH TWO HOLES IN IT AND MAKE IT INTO SOME-
THING ELSE WITH TWO HOLES IN IT WITHOUT
DESTROYING THE HOLES.

SO THAT WAS THE SECRET, AND THE BIG WORD
IS THINGS THAT ARE TOPOLOGICALLY EQUI-
VALENT TO THIS ONE OR THIS ONE ARE CALLED
A TORUS. THE TOPOLOGICAL EQUIVALENT TO A
TORUS.

Component III

PLANNING

AND

PEER TEACHING

In this component, you will plan a lesson using the Reception Model of Concept Attainment and then teach this lesson to a small group of peers, evaluating the lesson with the aid of the Teaching Analysis Guide.

Four steps in planning and organizing Concept Attainment lessons have been identified. Short discussions of the considerations involved in each of these steps are provided to guide you through the planning of a Concept Attainment lesson. The four planning steps are:

1. selecting the concept
2. analyzing the concept
3. determining objectives
4. preparing exemplars

The sections on these planning steps should be read in conjunction with the preparation of the peer teaching lesson and the completion of the Planning Guide at the end of this section. Planning step 2 (analyzing the concept) corresponds to Parts I and II of the Planning Guide; Step 3 (determining objectives) corresponds to Part III; and Step 4 (preparing exemplars) corresponds to Part IV. As you read each of these sections, you are asked to carry out that step and complete the corresponding part of the Planning Guide.

Step 1 (selecting the concept) details possible criteria for determining the appropriateness, worth, and difficulty of a concept. If you already have in mind a concept to teach and you feel comfortable that you can readily identify the concepts in your subject area, feel free to skip this discussion and proceed to the discussion of Step 2. However, at some point you should return to this material, for it will assist you in long-term curriculum planning efforts and help you make choices among concepts to teach or to emphasize through Concept Attainment activities.

The planning sequence in this component is based on the Reception Model of Concept Attainment. We feel that if you can plan in terms of the Reception Model, you should be able to transfer those skills to the Selection Model and to the analysis of concepts in unorganized data.

After you plan the lesson you will peer teach it to a small group of colleagues. Select a topic (concept) that is appropriate for adults, but if you wish, one that may also be used later when you microteach with students. We recommend this because if the topic is too easy, the peer teaching will not reflect the realities of the model. On the other hand, some concepts that seem simple at first aren't so easy in actuality. It shouldn't be difficult to find concepts suitable for both adults and students.

A summary of the sequence of activities in this component includes:

I. Planning the lesson
   Step 1: selecting the concept (optional reading)
   Step 2: analyzing the concept (reading; completing the Planning Guide)
   Step 3: determining objectives (reading; completing the Planning Guide)
   Step 4: preparing exemplars (reading; completing the Planning Guide)
II. Peer teaching
III. Analyzing the peer teaching using the Teaching Analysis Guide
IV. Microteaching

SELECTING THE CONCEPT

Four activities are involved in selecting a concept:

1. locating a concept
2. determining if it is a concept
3. deciding if it is worth teaching
4. deciding if it is appropriate for the learner(s)

Each of these activities is treated in the following discussion.

Locating Concepts

In reality, most teachers do not choose the concepts they teach. The selection is determined by the authors of textbooks or curriculum guides. However, we feel that as more and more teachers become aware of conceptual learning and the nature of concepts, they will become better able to design their own units of study or to determine which of the many concepts covered in the prescribed curriculum warrant special instruction by means of Concept Attainment activities. Textbooks and curriculum guides are notorious for "concept overload." Where this occurs, students are not exposed to the attributes of the concepts or to a variety of exemplars; they are not given sufficient instruction in attaining and applying the concept.

For most of you, the task of selecting a concept is the task of recognizing the concepts you are already teaching and then deciding which ones are of most worth and relevance. Each discipline or subject area has a conceptual framework that embraces the major concepts in that field of study. These concepts consist of the key ideas or terms that are used repeatedly by scholars to describe the phenomena they study, whether these are human social behaviors, small animals, chemical reactions, novels, mathematics, or the elements of grammar. As an example, Figure 1 presents a list of key concepts in several subject areas.

Literature	Math	Economics
mood	sets	economic activities
theme	numbers	production
plot	order	consumption
character	relations	exchange
antagonist	operations	distribution
protagonist	measurement	capital accumulation
style	base	economic analysis
	place	supply
	equations	demand
	mathematical systems	scarcity
		wants
		needs
		goods
		services

Figure 1. *A Selection of Key Concepts.*

Not all the concepts we teach come from the key concepts of the disciplines. Some refer to common objects, events, and relationships in the environment— concepts such as "newspaper," "over-under," "above-below," "festival," and "holiday." Other concepts come from applied fields that we do not think of as disciplines, such as concepts of law—"justice," "due process," "equality," and "the Constitution." Still other concepts are cross-disciplinary, particularly those related to social problems.

Figure 2 presents a list of concepts that James Banks, a noted leader in the ethnic studies field, recommends be included in an approach to the topic of ethnic studies.[1]

One line of thinking holds that the key concepts in a subject area are the most powerful concepts—they explain more phenomena—and therefore the ones we should be teaching. In the next few pages we discuss some of the factors you might

Discipline	Key Concepts	Discipline	Key Concepts
Anthropology	culture	History	immigration
	culture diversity		migration
	acculturation		change
	forced acculturation	Political Science	power
	cultural assimilation		powerless
	race		separatism
	racial mixture		oppression
	subculture		social protest
	syncretism		interest group
	melting pot		legitimacy
	cultural genocide		authority
	ethnocentrism		power elite
Economics	scarcity		colony
	poverty		colonized
	production		rebellion
	consumption	Psychology	identity
	capitalism		aggression
	economic exploitation		repression
Geography	ethnic enclave		displacement
	region	Sociology	discrimination
	ghetto		ethnic group
	inner city		ethnic minority group
	location		prejudice
			racism
			socialization
			status
			values

Figure 2. *Organizing Concepts for Ethnic Studies Curriculums (from James A. Banks,* Teaching Strategies for Ethnic Studies, *Boston: Allyn and Bacon, 1975, p. 64).*

[1]Identifying and organizing historical concepts is especially difficult because history does not possess unique concepts but uses concepts from *all* social science disciplines to study human behavior in the *past*. For a further discussion of this point, see James A. Banks, "Teaching Black History with a Focus on Decision-Making," *Social Education*, 35 (November 1971), 740-45, 820-21. Reprinted with permission of the National Council for the Social Studies and James A Banks.

want to consider in selecting concepts, but first, reflect on your subject area(s). In the space below, list some of the concepts you are already teaching. As each factor is discussed, you can relate that factor to your list of concepts.

EXERCISE 1

List here ten concepts you are presently teaching in any *one* subject area. If you teach more than one subject, select concepts from one subject area. Then, select one of these concepts (or a concept not listed) to peer teach. Record the concept you have chosen to teach on the Planning Guide.

1.
2.
3.
4.
5.
6.
7.
8.
9.
10.

Is It a Concept?

One of the most common planning mistakes of teachers who are trying out the Concept Attainment Model for the first time is their selection of a generalization instead of a concept. Using the model as we have explained it, students would have difficulty attaining a generalization. For this reason, we are asking you to make sure that your idea is, indeed, a concept. Remember that a generalization states a relationship among several concepts. The statement in the following example is a generalization. The concepts included in the generalization appear below it.

Statement: *Prices* are determined by *supply* and *demand.*
Concepts: prices
                supply
                demand

Look again at the "idea" you selected to peer teach. Is it a concept or a generalization?

Is the Concept Worth Teaching?

There are probably many ways to determine the worth of a concept. Objectively speaking, no one way is any better than another. Timeliness, significance in the student's current or past life experience, and usefulness are all possible considerations. The criteria we will introduce here, however, have to do with the body of knowledge from which the concept is drawn. In using these criteria, we are acknowledging our belief that it is important to teach the key concepts of a discipline or quasi-discipline.

As we mentioned earlier, each subject area has its own conceptual structure.

The concepts in a subject area can be organized into related hierarchical clusters, the broadest, most inclusive concepts appearing at the top of the hierarchy. As an example, Figure 3 lists some major concepts within the discipline of anthropology.

Level I	Level II	Level III
culture	human ecology	
	culture type	material culture
		nonmaterial culture
		secular culture
		traditional culture
		peasant culture
		urban culture
		monastic culture
		preliterate culture
	culture change	diffusion
		assimilation
		invention
		isolation
		migration
		accultural
		adaptation
		culture lag
	belief systems	mores
		folkways
		myths
		values
		norms
		goals
		symbols
		attitudes
		customs
	cultural organizations	
	art	

Figure 3. *Some Key Concepts of Anthropology (From: Clinton E. Boutwell,* Getting It All Together, *San Rafael, Calif.: Leswing Press, 1977, pp. 196-224).*

Notice that the major concept of anthropology is culture. This is the most inclusive concept. The field is then further subdivided into six concept areas— human ecology, culture type, culture change, belief systems, culture organizations, and art. These are the Level II concepts. Each Level II concept embraces its own subset of concepts, which are classified as Level III concepts, which can then be further subdivided.

According to Edith West, the importance of a concept is determined by the following criteria (see Figure 4):

1. The scope of the concept: how many concepts are subsumed under it or related to it?
2. The number of generalizations relating one concept to other concepts.
3. The significance of the generalization that uses the concepts.

Units or chapters of textbooks and curriculum guides are often organized around a generalization. The choice of concepts to teach can be determined by these generalizations, or, as West suggests, the generalizations themselves can be evaluated. Often, the most inclusive concept—such as "culture" or "socialization"—is introduced early and needs to be further clarified and deepened as more and more subordinate concepts are taught. Thus, the teacher may use the same concept in building several progressively more complex concept attainment tasks over a period of time.

Look over the list of ten concepts you identified earlier. Using West's three criteria, see if you can determine the worth of the concepts.

Unimportant	Of More Importance	Of Great Importance
Limited scope	Broader scope	Very broad scope
Few generalizations using concept	A number of generalizations using concept	Many generalizations using concept
Generalizations using concept of little significance:	Generalizations using concept of some significance:	Generalizations using concept of great significance:
a. Nonexplanatory or predictive	a. Explanatory (and probabilistic)	a. Explanatory and predictive
b. Empirical	b. Theoretical	b. Part of a narrow- or broad-gauge theory

Figure 4. *Scale of Significance of Concepts (From Edith West, "Concepts, Generalizations, and Theories: Background Paper 3," unpublished paper, Project Social Studies, University of Minnesota, no date, p. 10). Used by permission.*

Is the Concept Appropriate to the Learner?

As with the issue of what concept is worth teaching, many criteria can be applied to determine appropriateness. It is possible to consider this question from a developmental point of view, a life-experience point of view, and/or a cultural-heritage point of view.

West uses a combination of six criteria. Her scale of difficulty for each of these criteria appears in Figure 5. These criteria must be considered together, not separately:

1. distance from child's experience
2. distance from observed referents
3. scope of concept

Criteria of Difficulty	Scale of Difficulty		
	Easy	More Difficult	Very Difficult
Distance from child's experience	Within direct experience	Within vicarious experience	Unrelated to past direct or vicarious experience
Distance from observed referents	Referents are phenomena that can be perceived through senses — Physical objects / Relationships / Processes	Referents are idealized types which do not exist in actuality	Referents are phenomena which must be inferred from observations of other phenomena (constructs) — Predispositions / Configurations / Processes
Scope of concept	Narrow scope — Few concepts subsumed under it / Relates few concepts	Broader scope	Very broad scope — Many concepts subsumed under it / Relates many concepts
Certainty of presence of defining attributes	Always present	Always present	Tendency
Open-endedness of concept	Closed, and so reliable	Not completely closed; somewhat unreliable	Open-ended; vague boundaries; unreliable
Way in which attributes of concept are related	Conjunctive (joint presence of several attributes)	Disjunctive (presence of one or another attribute)	Relational — Specified relationship (ratio, product, verbal) / Comparative — One attribute affects another / All attributes interact

Figure 5. *Difficulty of Concepts (From Edith West, "Concepts, Generalizations, and Theories: Background Paper 3," unpublished paper, Project Social Studies, University of Minnesota, no date, p. 8). Used by permission.*

4. certainty of presence of defining attributes
5. open-endedness of concept
6. way in which the attributes of the concept are related[2]

Once again look over the ten concepts you listed in Exercise 1 at the beginning of this section. Scale them according to order of difficulty and then determine the appropriateness of each for the learner. (Score them on each of the six criteria. For each criteria, score 1 point if the concept falls in the "easy" category, 2 points in the "more difficult" category, and 3 points in the "very difficult" category. Total the score for all six criteria.)

This scale of difficulty may be useful as a means of sequencing instructional planning over a period of time, or as a way of providing for individual differences by matching difficulty of concepts to the ability of the students. For example, you may choose to present closed concepts first for some students, or those that are narrow in scope, or perhaps only conjunctive concepts. Using the scale, you can grade any concept for its difficulty in terms of the six criteria.

An interesting problem is that it does not make sense to consider the appropriateness of a concept for the learner (as determined from the scale of difficulty) totally outside the context of the body of knowledge (as manifested in the structure of its key concepts). In fact, the most powerful, inclusive concepts in a discipline are the broadest in scope, and therefore very difficult in terms of the criterion of scope. Sometimes, however, the important instructional variant may be not so much what concept is taught as the way it is taught—the medium of the exemplars, the difficulty of the exemplars, and so on.

Bruner, in one of his later works, *The Process of Education*,[3] maintains that any concept can be taught to any student at any age if done so in an intellectually meaningful way. There is probably some question whether a complex, abstract concept such as capitalism should be taught in the elementary grades. On the other hand, Bruner's statement did cause educators to realize that many concepts, perhaps the most powerful ones in each discipline, did not have to be withheld from students until junior and senior high, or perhaps even college. With adequate instructional models of conceptual activity, and with data or information that is within young children's experience, many concepts can be taught in the early grades. David Ausubel, who developed the Advance Organizer Model, suggests starting with the most inclusive concept. With very young children, it is necessary to use examples that can be directly experienced. He concedes that, at times, middle-range concepts may be more appropriate to the learner's intellectual development than the most inclusive ones.[4]

ANALYZING THE CONCEPT

The second step in planning Concept Attainment lessons is to analyze the concept in terms of (1) its essential and nonessential attributes, and (2) its type (conjunctive, disjunctive, or relational; observed, inferred, or ideal-type). Remem-

---

[2]Edith West, "Concepts, Generalizations, and Theories: Background Paper 3" (unpublished paper, Project Social Studies, University of Minnesota, no date), p. 8.
[3]Jerome Bruner, *The Process of Education* (New York: Vintage Books, 1963).
[4]David Ausubel, *The Psychology of Meaningful Verbal Learning* (New York: Grune and Stratton, 1963).

ber that the type of concept affects the nature of the defining attributes, the modality of the exemplars, and possibly the ultimate objectives of the lesson. For example, with inferred and ideal-type concepts, we cannot be certain of the presence of defining attributes in all positive examples of the concept. Also, these types of concepts are somewhat open-ended: they merge with or overlap other concepts. "Anger" and "hostility" (inferred concepts) and "liberal" and "radical" (ideal-type concepts) are two pairs of overlapping concepts; that is, they share many common attributes.

At this point, complete Parts I and II of the Planning Guide, which call for the name, attributes, rule (if there is one), and type of the concept you have chosen to teach.

DETERMINING OBJECTIVES

Concept Attainment models can be employed toward several educational ends. They can be used to:

1. teach a new concept
2. clarify and increase understanding of a known concept (perhaps a complex or abstract one)
3. increase awareness of and improve thinking processes
4. expose value assumptions and engage in value clarification of ideal-type and abstract concepts (justice, capitalism)
5. teach the nature of conceptual activity and increase students' utilization of conceptual activity

The use of a particular variation of Concept Attainment will depend on the primary educational objective. The Reception Model is probably best for introducing students to conceptual activity and its terminology, and for teaching a new concept in which the attributes are relatively certain. It is also appropriate for clarifying a complex or abstract concept, even if its attributes are less clear. The Selection Model, on the other hand, is essential for helping students become autonomous in their use of conceptual thinking, and for increasing their awareness of their thought processes. The Reception and Unorganized-Material strategies, particularly the latter, are useful for exposing value differences and assumptions.

The five objectives mentioned above are rather broad and can be developed into specific behavioral objectives. For example, "teaching a new concept" may mean any or all of the following behaviors:

1. Students will correctly recognize unlabeled examples.
2. Each student will generate three new examples of the concept.
3. Each student will locate three examples of the concept in textbooks or other resources.
4. Students will locate an example of the concept and describe the essential attribute-values as they appear in this new concept.
5. Students will state the concept rule.
6. Students will be able to state the attributes of the concept.

The first two of these behaviors would occur naturally in the course of the Reception of Model Concept Attainment, especially in Phase Two. The remaining objectives would involve follow-up educational activities, transfer tasks, or paper-and-pencil exercises. Ideally, the behavioral objective incorporates not only the goal of the educational activity but also the evaluation of the objective.

You may want to develop a list of specific objectives for *each* of the five broad objectives mentioned above. Remember, there are different levels of Concept Attainment activity; the objectives you develop should reflect increasing complexity in the process of Concept Attainment.

EXERCISE 2

Look now at the concept you selected and analyzed in Exercise 1. Determine the broad objective(s) of the lesson you wish to teach, and list three specific objectives. Record these in Part III of the Planning Guide.

Optional Activity

With a group of peers, generate a list of specific objectives for each of the five educational goals discussed earlier. Divide into small groups, comparing and contrasting the list of each group; or assign one educational goal to each group.

PREPARING EXEMPLARS

Researchers of concept learning have experimented with alternative types of exemplars and have studied the factors related to them that increase or decrease the student's difficulty in attaining a concept. Unfortunately, there are few hard and fast rules for any one of these factors. In this section, we want to familiarize you with guidelines that you can use to select and organize exemplars. We explore the following questions:

1. Media: Which is best for this concept?

2. "Yes" exemplars: Do they contain all the attributes? Do they exhibit a range of values?

3. "No" exemplars: Do some of them have none of the attributes? One attribute? Two or more attributes?

4. Noise: Is there a minimum of extraneous cues or information that are not related to the essential attributes?

5. Sequencing the presentation of exemplars: Do you have a "yes" exemplar first if it is a conjuncture concept and a "no" exemplar first if it is a disjunctive concept?

6. Unlabeled exemplars: Have you prepared enough exemplars for students to identify some as "yes" and some as "no"?

7. Presentation: How will you present the exemplars? Is there room for all of them? Can they be seen? How will you and the students keep track of the essential and nonessential attributes as they are identified?

Selecting the Medium

The problem here is to determine which medium reveals the attributes of the concept most adequately. If the concept is concrete (if it can be seen and/or touched), objects or still pictures are ideal. Similarly, such specialized concepts as types of poetry, painting, and music require the medium of the discipline—poems, paintings, and music. The real difficulty is with complex, abstract concepts—concepts of human behavior or social processes, of scientific events, of processes that may occur over time and involve attributes of motion, of social structure (government, family), and of function and relationship. If the concept concerns human behavior, a short film clip is perfect (for we can then observe the behavior), but it is rare that teachers have the time or resources to put together such an elaborate example. Sometimes verbal descriptions in the form of paragraphs can be constructed so that all attributes are included and explicit.

A common tendency in developing a Concept Attainment lesson is to select examples that "represent" the concept—for instance, selecting a picture of a church for the concept of Catholicism. However, Catholicism involves more than a building to meet in. When examples "represent" concepts, all the attributes of the concept cannot be experienced directly and immediately by the students. Consequently, they have to rely on their memories of previous experience. It becomes difficult for the teacher to tell what features of the concept students are focusing on in order to distinguish the "yeses" from the "nos," and whether each student is experiencing all the attributes of the concept.

One way to overcome the difficulties is to create written exemplars in the form of descriptive paragraphs or dialogues. Creating your own exemplars gives you control over the attributes and the choice of the best way to illustrate them. You can systematically manipulate the negative exemplars to reflect the absence of critical attributes or to eliminate certain incorrect concept-hypotheses. When words or pictures are used to "represent" an idea, activity, or event, it is probably advisable to ask students to describe the characteristics of the exemplar. The collective verbal descriptions thus obtained serve to flesh out the actual features of the exemplar, which are represented only by the word or picture. Knowing what attributes are associated with the exemplar is especially important if the purpose of the lesson is to clarify or deepen understanding of a concept, less important if the purpose is to focus on thinking strategies. Stopping for verbal descriptions may cause some pacing problems if a record of these descriptions is to be kept.

Generating Exemplars

After you have decided on the optimal medium, the next step is to generate positive and negative exemplars of the concept. Remember that, except for relational concepts, positive exemplars must contain *all* the attributes of the concept. Negative exemplars contain less than all the attributes. Concept Attainment is most effective when the negative exemplars share some of the critical attributes of the positive exemplars, rather than containing none of them. Negative exemplars also differ from positive ones in that the attribute-values of their criterial attributes may be "out of range." Remember to generate enough exemplars so that some can be unlabeled exemplars for the students to identify.

Once you have generated positive and negative exemplars, see that there is a *minimum* of "noise"—that is, extraneous cues or information not related to the concept. Also, see that your positive exemplars represent all the varieties of illustrations of the concept. If "apple" is your concept, make sure all the varieties of apples are included as positive exemplars.

The presentation of exemplars should begin with a positive one, unless the concept is disjunctive, in which case the first exemplar should be a "no." After that, the exemplars can be ordered so that they systematically test the attributes. One way to do this is to list possible concept-hypotheses and then order the exemplars so that they gradually eliminate the incorrect hypotheses. Figure 6 shows how this is done. The vertical line indicates that the hypothesis is still plausible. Where the line stops, the hypothesis is no longer possible because the exemplar, either positive or negative, rules it out. See if you can follow the reasoning for each hypothesis. Imagine how you might rotate or substitute exemplars in order to keep the hypothesis going. By laying out your exemplars in this way before the lesson, you can arrange the sequence of their presentation. Also, in using this format you can vary attributes instead of examples of concepts.

Exemplars		1. Games	2. Entertainment	3. Sports	4. Culture
Baseball	YES				
Playing with dolls	YES				
Competitiveness	YES				
Sleeping	NO				
"Monopoly"	YES				
Measles	NO				
Dancing	YES				
Trees	NO				
Greek tragedy	YES				
Rocks	NO				
Television	YES				
Democracy	YES				
Lincoln Continental	YES				
Illegality of marijuana	YES				
Reproduction	NO				
Abortion laws	YES				
Hunger	NO				
Size of family	YES				

Figure 6. *Ordering Concept-hypotheses.*

Presenting the Exemplars

Before the lesson, some thought and planning must be given to the presentation of exemplars and the recording of attributes, especially in the Reception Model, which emphasizes the basic elements of a concept. There must be enough space for all students to view all exemplars simultaneously. Second, a means should be devised for recording the attributes and concept hypotheses as these are identified in Phase One of the model; a chalkboard, newsprint, or blackboard is probably best.

It is tempting to place all the "yes" exemplars in one group and all the "no" exemplars in another, as if there were only two concepts. However, the "no" exemplars should illustrate a diversity of concepts and should be used to examine the "yes" exemplars. Grouping the "yeses" and "nos" circumvents the kind of searching and hypothesizing we have been describing. The result of this tactic is much more akin to a process called concept formation than to the related process of concept attainment. Remember, then, to intersperse the "yes" and "no" exemplars. With conjunctive concepts, begin with a "yes" exemplar; with disjunctive concepts, begin with a "no."

SUMMARY OF PLANNING CONCEPT ATTAINMENT LESSONS

Step 1: Select a concept.
    A. Locate a concept.
    B. Determine if it is a concept.
    C. Decide if it is worth teaching.
    D. Decide if it is appropriate for the learner(s).

Step 2: Analyze the concept.
    A. Determine its essential and nonessential attributes.
    B. Is it conjunctive, disjunctive, or relational?
    C. Is it observed, inferred, or ideal-type?

Step 3: Determine objectives.
    A. Identify specific goal or goals.
    B. Generate behavioral objectives for the goal(s).

Step 4: Prepare exemplars.
    A. Determine the most appropriate medium for exemplars.
    B. Generate exemplars.
    C. Check exemplars for "noise."
    D. Check exemplars for variety.
    E. Sequence the presentation of exemplars.
    F. Organize the presentation of exemplars.

Step 5: Complete the Planning Guide.

Planning Guide for Concept Attainment Models

The Planning Guide for Concept Attainment follows. By now you should have completed Parts I-III of the Guide. Take the time now to complete Parts IV and V, which ask you to focus on the interactive teaching aspects of the model, in contrast with the planning and organization of the lesson. Some teachers find it very useful to write out the actual opening moves they will use to initiate each phase, and to think about ways of responding to the learners.

You may wish to show the completed Planning Guide to your instructor or to a peer before you teach the lesson. We have found that most of the problems teachers experience in their early attempts to use this model have to do with planning. This model is relatively easy to teach if the planning and organization of the lesson is in order.

PLANNING GUIDE FOR CONCEPT ATTAINMENT MODELS

I. Analysis of concept

   1. Name of concept:

   2. Essential attributes of concept:

      a.

      b.

      c.

      d.

      e.

   3. Nonessential attributes of concept:

      a.

      b.

      c.

      d.

   4. State the rule:

II. Type of Concept

   5. Circle one: conjunctive   disjunctive   relational

   6. If the concept is conjunctive or relational, do all the "yeses" contain all the essential attributes? YES _____ NO _____ Or, if the concept is disjunctive, do all the "yeses" contain at least one essential attribute? YES _____ NO _____

III. Objectives

   7. Write three behavioral objectives that students will accomplish in this lesson.

      a.

      b.

      c.

IV. Exemplars

   8. Describe the "yes" exemplars.

   9. Describe the "no" exemplars.

   10. Is the medium of presentation (pictures, words, paragraphs) suitable for the concept?

   11. Do you have a sufficient number of "yes" and "no" exemplars? How many "yeses"? _____ How many "nos"? _____

   12. How many of the "no" exemplars have none of the essential attributes? _____ How many of the "no" exemplars have one or more of the essential attributes? _____

PLANNING GUIDE FOR CONCEPT ATTAINMENT MODELS

V. Phases of the Model

13. Write your opening move for each phase of the model.

Phase One: Presentation of Data and Identification of the Concept

Phase Two: Testing of the Concept Attainment

Phase Three: Analysis of Thinking Strategies

14. For each essential attribute in your concept, write two questions that will elicit from students those characteristics in the exemplar.

a. Attribute
   Question(s)

b. Attribute
   Question(s)

c. Attribute
   Question(s)

d. Attribute
   Question(s)

ANALYZING THE PEER TEACHING LESSON

Organize a small group of peers (three or four is ideal) to teach the Concept Attainment lesson you have prepared. The lesson should not take more than thirty minutes. After you complete the lesson, analyze it by completing the Teaching Analysis Guide on the following pages. Duplicate as many copies of the Guide as you may need to analyze the peer teaching and microteaching of all group members.

We recommend that you microteach this lesson to a small group of students after you try it out in a peer teaching setting. Peer teaching is a good facsimile of the real teaching situation but it is not the same, especially when your peers are knowledgeable in the model! If possible, record the lesson on an audio tape so that you can analyze your teaching with the aid of the Teaching Analysis Guide.

TEACHING ANALYSIS GUIDE FOR THE RECEPTION MODEL OF CONCEPT ATTAINMENT

This Guide is designed to help you analyze the process of teaching as you practice the Reception Model of Concept Attainment. The analysis focuses on aspects of teaching that are important to the syntax of the model, the teacher's role, and specific teaching skills.

The Guide consists of a series of questions and phrases. As you observe a practice session (whether peer teaching or microteaching), analyze the teaching using the rating scale that appears opposite each question and statement. This scale uses the following items:

Thoroughly. This item signifies that the teacher engaged in the behavior to the point where students were responding comfortably and fluently. Appropriateness varies from situation to situation. For example, young children may need more assistance in describing the exemplars than older ones.

Partially. This item signifies that the teacher engaged in appropriate behavior, but not as thoroughly as possible. There is some doubt about whether the students are responding fully.

Missing. The teacher did not engage in the behavior; there appears to be a loss in student response or probably will be one.

Not Needed. The teacher did not explicitly manifest the behavior, but there is no loss. Either the behavior was included in others or the students began to respond appropriately without being led to.

For each question or statement in the Guide, circle the term that best describes the teacher's behavior.

PHASE ONE: Presentation of Data and Identification of the Concept

1. Did the teacher state the purpose of the game? Thoroughly Partially Missing Not Needed

2. Did the teacher explain the procedures of the game (how the "yeses" and "nos" function)? Thoroughly Partially Missing Not Needed

3. Did the initial "yes" clearly contain the essential attributes? Thoroughly Partially Missing Not Needed

4. If teaching a conjunctive concept, did the teacher begin with a "yes" exemplar? Thoroughly Partially Missing Not Needed

or

If teaching a disjunctive concept, did the teacher begin with a "no" exemplar followed by a "yes"? Thoroughly Partially Missing Not Needed

5. Did the teacher ask questions that focused students' thinking on the essential attributes? Thoroughly Partially Missing Not Needed

6. Did the teacher ask the students to compare the "yes" exemplars? Thoroughly Partially Missing Not Needed

7. Did the teacher ask the students to contrast the attributes of the "yes" exemplars with those of the "no" exemplars? Thoroughly Partially Missing Not Needed

8. Did the teacher present labeled exemplars? Thoroughly Partially Missing Not Needed

TEACHING ANALYSIS GUIDE FOR THE
RECEPTION MODEL OF CONCEPT ATTAINMENT

9. Did the teacher ask the students to generate and test hypotheses about the identity of the concept?   Thoroughly   Partially   Missing   Not Needed

10. Did the teacher ask the students to name the concept?   Thoroughly   Partially   Missing   Not Needed

11. Did the teacher ask the students to state the essential attributes of the concept?   Thoroughly   Partially   Missing   Not Needed

PHASE TWO: Testing Attainment of the Concept

12. After the concept was agreed upon, did the teacher present additional exemplars and ask whether they contained the concept?   Thoroughly   Partially   Missing   Not Needed

13. Did the teacher ask the students to justify their answers?   Thoroughly   Partially   Missing   Not Needed

14. Were the students able to supply their own exemplars to fit the concept?   Thoroughly   Partially   Missing   Not Needed

15. Did the teacher ask the students to justify their exemplars by identifying the essential attributes?   Thoroughly   Partially   Missing   Not Needed

PHASE THREE: Analysis of Thinking Strategies

16. Did the teacher ask the students to describe the thinking processes they used in attaining the concept?   Thoroughly   Partially   Missing   Not Needed

17. Did the teacher ask the students to reflect on the roles of attributes and concepts in their thinking strategies?   Thoroughly   Partially   Missing   Not Needed

18. Did the teacher ask the students to evaluate the effectiveness of their strategies?   Thoroughly   Partially   Missing   Not Needed

AFTER PEER TEACHING: MICROTEACHING

Peer teaching was an opportunity to "walk through" the pattern of activities of the model. It should have helped you identify areas of understanding or performance that were amiss for you!

Aside from the specifics of the Teaching Analysis Guide, we would like you to reflect intuitively on your peer teaching experience. Did you feel that the essence of Concept Attainment was incorporated into the learning activity? Were you able to maintain the teacher's role as you had anticipated?

As you prepare to teach your first lesson to a small group of students, identify aspects of the Concept Attainment activity that you want to improve upon or include. Usually, these aspects are such things as being more precise in your directions, clearly defining attributes, and providing sufficient examples. We suggest walking yourself mentally through the microteaching.

It is natural in microteaching to wonder, "Am I doing this right?" However, except for any glaring omissions or commissions that may emerge in your peer teaching, the pursuit of excellence in a model is more a matter of refinement, style, and personal goals for the teaching situation. If you have been operating in the "Did I get this right?" frame of mind, now is the time to change to "What do *I* want to get across or elicit in this first teaching situation? How will I go about doing that?" If you have internalized the *basic* goals, principles, and procedures of the model, now is the time to shift from an external way of thinking to an internal one. Build the variations that seem appropriate to you.

We suggest audio-taping the first microteaching session so that you can reflect on the lesson afterwards. Students will respond differently from your peers. It is a good idea to use the Teaching Analysis Guide with the microteaching lesson. You may also want to share the experience with your colleagues and receive their comments and suggestions.

The fourth and last component of the Concept Attainment Model suggests how to use the model over the course of a long-term curricular activity, and how to adapt curriculum materials to the model. The emphasis of your training in this model will gradually shift now from mastering the basic elements of teaching to curriculum design and application.

Component IV

ADAPTING
THE MODEL

Based on what you have learned so far, it is easy to form the impression that a Concept Attainment Model of teaching is a short lesson with relatively precise steps! In peer teaching and microteaching, you did not have to be concerned with curriculum continuity. However, now that you have mastered the key ideas and performance skills of the model, it is time to think about your curriculums and extended use of the model. In this component, we move from issues of training and teacher performance to curriculum application and long-term use of the model.

CURRICULUM POSSIBILITIES AND TRANSFORMATION

Every discipline and subject area contains major concepts that guide the thinking in that field. This holds true for tennis, auto mechanics, law, and career education as well as for physics, biology, and sociology. The Concept Attainment Model is an effective means of making the most powerful ideas stand out from the more concrete ones and from factual material. It insures that students learn the fundamental ideas in a conceptual way—that is, in a way that enables them to recognize new examples of the concept as they arise, or to generate new examples.

Although, for purposes of illustration, the training material in this system tended to use rather simple concepts (such as the "ăt" sound) and to emphsize social studies concepts, we hope everyone using this system realizes that *all* subject areas or topics have concepts. In the next few pages, we will illustrate some ways of locating these concepts and of using traditional textbook materials to facilitate the building of Concept Attainment lessons. We have tried to draw on a range of subject areas and grade levels. For the most part, we assume that the first three components of training have been effective enough so that you can transfer your competence in planning and performing the model to your own subject area. If we have succeeded in helping you learn the major ideas and skills of Concept Attainment, you are in a far better position than we are to be creative with this model in your own area.

The major tasks in applying the model to your particular classroom situation are:

1. to identify the concepts you teach or would like to teach
2. to analyze those concepts
3. to gather material for Concept Attainment lessons

We are assuming that most teachers and school systems rely heavily on one of the many textbook series in each of the subject areas. Consequently, our suggestions for curriculum application will draw on these sources. As we all know, textbooks share many disadvantages as well as advantages. We are not advocating textbooks as the sole support system, but they are what most teachers presently happen to work with, and we want to enable you to perceive and plan Concept Attainment lessons from these materials.

It happens, coincidentally, that a good basic text in a subject area is usually the quickest way to locate the major concepts and propositions in that area. Though varying somewhat in treatment, style, and approach, the basic texts in a given area usually cover the same topics. One of the problems with texts, however, is that they do not adequately define and exemplify concepts; most students are not truly able to develop a conceptual approach just from the exemplars in the text. Frequently, it is necessary to plan individual Concept Attainment lessons that reinforce the essential attributes of the concept and give the students opportunity to contrast negative examples of the concept with positive ones. This often requires transformation of or additions to the existing curriculum materials.

The major job of curricular application of the Concept Attainment Model is to *transform* existing materials and augment them with teacher-developed materials. Some materials, as you will see, are already set up as exemplars. This, not surprisingly, is more true in early childhood and elementary materials, where pictures are a predominant medium.

Using the Table of Contents and Introductory Materials To Identify Concepts

One of the first means of identifying significant concepts in curriculum materials is simply to read the table of contents. Some chapter headings will reveal that the material is concerned with explaining or exemplifying generalizations or principles; other chapter headings clearly indicate that a concept is being taught. In the next few pages, parts of the table of contents from several elementary and secondary textbook series, covering a range of subject matter, are presented. Concepts that might be used in building Concept Attainment lessons are circled. Read through the selections. Do you agree with our identification of concepts? Can you identify others? Look through your own curricular materials, and identify some of the major concepts.

CONTENTS

John R. Mayor, John A. Brown, Bona Lunn Gordey, and Dorothy Sward, *Contemporary Mathematics: First Course* (Englewood Cliffs: Prentice-Hall, Inc., 1964). Reprinted by permission.

Contents

Paul G. Hewitt, *Instructor's Manual to Accompany: Conceptual Physics—A New Introduction to Your Environment* (Boston: Little, Brown, 1974). Reprinted by permission.

CONTENTS

Boyd C. Shafer, Richard A. McLemore, Everett Augspurger, and Milton Finkelstein, *A High School History of Modern America* (River Forest, Ill.: Laidlaw Brothers, 1966), pp. 5, 6. Reprinted by permission.

People and Their Social Actions

The *Man in Action Series* provides a comprehensive program in the social sciences for the elementary grades. This program is based on six fundamental principles:

That knowledge of all of the social science disciplines is crucial to effective functioning in the social environment.

That it is important for children to learn the key ideas of the social sciences in the elementary grades so that they are able to function more effectively through the remaining school years and in the adult world.

That the emphasis should be placed on acquiring concepts which organize a wide range of data and thus promote the learning and retention of information and the application of knowledge to new circumstances.

That the selection and placement of concepts should be determined by knowledge of child development and by a logical structure of the social science disciplines.

That the activities and materials chosen for the curriculum should foster in students the development of generalized mental skills which can serve in the solution of many types of problems.

That students should participate actively in the learning situation and should be encouraged to apply learned concepts to new situations.

People and Their Social Actions, Level B in the program, builds on the major social science concepts initially introduced in Level A. The approach and the content of this book reflect the broadening interests and increasing maturity of the student.

The work of Level B is organized into seven units, each consisting of from four to twenty-one activities. In most cases each picture in this book provides the core of a separate activity. Completing any one activity may require only one class period, or it may stretch over several days' time. Following is a brief notation of the title of each unit, the pages it covers in this book, and its subject.

Unit One SOCIAL INTERACTION, Pages 1–29: A study is made of what interactions are and of some factors which regulate or affect them.

Unit Two SOCIAL GROUPS, Pages 30–41: The distinguishing characteristics of a social group are investigated.

Unit Three POLITICAL SYSTEMS, Pages 42–45: A study is made of how and why interactions are organized into political systems to achieve social goals.

Unit Four ECONOMIC SYSTEMS, Pages 46–63: Some basic economic ideas and terms are introduced, and a study is made of some characteristics of social groups engaged in economic activity.

Unit Five COMMUNICATION, Pages 64–78: Attention is devoted to the role of symbols in interactions which are concerned with communication.

Unit Six POINT OF VIEW, Pages 79–83: Practice is given in studying situations or problems from more than one point of view.

Unit Seven SOCIAL ACTIONS IN MEXICO, Pages 84–91: Concepts learned in the first six units are applied in the study of social actions in another culture group.

Vincent Presno and Carol Presno, *Man In Action Series: People and their Social Actions* (Englewood Cliffs: Prentice-Hall, Inc., 1967). Reprinted by permission.

EXERCISE 1

Were you able to identify other concepts from the preceding pages? You might want to list some concepts under the following headings:

Social Studies

Math

Science

Reading

You may want to pause at this point and try to find examples of concepts in the textbooks that you use.

In the following selection from *Growing with Music*, we have marked several pages for key concepts, definitions, subconcepts, exemplars, and attributes. Can you identify other examples of these in subsequent pages of the sample material, or in pages from your own text? Take a few minutes, now, to do so.

Contents—Book 5

Harry R. Wilson, Walter Ehret, Alice M. Knuth, Edward J. Hermann, Albert A. Renna, *Growing With Music*, Teacher's Edition 5 (Englewood Cliffs: Prentice-Hall, Inc., 1970), pp. iii, viii. Reprinted by permission.

ORGANIZATION OF SERIES

The emphasis of the GROWING WITH MUSIC series is on the study of music as a significant learning. The intrinsic values of music and the contribution music makes to personality fulfillment have been given primary consideration in organizing these books. At the same time, the extrinsic values of music education—recreational, social, and enrichment—are given proper recognition. For example, among the titles at the left, those illustrating intrinsic values are "Mood in Music," "Melody in Music," and "The World of Sound." Extrinsic values are represented by "Songs for Special Days."

As children grow with music, they develop a growing understanding of music. This assumes a study of the elements of which music is made. Since GROWING WITH MUSIC is a song series, these musical elements are presented in the context of song material which has been chosen for its high musical quality and its genuine appeal to children.

Musical elements with which this series is concerned are Mood, Tone, Text, Melody, Rhythm, Form, and Harmony. Since music exists only through a proper balance and interrelationship of these elements, great care has been given to the organization of these books. The emphasis may vary with the grade level, but a growing understanding of all elements is assured throughout the series. The chapter titles at the left should be examined carefully in this context.

Consideration of "Mood" and "Melody" is given first importance during the intermediate grades. "Harmony," which was introduced in Book Three as "Tones Sounding Together," receives increasing emphasis in Books Four to Six. Older children still move to music and take part in "Dramatizing Songs;" but movement is increasingly patterned. Opportunities for such movement are provided in "Rhythm and Dance." As the capability for both hearing and acting out patterns develops, "Form in Music" is given increasing importance.

Musical learnings have been reinforced by the planned development of musical skills in the GROWING WITH MUSIC series. The experiences offered at each level in "Reading Music" and "Making Up Music" have been carefully graduated. It is the intention of the authors that these be extended by general application throughout.

THINGS TO LEARN

ABOUT MOOD

— Definition

Mood is the feeling which music creates in us as we sing, play or listen. Some music makes us feel light-hearted and gay, while other music makes us feel sad or serious.

Throughout the intermediate grades, boys and girls become increasingly able to recognize some of the more obvious devices that a composer uses to create a mood. In writing a gay, lively song, for example, he may use quick notes, strongly felt uneven rhythms, and a rapid tempo. By using many wide leaps and upward movement, he may give his melody a lilting, carefree feeling. *Subconcept*

In writing a somber, reflective song, a composer may use a slow tempo, regular rhythms, and an even note pattern. His melody may have a falling line. Use of the minor scale may heighten the melancholy effect (although many gay songs are also written in minor); or dark-sounding harmonies may be utilized in the accompaniment.

Boys and girls in the intermediate grades should not only be able to identify the predominant mood of a song; but should also be able to *project this mood* as they sing or play the song. A lullaby should be made to sound tender and soothing. A fun song, on the other hand, should have a light-hearted sound.

The following songs may be used for discovering various means chosen by composers in creating moods.

Examples of contrasting moods:

Exemplars

GAY, BRIGHT, LIVELY	QUIET, SOMBER, REFLECTIVE
A Murmuring Brook, 28	All Through the Night, 46
Awake! 49	Fall Leaves, 13
Bahar Bagai, 18	Falling Snow, 89
Carolina in the Morning, 84	Letter Song, The, 140
Cheers for la Canadienne, 6	Lonesome Road, 2
Dixie, 190	Lord's My Shepherd, The, 154
Let Us All Sing! 1	Magyar Maid, The, 11
Sacramento, 8	Sailor's Farewell, A, 71
Springtime in the Tyrol, 42	Scotch Lullaby, 7
Waltz Song, 78	Trees, 213

ABOUT TONE

Definition

Tone is the unique building material of music. Tone is distinguished from noise by a regularity of vibrations which results in definite pitch. Composers make music by *organizing tone in expressive ways.*

Children should become increasingly aware of these basic characteristics of tone:

attributes

Pitch	high or low
Duration	long or short
Intensity	loud or soft
Quality	tone color or timbre

The elements of tone are explained acoustically as follows:

Pitch . . . All sound is produced by vibration. The faster the vibration, the higher the pitch; the slower the vibration, the lower the pitch. *attribute-Values*

Duration . . . Tones in music last for specific periods of time. In music, symbols called notes represent tones of varying lengths. For example, a whole note (**o**) represents a tone of longer duration than another tone represented by an eighth note (♪).

Intensity . . . The degree of loudness or softness of musical tones depends upon the size of the vibration. Big vibrations produce loud tones; small vibrations soft ones.

Quality . . . Quality is the difference in the way that various voices and instruments sound. We can recognize the difference between the soprano and the bass voice even though both are singing middle C. Similarly, we can distinguish between the sound of the flute and the violin playing the same pitch. We can hear that the sound of melody bells is different from the sound of a singing voice.

Songs illustrating outstanding expressive features of

Examples

DURATION OF NOTES	LOUD AND SOFT	USE OF PITCH
Aura Lee, 62	Hunter's Horn, The, 115	All Through the Night, 46
Cotton Needs Pickin', 80	Masters in this Hall, 210	Chopsticks, 124
God Be in My Head, 3	Secret, The, 86	Kerry Lad, The, 20
Trees, 213	Sing and Dance, 67	Lonesome Valley, 14
Zum-ta-di-ya, 110	Slumber Song of the Child Jesus, 209	Shore Dinners, 66

Using the Material as Exemplars

One of the problems with the introduction of concepts in curricular materials is that the attributes are not always specified, either in a definition or in the examples. Often, negative examples are not presented, only positive ones.

In the elementary materials on biology that are reproduced on the following pages, the authors present the concept of living things. Many examples of the concept are presented, and attributes of it are discussed. Finally, the concept label, "organism," is provided. There are, however, some aspects of Concept Attainment theory that are omitted. For instance, there are no negative examples, and the attributes that are identified are not necessarily the critical attributes. What are the essential features that distinguish living things from nonliving things? Nevertheless, we like these materials because they are clear and easy to arrange. Teachers can provide additional exemplars and highlight the essential attributes. Look them over and see if you agree with our analysis. Comment on each of the aspects listed below.

Concept label

Negative example

Positive examples

Definition

Essential attributes

Nonessential attributes

Idea 2
Evolution

Investigation 1

You Can't Help but Bump Into One

Where do you live? Do you live in the city? Or do you live in the country? Wherever you live, you will find living things all around.

Harry K. Wong and Marvin Dolmatz, *Biology Idea 2; Evolution, Ideas and Investigations in Science Series* (Englewood Cliffs: Prentice-Hall, Inc., 1971), pp. 41-44. Reprinted by permission.

Ameba

Giraffe

Living things differ in their color. Some are black; some are brown; and others are white.

Living things come in many different shapes and forms. Some living things do not have a definite shape. Others have a very definite shape.

The scientist calls a living thing an *organism*. Ten different organisms are pictured below. Describe each organism in your data sheet. Imagine that you are talking to someone on another planet who has never seen these organisms. Try to give a complete description.

Koala Bear

Fir Tree

Lobster

Earthworm

Bat

113

Bighorn Sheep

Living things like bighorn sheep can be found on mountains. Others like blind cave salamanders live in caves.

Blind Cave
Salamander

Living things vary in size. Some are large like this whale. Others are very small like these bacteria.

Whale

Living things differ in how they move.

Bacteria

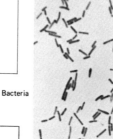

Some run . . .   some fly . . .

some crawl . . .   and some swim.

The pamphlet *Propaganda, Polls, and Public Opinion* in a series titled "Inquiry into Crucial American Problems"[1] (not reproduced here) presents an exciting opportunity for teachers to build a Concept Attainment lesson. Unlike many secondary materials where exemplars are mentioned but not provided, this one includes samples of many types of propaganda. For instance, it includes a song from the American Revolution, excerpts from public speeches, posters, leaflets, newsletters, and excerpts from novels. The material is set up beautifully, with the examples first and a didactic discussion of the concept of propaganda and its characteristics afterwards, separate from the examples. Finally, a series of unlabeled exemplars is provided in the discussion of political symbols. One drawback is that there are no negative exemplars, but the teacher can supply these. Building a Concept Attainment lesson from this source would involve very little transformation of materials.

Other materials have both negative and positive examples but omit the attributes. Primary grade materials omit discussion of attributes for an obvious reason: the students cannot yet read. But the materials are all there for the teacher to build a Concept Attainment lesson around the concept of action, which the authors define in their introductory material as "goal-directed human movement."

[1] Malcolm G. Mitchell, *Propaganda, Polls, and Public Opinion*, from "Inquiry Into Crucial American Problems," Jack R. Fraenkel (ed.) (Englewood Cliffs: Prentice-Hall, Inc., 1970), pp. 13-28.

A President interacts with many people.
Which objects might he use?

Vincent Presno and Carol Presno, *Man In Action Series: People and Their Social Actions* (Englewood Cliffs: Prentice-Hall, Inc., 1967), pp. 16, 17. Reprinted by permission.

An astronaut interacts with many people.
Who might an astronaut interact with?

A LONG-TERM PLAN

In the next section we shall discuss long-term planning in terms of combining Concept Attainment with other models of teaching. In this section we discuss the development of the pupil's concept attainment skills over a period of time, as well as the idea of "stretching" the model.

No matter what the model of teaching, we envision making it transparent to the students—its terminology, phases, and purposes. Gradually, we assume students will take over the initiation of the phases of the model, as well as using it on their own. It has been our experience that when teachers share the ideas behind the model and use it several times, the students become familiar with the sequence. This early familiarity with the model may be superficial, but we believe that students can be taught the more complex ideas behind the model. Of course, success in doing this varies from model to model, but it is not an unrealistic goal, especially from the upper elementary grades on.

Student Skill Development

One of the major purposes of using the Concept Attainment Model(s) over a long period of time, we feel, is to teach students the nature of conceptual activity and to increase their utilization of it. This means sharing with them Bruner's theory of concepts—the definition, elements, and types of concepts. To us, student skill development in the Concept Attainment Model entails increasing sophistication, awareness, utilization, and accuracy in conceptual activity. In other words, we are concerned with transmitting the *process* of concept attainment rather than the content of a particular concept. Content is important too, but our priority is to have students know that there is such a thing as a concept, what it is, and how it operates to help us organize information.

There are several ways to view the development of student skills in conceptual activity. As we noted earlier, the three variations of the Concept Attainment Model— reception conditions, selection conditions, and unorganized data—seem to us to represent an increasing order of difficulty in conceptual activity. The activities (phases) and skills attendant to each of these variations are sources for a developmental profile of pupil skills. For example, with very young children, understanding how the "nos" "cancel out" or "confirm" the "yeses" may be the first important skill to stress and, perhaps, teach directly prior to going through all the phases. One way to talk about models and skill development, then, is to identify the so-called prerequisite skills, which may be practiced apart from the entire model.

Increasing proficiency with different types of concepts and modalities is another way of viewing student skill development. We know that relational and disjunctive concepts are more difficult than conjunctive concepts. According to developmental psychology, relational and disjunctive concepts may be impossible for very young children. Similarly, abstract, symbolic material (words, paragraphs) is a more advanced learning modality than three-dimensional, manipulable objects or two-dimensional pictures. Inferred and ideal-type concepts are more difficult than observed concepts.

Another way to consider student skill development is in terms of the skills of conceptual activity. We envision three stages of conceptual activity: (1) working with the basic elements; (2) using concept terminology and focusing on thought processes; and (3) independent application of conceptual activity. Student skills in the first stage include identifying attributes, using "yes" and "no" exemplars, generating labels, generating exemplars, and stating rules (or definitions). A more advanced stage of conceptual activity includes the use of concept terminology and reflection on thinking processes. The latter activity involves describing the thinking strategy, identifying the strategy, evaluating the strategy, and trying alternative strategies. Finally, in the most advanced stage, students internalize the Concept Attainment Model and employ it independent of the model and the teacher. These independent activities might include looking for concepts in unorganized data and/ or learning activities; speaking of concepts and their attributes and/or data; and planning and carrying out Concept Attainment activities.

Figure 1 summarizes these factors and the related skills. It is possible to plan sequences of learning activities that take each of these factors into account, and that track student success in reaching the advanced levels.

There may be other student skills involved in Concept Attainment, and other ways of conceptualizing them. We merely present this outline as heuristic. There is some evidence for believing in the stages and factors that we have discussed, but they have not been validated empirically. What does seem clear is that teachers cannot expect all these skills to appear in the first few exposures of students to the

Factor	Beginning	Advanced	More Advanced
Type of Concept	observed	inferred	ideal-type
Learning Modality	concrete, manipulatable	still or motion pictures	symbolic material
Type of Concept	conjunctive	disjunctive	relational
Type of Model	reception	selection	unorganized data
Conceptual Activity	working with basic elements: identifying attributes / correct using of "yes" and "no" exemplars / generating labels / generating exemplars / stating rules (definitions)	use of concept terminology / thinking processes: reflecting on thinking / identifying the strategy	independently looking for concepts in learning activities and/or unorganized data / planning and carrying out Concept Attainment activities / speaking of concepts and their attributes / speaking of concepts and data

Figure 1. *Stages of Conceptual Activity.*

model; they probably can be developed with practice and by varying the use of the model. For example, the teacher can concentrate on one phase of the model more than on others, or plan new learning activities that require students to use their skills independent of the teacher and the original syntax.

Stretching the Model

By stretching the model, we mean two things: first, breaking out of the original syntax and applying the essence of the theory in other contexts; second, lengthening the activities of each phase, perhaps to several days or weeks.

In the first case, the essence of the Concept Attainment Model is the identification of a concept, the search for its attributes, and the use of labels. Regardless of the content or the teaching strategy, the teacher can always probe the students on their application of a concept or its specifying attributes. Diagnostically, the teacher can be aware when students have attained a concept but not its label, or when they are not clear about a concept's attributes. She can probe or explain in terms of attributes, or she can supply the label. Some people would call the latter situation the "teachable moment."

Second, we would like to encourage teachers to spend time on each of the phases, more time than just one session. Thus, you may want to spend several days on Phase One (identifying the concept), progressively adding more exemplars. If the setting is an open classroom, students can work on their own, identifying attributes and generating hypotheses. It seems to us that Phase One inquiry could go on for several sessions. Similarly, depending on the concept, students could spend several days or weeks testing concept attainment. They could be directed to search for and develop exemplars from several settings (for example, roles in school, roles in the family, or roles in the office) or in several modalities. The key here is seeing the model and each of its phases as principles for designing multiple learning situations.

COMBINING CONCEPT ATTAINMENT WITH OTHER MODELS OF TEACHING

When we begin studying a model of teaching, it is necessary that demonstrations and practice take place in relatively short periods of time, and cover relatively simple instructional materials. This is simply a matter of convenience. A short demonstration reveals to us the essence of the model, and short practice sessions help us master its basic skills. However, most of our use of models of teaching is in longer curricular activities, which may be built primarily around one model of teaching but generally combine several of them. A science unit, for example, may begin with a Concept Attainment exercise that establishes a basic idea that will be explored for several weeks. That idea may then function as an Advance Organizer for readings and experiments. Inductive models of teaching, such as Concept Learning and Inquiry Training, may then be used to guide laboratory sessions and other activities. As we mentioned earlier, one model may dominate a unit and provide most of the elements of its design, or it may be that several models will be sequenced in a unit.

In this section, we briefly consider three ways to combine Concept Attainment with other models of teaching in curricular activities:

1. organizing personal feelings generated by personalistic models of teaching
2. evaluating learning that has resulted in curricular units
3. introducing inquiry into new areas

Organizing Personal Experience

Models such as Role Playing and Simulation generally arouse considerable affect from students. For example, teachers use Role Playing to help students explore their feelings about conflict situations and to clarify their values. Concept Attainment can be useful when it is time to categorize various ways of approaching conflict situations, and to compare and contrast them. For example, a series of role playing situations might be used with young children as a means of exploring ways of dealing with peer conflict, say in play situations. A series of problem situations could be explored, and students could role-play several possibilities for managing them. These solutions could then be listed, and Concept Attainment could be used to make clear such concepts as negotiating, mediating, confronting, withdrawing, or other solutions suggested. Thus used, Concept Attainment helps provide students with conceptual handles for dealing with the material generated in the less structured role playing situations.

Evaluating the Material Learned

Deductive models such as the Advance Organizer are designed to teach children material in the form of a conceptual structure. Major ideas (Advance Organizers) are presented to the students, who then read material, conduct experiments, or otherwise gain experience that is to be organized around these ideas. Concept Attainment exercises can be used to determine whether the students are indeed mastering the major concept and arranging the facts and lesser concepts around it. For example, a major idea about poetry can be introduced to the students, who then study a variety of poems. Concept Attainment can be used to determine whether the students are in fact discriminating the poems according to the major idea. In general, Concept Attainment is an excellent evaluation model when one wishes to determine whether important ideas have been mastered.

Introducing a Fresh Line of Inquiry

By opening up a new conceptual area, Concept Attainment can initiate a sequence of individual or group inquiries. Suppose a teacher wishes to open up a unit exploring the concept of culture. A series of Concept Attainment lessons could introduce students to the concept of culture itself. This could be followed by the use of the simulation game *Bafa*, in which students experience the problems that persons of one culture have when they are first introduced to members of a different culture. (For a demonstration of *Bafa*, see the Simulation Model in *Social Models of Teaching* in this series.)

Further Concept Attainment activities could help students to analyze the experience gained during *Bafa* and to develop preliminary concepts about the relationships between cultures. Out of these experiences, students could begin to organize themselves to read about different cultures and to gather data that could be organized into Concept Attainment activities designed to further clarify and extend the ideas obtained from their study.

Thus, the Concept Attainment Model not only can introduce extended series of inquiries into important areas, but can also augment ongoing inductive study. Concept Attainment lessons providing important concepts can be interspersed throughout more inductive activity. Used in this way, it "boosts" the conceptual level of ongoing units of study, and stimulates a higher level of inquiry. For example, in social studies units, concepts such as "democracy," "socialism," "capitalism," and "due process" can be interjected periodically into units that otherwise depend on student reading and reporting. If a concept is controversial, the teacher can present one interpretation of it, which the students can then debate. Democracy, for example, is interpretable in a variety of ways, and the teacher can present some of the controversial interpretations in order to stimulate debate and discussion. In addition, the debates over the essential characteristics of such a concepts are usually great motivators for further inquiry into the subject matter in question.

INQUIRY TRAINING MODEL

SCENARIO FOR INQUIRY TRAINING

One morning, as Mrs. Harrison's fourth-grade class is settling down to their arithmetic workbooks, she calls their attention. As they raise their eyes toward her, a light bulb directly over Mrs. Harrison's desk blows out, and the room darkens.

"What happened?" asks one of the children.

"Can't you see, dopey?" says another. "The light bulb blew out."

"Yeah," says another, "but what does that mean?"

"What do you mean, 'What does that mean'?"

"Just that. We have all seen a lot of light bulbs blow out, but what does that really mean? What happens?"

Mrs. Harrison unscrews the light bulb and holds it up. The children gather around and she passes it among them. After she has it back, she says, "Well, why don't you see if you can develop a hypothesis about what happened."

"What's inside the glass?" asks one of the children.

"I'm afraid I can't answer that," she says. "Can you put it another way?"

"Is there air inside the glass?" asks one of the children.

"No," says Mrs. Harrison.

"Is there a gas inside?" asks another.

"No," says Mrs. Harrison. The children look at one another in puzzlement. Finally, one asks, "Is it a vacuum?"

"Yes," says Mrs. Harrison.

"Is it a complete vacuum?" asks one of the children.

"Almost," says Mrs. Harrison.

"What is that little wire made of?" asks another student.

"I can't answer that," says Mrs. Harrison. "Can you put it another way?"

"Is the little wire made of metal?"

"Yes," she says.

Asking questions such as these, the children gradually identify the materials that make up the light bulb and the events that took place. Finally, they begin to venture hypotheses about what happened. After they have generated four or five of these, they search through reference books in an effort to verify them.

Mrs. Harrison's class has been prepared to carry out a model of teaching that we call Inquiry Training. Normally, the class uses Inquiry Training to explore preselected areas. That is, either Mrs. Harrison organizes a unit of instruction or the children identify a topic that they are going to explore. In this case, the children used the techniques of Inquiry Training to try to formulate theories about an event that was familiar to all of them, and yet puzzled them, for none of them had previously developed ideas about what really went on when a light bulb blew out.

OUTLINE OF ACTIVITIES FOR THE INQUIRY TRAINING MODEL

Objective	Materials	Activity
COMPONENT I: DESCRIBING AND UNDERSTANDING THE MODEL		
1. To recognize the goals, assumptions, and procedures of the Inquiry Training Model and to recognize elements of the inquiry process.	Theory and Overview	Reading
2. To gain a sense of the model in action	Theory in Practice	Reading
3. To recognize and generate theorizing and data-gathering questions	Taking Theory into Action	Reading/Writing
4. To evaluate your understanding of the Inquiry Training theory.	Theory Checkup	Writing
COMPONENT II: VIEWING THE MODEL		
1. To become familiar with the Teaching Analysis Guide and identify items that you do not understand.	Teaching Analysis Guide	Reading
2. To identify phases of the model and comment on the lesson.	Demonstration Transcript	Reading/Writing/Discussion
3. **Option:** To apply the Teaching Analysis Guide to the alternative demonstrations.	Video tape or live demonstration/Teaching Analysis Guide	Viewing/Group discussion or individual analysis
COMPONENT III: PLANNING AND PEER TEACHING		
1. To select and formulate a discrepant event.	Selecting and Formulating a Discrepant Event	Reading
2. To develop behavioral objectives related to Inquiry Training.	Determining Educational Objectives	Reading/Writing
3. To plan an Inquiry Training lesson using the Planning Guide.	The Planning Guide	Writing
4. To peer teach the Inquiry Training Model.	3 to 4 peers, problem statement, Teacher Fact Sheet	Teaching
5. To analyze the Inquiry Training lesson using the Teaching Analysis Guide.	Teaching Analysis Guide	Writing/Group discussion

OUTLINE OF ACTIVITIES FOR THE INQUIRY TRAINING MODEL

Objective	Materials	Activity
6. **Optional:** To teach the Inquiry Training Model to a small group of students.	Small group of students, problem statement, Teacher Fact Sheet, audio-cassette recorder, audio-cassette	Teaching/Taping
7. To analyze the microteaching lesson.	Teaching Analysis Guide	Individual or group listening to audio tape/Writing

COMPONENT IV: ADAPTING THE MODEL

Objective	Materials	Activity
1. To recognize possible Inquiry Training lessons in existing curricular materials and make any necessary changes.	Curriculum Possibilities and Transformations	Reading
2. To plan the use of Inquiry Training for long-term development of pupil and teacher skills.	Long-Term Plans	Reading
3. To be aware of the possibilities of combining Inquiry Training with other models of teaching.	Combining Inquiry Training with Other Models of Teaching	Reading

Component I

DESCRIBING
AND UNDERSTANDING
THE MODEL

THEORY AND OVERVIEW

The Inquiry Training Model was developed by Richard Suchman. It contrasts interestingly with other models of teaching within the information processing family. Hilda Taba (Inductive Thinking Model) and David Ausubel (Advance Organizer Model) are both concerned with concepts. Taba teaches children how to organize data and how to build concepts independently. Ausubel presents children with concepts and then with data that they can organize around those concepts. Suchman's Inquiry Training Model helps students establish facts, build concepts, and then generate explanations or theories that explain the phenomenon under consideration. His model takes students through, in miniature, the kinds of procedures that scholars use in order to organize knowledge and generate principles that explain causation.

Suchman developed his model of scientific inquiry by analyzing methods employed by creative research personnel, especially physical scientists. As he identified the elements of their inquiry processes, he generated the instructional model called Inquiry Training. Suchman has experimented with this model and identified many of the problems involved in training children to inquire scientifically. He has also developed sets of curriculum materials that are appropriate for inquiry training.

Goals and Assumptions of the Model

The goals of Inquiry Training are to help students develop the intellectual discipline necessary to search out data, process it, and apply logic to it. Suchman is interested in helping students to inquire independently, but in a disciplined way. Sheer independent learning is not his goal. He wants students to question why events happen as they do, and to develop intellectual strategies that they can use to determine causal relationships among phenomena.

Inquiry Training begins with a puzzling event. Suchman believes that individuals, faced with a puzzling situation, are motivated to pursue meaning in it. They naturally seek to understand what they encounter. In order to understand puzzling situations, they must increase the complexity of their thinking and understand better how to link data into concepts and how to apply those concepts toward the identification of principles of causation. Thus, the underlying assumption of the model is that individuals, when puzzled, need to explore the data surrounding the puzzlement and put these data together in new ways. They inquire and as they inquire, they reorganize their knowledge.

Like Bruner, Taba, and Ausubel, Suchman believes that students can become more and more conscious of the process of inquiry, and that this process can be taught to them directly. He sees conscious awareness of the process and strategies of inquiry as an essential aspect of autonomous inquiry. All of us often inquire intuitively; however, Suchman feels we cannot analyze and improve our thinking unless we are consciously aware of it. In his training program, Suchman teaches students directly about their processes of inquiry by introducing them to the language and operations of inquiry as they are in the midst of inquiring, and by having them reflect on their thinking.

Suchman believes, further, that it is important to convey to students the attitude that *all knowledge is tentative*. Scholars generate theories and explanations; years later, these are pushed aside by new theories. There is no one answer. We can always be more sophisticated in our explanations, and most problems are amenable to several equally plausible explanations. Students should recognize and be comfortable with the ambiguity that genuine inquiry entails. They should also be aware that "two heads are better than one." The development of knowledge is facilitated by help and ideas from colleagues.

An Overview of the Teaching Strategy

Embodying Suchman's belief that individuals have a natural motivation to inquire, the Inquiry Training Model is built upon intellectual confrontations. The student is presented with a puzzling situation—a discrepancy—and inquires into it. In the following example, the bending of a metallic strip when it is held over a flame is an episode that confronts the learner and begins the inquiry cycle.

The strip is made of a lamination of unlike strips of metal (usually steel and brass) that have been welded together to form a single blade. With a handle at one end it has the appearance of a narrow knife or spatula. When this apparatus is heated, the metal in it expands, but the rate of expansion is not the same in the two metals. Consequently, half of the thickness of this laminated strip becomes slightly longer than the other half and since the two halves are attached to each other the internal stresses force the blade to assume a curve of which the outer circumference is occupied by the metal which has expanded the most.[1]

Suchman deliberately selects episodes that have sufficiently surprising outcomes to make it difficult for students to remain indifferent to the encounter. The learners cannot dismiss the solution as obvious; they have to work to explain the situation, and the product of that work is a new insight into the phenomenon, new concepts, new theories.

After the presentation of the puzzling situation, the student proceeds to ask questions of the teacher, and the teacher attempts to respond to the questions. However, the teacher structures the situation so that the questions must be answerable by a "yes" or a "no." This eliminates open-ended questions. Students may not ask the teacher to explain the phenomenon to them. They have to focus and structure their probes in order to solve the problem. In this sense, each question becomes a limited hypothesis of a sort. Thus, the student may not ask, "How did the heat affect the metal?" but may ask, "Was the heat greater than the melting point of the metal?" The first type of question is not a specific statement of what information is wanted; it asks the teacher to do the conceptualizing. The second question requires the student to put several factors together—heat, metal, change, liquid. The student has to ask the teacher to verify the hypothesis that he or she has developed (the heat caused the metal to change into a liquid).

The students continue to ask questions. Whenever they phrase one that cannot be answered by a "yes" or a "no," the teacher reminds them of the rules of the game and waits until they find a way of stating the question in proper form. Comments such as "Can you restate this question so that I can answer it with a 'yes' or a 'no'?" are common teacher responses when students step out of the inquiry mode.

The teacher may guide the students to a strategy whereby their early questions are confined to analyzing and verifying the situation they have observed—trying to find out the nature and identity of the objects, the events, and the conditions surrounding the puzzling situation. Thus, the students are taught through experience that the first stage in a series of questions is to verify the facts of the situation. The question "Was the strip made of metal?" helps verify the facts of the situation—in this case, a property of the object. As the students become aware of the properties of the data, hypotheses should come to mind and guide further inquiry. Using their knowledge about the behavior of the objects, students can turn their questions to the relationships among the variables in the situation. They can conduct verbal or actual experiments to test these causal relationships, selecting new data or organizing the existing data in new ways to see what will happen if things are done differently. For example, they could ask, "If I turn the flame down, will the bend-

[1] J. Richard Suchman, *The Elementary School Training Program in Scientific Inquiry*, Report to the U.S. Office of Education, Project Title VIII, Project 216 (Urbana, Ill.: University of Illinois Publications Office, 1962), p. 28.

ing still occur?" Better yet, they could actually do this! By introducing a new condition or altering an existing one, students isolate variables and perceive how they affect one another.

It is important for students and teachers to recognize the difference between questions that attempt to verify "what is" and questions or activities that "experiment" with the relationships among variables. Each of these data-gathering processes is essential to theory development. However, unless sufficient information about the nature of the problem situation and its elements is verified, students are likely to be overwhelmed by the many possible causal relationships.

> If the child immediately tries to hypothesize complex relationships among all the variables that seem relevant to him, he could go on testing indefinitely without any noticeable progress, but by isolating variables and testing them singly, he can eliminate the irrelevant ones and discover the relationships that exist between each relevant independent variable (such as the temperature of the blade) and the dependent variable (which in this case is the bending of the blade).[2]

Finally, the students try to develop causal hypotheses that will fully explain what happened. (For instance, "The strip was made of two metals that were fastened together somehow. They expand at different rates, and when they were heated, the one that expanded the most exerted pressure on the other one so that the two bent over together.") Even after lengthy and rich verification and experimentation activities, many explanations may be possible. Also, although students may zero in on the primary causal relationships, they can express these theories with different levels of sophistication and specificity.

Inquiry cannot be programmed, and the range of productive inquiry strategies is vast. For the most part, students should:

> experiment freely with their own questions, structuring and sequencing [the inquiry session]...Nevertheless, inquiry can be divided into broad phrases which, on the whole, should be taken in logical order simply because they build upon one another. Failure to adhere to this order leads either to erroneous assumptions or to low efficiency and duplication of effort.[3]

We have taken Suchman's point into account in extrapolating the syntax of the Inquiry Training Model. We have incorporated the operations and a sequence of inquiry into the syntax through the distinction and ordering of phases. The syntax thus includes five stages—the initial encounter with the problem, the three stages of inquiry (verification, experimentation, and explanation), followed by the postmortem process (the analysis of the inquiry). Figure 1 provides an outline of this syntax.

The emphasis in this model is clearly on becoming aware of and mastering the inquiry process, not on the content and explanation of any particular problem situation. Although the model should also be enormously appealing and effective as

---

[2]Ibid., pp. 15-16.
[3]Ibid., p. 38.

Phase One: Encounter with the Problem	Phase Two: Data Gathering: Verification	Phase Three: Data Gathering: Experimentation	Phase Four: Formulating an Explanation	Phase Five: Analysis of the Inquiry Process
Explain inquiry procedures. Present discrepant event.	Verify the nature of objects and conditions. Verify the occurrence of the problem situation.	Isolate relevant variables. Hypothesize (and test) causal relationships.	Formulate rules or explanations.	Determine inquiry strategy and develop more effective ones.

Figure 1. *Syntax of the Inquiry Training Model.*

a mode of acquiring and using information, the teacher cannot be too concerned with subject-matter coverage or "correctness." In fact, this would violate the whole spirit of scientific inquiry, which envisions a community of scholars searching together for more accurate and powerful explanations for everyday phenomena.

Tips for Teachers

Suchman points out that students frequently are puzzled when they begin Inquiry Training. They are unaccustomed to guiding their own intellectual study and to asking questions. Suchman advises teachers to get into the problem situation as quickly as possible, and not to dwell on the terminology of inquiry or give direct instruction as to its nature and stages. Teachers are cautioned to let the students take the initiative. Inquiring involves risk taking, and some individuals will withdraw in silence at first. Eventually, when they are ready, they will become active participants. A second suggestion is for teachers to model the inquiry process by proposing a theory and then generating and answering "yes" and "no" questions to test it.

As the students become more comfortable with the inquiry process, the teacher should begin to teach the terminology of inquiry and suggest subsequent steps: "That's an interesting theory; how would you go about testing it?" When a student experiments, verifies conditions, or isolates variables, these processes should be identified: "Are there any more objects you should identify? Are there any more conditions you want to explore?" Gradually, the teacher indirectly helps the students learn the terminology for what they are doing by using that language as they inquire. When the students become familiar with the language of inquiry by virtue of encountering many problem situations in which the teacher has labeled the operations, they may be ready to think and talk about inquiry directly. They might consider such topics as: What is theory? What are the origins of theories? What are the optimal strategies for inquiry?

As a last tip, we are told that when first introducing students to the inquiry process, it is good to select problems that do not require formal academic training or information. Suchman's Inquiry Box (see Figure 2) is a nice example of such a strategy:

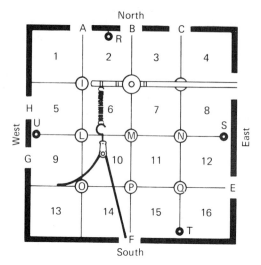

PROBLEM LINKAGE 1.
Level C

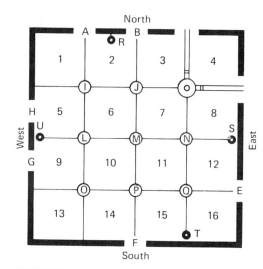

PROBLEM LINKAGE 2.
Level A.

Figure 2. *Suchman's Inquiry Box.*

The Inquiry Box is a device that poses problems for inquiry. Inside the box, various pieces of apparatus can be assembled in a mechanical linkage which is almost completely concealed. Part of the linkage extends outside the box. The student manipulates this part and observes the consequences of what he does. In other words, he observes the output of the box in response to his input.

The box poses the problem: what pieces are inside, where are they located, and how are they hooked together? The inquirer can gather information about this problem in two ways: by manipulating the external portion of the linkage and observing the results, and by probing into the box with a stick to test theories about the location of objects.[4]

Creating the Climate for Inquiry: A Set of Procedures

The chief purpose of Inquiry Training is to make children more autonomous learners. It is essential that teachers concern themselves primarily with creating a climate that aids inquiry. For many teachers, this means radiating a less directive instructional role and adopting the attitude that all knowledge is tentative—there is no one answer. To facilitate this climate for inquiry, Suchman provides us with six rules for conducting the inquiry session:

Rule 1: The questions should be phrased in such a way that they can be answered "yes" or "no." This rule does two things: it requires more precise thinking on the part of students, and it prevents them from putting the burden of thinking on the teacher through open-ended questions.

[4]J. Richard Suchman, *Inquiry Box: Teachers Handbook* (Chicago: Science Research Associates, 1967), pp. 1-2. Reprinted by permission of the publisher.

"Rule 2: Once called upon, a student may ask as many questions as he or she wishes before yielding the floor. . . ."[5] Creative thinking takes time and continuity. Students should not feel pressured by other students eager to inquire.

"Rule 3: The teacher does not answer "yes" or "no" to statements of theories, or to questions that attempt to obtain the teacher's approval of a theory."[6] Theories are only starting points for inquiries; the teacher should encourage students to go beyond their theories, to experiment and test them. There are no final answers in science. Scientists are always searching for better theories. Also, there are many lessons regarding sophistication in expressing a theory; students' explanations can usually be refined. For example, the last three rules reflect the notion that scientific inquiry is a mutual activity among a community of scholars. The procedures for inquiry should encourage students to cooperate with one another and to build upon the groundwork of others.

Rule 4: Any student can test any theory at any time. Students should argue the merits of one another's theories and feel free to test all theories that have been advanced.

Rule 5: Anytime the students feel a need to confer with one another without the teacher's presence, they should be free to call a conference. Conferences should be brief, about a minute. Their purpose is to help students who are reluctant to expose their ideas to a teacher, and to facilitate the cross-fertilization of ideas.

Rule 6: Inquirers should be able to work with experimental kits, idea books, or resource books at any time they feel. These are source materials developed as part of Suchman's training program. The point here is that the environment should provide information to students. If this is done, the students can develop more sophisticated explanations. They can read about theories such as molecular theory and begin to connect the relationship they discover to the problem they are trying to solve.

Classroom Application

Although Inquiry Training was originally developed in the context of the natural sciences, its procedures have wide applicability in all subject areas. Any topic that can be formulated as a puzzling situation is a candidate for Inquiry Training. In literature, murder mysteries and science fiction stories or plots make excellent puzzling situations. Newspaper articles about bizarre or improbable situations are grist for constructing stimulus events. One of the authors was at a Chinese restaurant not too long ago and puzzled over the question, "How is the fortune put into the fortune cookie, since it did not appear burned or cooked in any way?" It occurred to us that this would make an excellent Inquiry Training topic for young children.

The social sciences also offer numerous possibilities for Inquiry Training. Component III of this model presents sample problems from this area. One asks students to explain the failure of a Peace Corps volunteer's efforts to institute new latrines in a small Indian village. Another asks for explanations for the internment of Japanese-Americans by the United States during World War II.

The construction of puzzling situations is relatively easy. When objects and

[5]J. Richard Suchman, *Inquiry Development Program: Developing Inquiry* (Chicago: Science Research Associates, 1966), p. 11. Reprinted by permission of the publisher.
[6]Ibid., p. 12.

other materials are not available or appropriate to the problem situation, we recommend that teachers make up a *problem statement* for students and a *fact sheet* for themselves (as in the anthropological problem described in the Demonstration Transcript in Component II). The problem statement provides the information that is shared initially with the students. It describes the discrepant event. The fact sheet gives the teacher further information about the problem under consideration. The teacher draws on the information in the fact sheet to respond to the students' questions.

The anthropological problem in the transcript in Component II represents an important but subtle distinction between discovery and inquiry. Discovery can occur whenever the explanation is not readily apparent. Inquiry requires a highly inferential hypothesis about causation; it is built around a theory that explains apparently disparate facts. Inquiry includes discovery but goes beyond it. Discovery problems are not necessarily problems of causation. They can simply be situations where the answer or explanation is not readily apparent. Theories of causation are not necessarily part of the explanation. If one of your students is absent for three days and you want to find out why, you have a discovery problem. If his family suddenly disappears without apparent reason and you cannot obtain a definitive explanation, you have an inquiry problem that involves inferential explanations of causation.

Inquiry Training as a Model of Teaching

Syntax of the Model

Inquiry Training has five phases. The first phase is the student's confrontation with the puzzling situation. Phases Two and Three are the data-gathering operations of verification and experimentation. These phases require the students to ask a series of questions to which the teacher can answer by "yes" or "no," and to conduct a series of experiments on the environment of the problem situation. There are three distinguishable steps within these data-gathering operations: (1) verifying the nature of objects, conditions, and properties and the occurrence of events; (2) isolating the relevant variables and conditions through experimentation; and (3) hypothesizing and testing causal relationships through experimentation. Beginning in the third phase and continuing in subsequent activities, a systematic scheme for approaching puzzling situations may be taught. In the fourth phase, the students extract the information from their data gathering and explain the problem as best they can. In the fifth phase, the teacher and the students work together to analyze one another's strategies; the emphasis here is on the consequences of particular strategies. This analysis attempts to help the students become more causal in their questioning and to follow a general scheme of (1) establishing the facts, (2) determining what is relevant, and (3) building concepts of explanation or relationship.

Principles of Reaction

The most important reactions of the teacher take place during the second and third phases. During the second phase the teacher's task is to help the students to inquire, but not to do the inquiry for them. If the teacher is asked questions that cannot be answered by a "yes" or a "no," she must ask the students to rephrase the questions so as to further their own attempt to collect data and relate it to the problem situation. The teacher can, if necessary, keep the inquiry moving by making new information available to the group and by focusing on particular problem events or by raising questions. During the last phase, the teacher's task is to keep the inquiry directed toward the process of investigation itself. Specific principles of reaction include:

1. Insuring that questions are phrased so they can be answered by a "yes" or a "no"
2. Asking students to rephrase invalid questions
3. Pointing out unvalidated statements—for example, "We haven't yet established that this is liquid."
4. Using the language of the inquiry process—for instance, identifying student questions as theories and inviting testing (experimenting)
5. Neither approving nor rejecting student theories
6. Pressing students for clearer statements of theories and more support for generalizations
7. Encouraging interaction among students

Social System

Suchman's intention is that the social system be cooperative and rigorous. Although the Inquiry Training Model can be quite highly structured, with the social system controlled largely by the teacher, the intellectual environment is open to all relevant ideas; teachers and students participate as equals where ideas are concerned. Moreover, the teacher should encourage students to initiate inquiry as much as possible. As the students learn the principles of inquiry, the structure can be relaxed, so that in their pursuit of the explanation for a problem situation they can alternate, in an open environment and time frame, between resource material, dialogue with other students, experimentation, and discussion with the teacher.

The Teacher's Role. The teacher's role in this model is to select (or construct) the problem situation, to referee the inquiry according to inquiry procedures, to respond to students' inquiry probes with the necessary information, to help beginning inquirers establish a focus in their inquiry, and to facilitate discussion of the problem situation among the students. Although the teacher also acts as a recorder, keeping track of the inquiry by recording theories and types of questions on the blackboard, we do not recommend recording at first, since it will probably interfere with the natural flow and pace of the inquiry.

After a period of time and practice in teacher-structured inquiry sessions, students can undertake inquiry in more student-controlled settings. A stimulating event can be set up in the room, and students can inquire on their own or in informal groups, alternating between open-ended inquiry sessions and data gathering with the aid of resource materials available in the class environment. In this way, the students can move back and forth between active inquiry and study. This utilization of the Inquiry Training Model is especially suited to the open classroom setting. In this situation, the teacher's role is one of instructional manager and monitor.

Support System. The optimal support is a set of confronting materials, a teacher who understands the intellectual processes and strategies of inquiry, and resource materials bearing on the problem. It is relatively easy for teachers to develop inquiry materials themselves. Procedures for doing this are discussed in Component III.

Summary

This reading has presented a brief overview of the Inquiry Training Model—its goals, assumptions, and procedures. It has also provided an introduction to the elements of inquiry. Further discussion and training in the stages and elements of inquiry will be presented in the next reading of this component (Taking Theory Into Action).

SUMMARY CHART: THE INQUIRY TRAINING MODEL

Syntax

Phase One: Encounter with the Problem
        Explain inquiry procedures.
        Present discrepant event.

Phase Two: Data Gathering: Verification
        Verify the nature of objects and conditions.
        Verify the occurrence of the problem situation.

Phase Three: Data Gathering: Experimentation
        Isolate relevant variables.
        Hypothesize (and test) causal relationships.

Phase Four: Formulation of an Explanation
        Formulate rules or explanations.

Phase Five: Analysis of the Inquiry Process
        Determine inquiry strategy and develop more effective ones.

Principles of Reaction

1. Insure that questions are phrased so they can be answered with a "yes" or a "no," and that their substance doesn't require the teacher to do the inquiry.

2. Ask student to rephrase invalid questions.

3. Point out unvalidated points—for example, "We have not established that this is liquid."

4. Use the language of the inquiry process—for instance, identify student questions as theories and invite testing (experimenting).

5. Try to provide a free intellectual environment by not evaluating student theories.

6. Press student to make clearer statements of theories and provide support for their generalization.

7. Encourage interaction among students.

Social System

The Inquiry Training Model can be highly structured, with the teacher controlling the inter-action and prescribing the inquiry procedures. However, the norms of inquiry are those of co-operation, intellectual freedom, and equality. Interaction among students should be encouraged. The intellectual environment is open to all relevant ideas, and teachers and students should participate as equals where ideas are concerned.

Support System

The optimal support is a set of confronting materials, a teacher who understands the intellec-tual processes and strategies of inquiry, and resource materials bearing on the problem.

THEORY IN PRACTICE

No amount of description can convey a sense of a model of teaching as well as an example of the model in practice. In fact, reading too much theory before gaining a rough "image" of the practice can be confusing and, for some people, frustrating and discouraging. So we encourage you, at this point of your study of the Inquiry Training Model, to read the following abbreviated transcript of an actual classroom session. We suggest that you first read only the teacher-student dialogue and then go back to note the annotations. Remember, the goal at this point in your training is to gain a sense of the model—its flow and feeling—not to master the techniques of implementation.

The following transcript illustrates the Inquiry Training Model of Teaching using a physical science problem. The lesson was taught by an experienced teacher to fifth-grade students. To our knowledge, it was the students' first exposure to the Inquiry Training method.

Phase I: Encounter With Problem and Episode Analysis

(The teacher presents the class with the discrepant event. She shows the students two large glass measuring cups. Each contains precisely one cup of clear liquid. The class observes the teacher pouring the contents of one measuring cup into the other and mixing the results thoroughly. The volume of the combined liquids (1 cup + 1 cup) is 1 3/4 cups, 1/4 cup less than the total of the two liquids taken separately.)

S: WHAT HAPPENED TO THE MISSING LIQUID?

T: TO FIND OUT WHAT HAPPENED, YOU CAN ASK ME QUESTIONS. BUT YOU CAN ONLY ASK QUES-TIONS TO WHICH I CAN ANSWER EITHER "YES" OR "NO." TO START, ASK ME QUESTIONS ABOUT WHAT YOU SAW HAPPEN AND ABOUT THE OBJECTS THAT WERE USED, TO MAKE SURE YOU REALLY UNDERSTAND WHAT HAPPENED.

The teacher explains the inquiry procedures—"yes" or "no" questions—and the particular inquiry process—verification of objects and events.

S: ARE BOTH MEASURING CUPS THE SAME?

Phase II: Data Gathering (Verification)

T: YES.

S: IS THERE A CRACK IN ONE OF THE CUPS?

T: NO.

S: IS THE LIQUID WATER?

T: YOU WILL HAVE TO BE MORE SPECIFIC.

The teacher reminds the students of the need for specificity in questions.

S: ARE THE LIQUIDS DIFFERENT?

T: YES.

S: IS ONE WATER?

T: YES.

S: IS THE OTHER VINEGAR?

T: NO.

S: IT IS ALCOHOL. IT SMELLS LIKE IT. IS IT?

T: YES.

S: DID ONE OF THE LIQUIDS SPILL OR LEAK OUT WHEN YOU MIXED THEM?

T: NO.

S: IS THERE SOMETHING SPECIAL OR DIFFERENT ABOUT THE MEASURING CUP?

T: NO.

S: WERE THE LIQUIDS THE SAME TEMPERATURE?

T: YES.

S: WERE THEY HOT?

T: NO.

S: WERE THEY ROOM TEMPERATURE?

T: YES. SUPPOSE YOU SUMMARIZE THE INFORMATION YOU NOW HAVE AND STATE THE PROBLEM. WHAT HAVE YOU FOUND OUT?

The teacher invites the students to summarize and synthesize the information into a problem. She did not state the problem at the outset and is instead asking the students to formulate the problem.

S: WELL, YOU TOOK ONE CUP OF WATER AND ONE CUP OF ALCOHOL AND MIXED THEM TOGETHER AND STIRRED THEM UP. WHEN YOU MIXED THEM TOGETHER, THE ONE CUP AND THE ONE CUP MADE 1 3/4 CUPS. WE WANT TO FIND OUT WHY IT DID NOT EQUAL TWO CUPS.

S: WE KNOW THAT THERE WAS NOTHING WRONG IN THE MEASURING CUPS. AND NOTHING SPILLED OUT WHEN THE LIQUIDS WERE MIXED TOGETHER.

S: AND THE LIQUIDS WERE BOTH AT ROOM TEMPERATURE.

S: SO, THE PROBLEM IS: WHERE DID THE 1/4 CUP OF LIQUID GO?

S: DID EVAPORATION CAUSE THE LIQUID TO DISAPPEAR?

Phase III: Data Gathering (Experimentation)

T: HOW COULD YOU FIND OUT?

The teacher invites experimentation. The students test a causal relationship and eliminate a relevant variable.

S: WE COULD TEST TO SEE HOW MUCH EVAPORATION OF WATER AND ALCOHOL TAKES PLACE IN A FEW MINUTES. (The students carry out the demonstration.)

S: WELL, IT WAS NOT BECAUSE OF EVAPORATION.

S: IS THE LOSS OF LIQUID BECAUSE OF THE DROPS OF ALCOHOL LEFT INSIDE THE EMPTIED CUP?

S: THERE DOES NOT SEEM TO BE THAT MUCH LEFT INSIDE THE CUP. JUST A FEW DROPS.

S: LET'S MIX TWO CUPS OF WATER TOGETHER AND SEE WHAT HAPPENS. (The students carry out the task.)

S: IT IS TWO CUPS.

S: LET'S MIX OTHER THINGS. (The students mix coke and water, ginger ale and water, milk and coke.)

S: THEY ALL EQUAL ABOUT TWO CUPS WHEN WE MIX THEM TOGETHER.

S: DOES THIS HAPPEN ONLY WHEN WE MIX ALCOHOL AND WATER?

    A student verifies a property.

T: NO.

S: DOES IT HAPPEN BECAUSE THEY ARE MIXED?

    Theorizing: linear causation. The teacher does not stop here, and another student presents a clearer explanation.

T: YES.

S: WHEN YOU MIX ALCOHOL AND WATER TOGETHER, YOU DO NOT GET WHAT YOU THINK: 1 CUP + 1 CUP = 2 CUPS.

S: IF WE MIXED 1/2 CUP OF WATER AND 1/2 CUP OF ALCOHOL, WOULD WE GET LESS THAN 1 CUP?

    Experimentation question.

T: YES.

S: LET US SEE WHAT HAPPENS. (The students demonstrate.)

S: IT IS LESS THAN ONE CUP. IT IS BETWEEN THE 3/4- AND 1-CUP LINE. WHEN WE MIXED THE OTHER LIQUIDS, SOMETIMES THEY DID NOT REACH THE RED LINE.

S: BUT NOT LIKE THE WATER AND ALCOHOL.

    Notice the student/student interaction.

S: DOES THIS MEAN THAT SOME THINGS, WHEN MIXED TOGETHER, DO NOT EQUAL WHAT YOU THINK THEY SHOULD?

S: BUT WHY?

T: DO YOU THINK YOU COULD USE SOME OF THESE MATERIALS TO ANSWER YOUR OWN QUESTION? (Materials include various kinds of liquids, sugar, salt, sand, pebbles, graduated cylinders. Students measure, mix, and observe.)

    Teacher invites students to experiment and cues them.

S: HERE IT HAPPENED! WHEN I MIXED 1 CUP OF SUGAR AND 1 CUP OF WATER, IT DID NOT EQUAL TWO CUPS EITHER.

S: YEAH, THE WATER GOES BETWEEN THE SUGAR. IT FITS INTO THE SUGAR.

    Phase IV: Formulation of Principles or Rules that Express the Relationship Among Variables Observed in the Event

S: IT HAPPENS WHEN YOU MIX WATER AND SALT, TOO.

S: AND THE SAND AND THE PEBBLES.

S: AND WHEN YOU MIX IT, THE WATER FITS IN MORE AND THE VOLUME KEEPS GETTING LESS.

T: AND WHAT ABOUT THE WATER AND THE ALCOHOL?

S: THAT IS WHAT MUST HAVE HAPPENED WHEN YOU MIXED THE ALCOHOL AND THE WATER. WHEN YOU MIX THEM TOGETHER, THE MOLECULES OF THE WATER AND THE MOLECULES OF THE ALCOHOL FIT INTO EACH OTHER. WATER MOLECULES FIND ROOM BETWEEN THE ALCOHOL MOLECULES.

    A theory!

T: WHAT ARE YOU SAYING ABOUT MOLECULES, THEN?

    The teacher presses for a clearer statement of the theory.

S: WELL, THINGS ARE MADE OF MOLECULES. AND WHEN YOU MIX SOME THINGS TOGETHER, THEY CAN FIT INTO THE MOLECULES OF EACH OTHER.

S: WE SAW THIS WHEN WE MIXED SUGAR AND WATER, AND THE SAND AND THE PEBBLES, AND THE WATER AND ALCOHOL.

T: WHAT ABOUT OTHER LIQUID MIXTURES?

The teacher continues pressing for further consideration of the theory, for a more general statement of it.

S: WHEN WE MIXED SOME OF THE LIQUIDS, IT WAS A LITTLE LESS.

S: NOT ALL THE TIME. IT WAS ONLY A LITTLE.

S: IT WAS HARD TO TELL. SOMETIMES WHEN WE MIXED LIQUIDS, IT WAS A LITTLE BELOW THE RED LINE IN THE CUP.

T: WHAT DO YOU HAVE TO DO, THEN, BEFORE YOU CAN SAY THAT THE MOLECULES OF ONE LIQUID FIT INTO THE MOLECULES OF ANOTHER?

The teacher invites testing that will validate the explanation.

S: LET'S MIX LIQUIDS AGAIN.

S: WE CAN USE DIFFERENT ONES, TOO.

S: THIS TIME, WE SHOULD USE THE GRADUATED CYLINDER. YOU REALLY CAN'T TELL IF THERE IS A DIFFERENCE, WITH THE MEASURING CUP.

S: YEAH, THE CYLINDER IS BETTER TO MEASURE WITH. (The students work at measuring carefully the results of mixing two liquids together.)

T: LET US STOP HERE AND THINK ABOUT WHAT WE HAVE DONE SO FAR. WHAT HAPPENED FIRST?

Phase V: Analysis of the Inquiry Process

S: YOU MIXED A CUP OF ALCOHOL AND A CUP OF WATER TOGETHER.

T: DID YOU KNOW THAT WAS WHAT I MIXED?

The teacher points out the invalid part of the student's theory.

S: NO. THEY BOTH LOOKED THE SAME. YOU DIDN'T TELL US.

S: YOU MIXED ONE CUP OF LIQUID AND ANOTHER CUP OF LIQUID TOGETHER AND YOU GOT 1 3/4 CUPS.

T: AND?

S: WE HAD TO EXPLAIN WHAT HAPPENED TO THE MISSING LIQUID.

T: SO, FIRST YOU SAW THE PROBLEM, OR THE PUZZLE, OR THE EVENT, AND THEN . . .

The teacher paraphrases.

S: WE ASKED QUESTIONS THAT YOU COULD ANSWER YES OR NO, AND WE DID SOME EXPERIMENTS.

T: WHAT KINDS OF QUESTIONS DID YOU ASK AT FIRST?

The teacher probes for clarity and accuracy.

S: WE ASKED IF THE LIQUIDS WERE WATER.

S: WE ASKED QUESTIONS TO FIND OUT WHAT THE LIQUIDS WERE.

S: WERE THE LIQUIDS THE SAME TEMPERATURE.

S: AND ABOUT THE MEASURING CUPS.

S: AND IF ANY WATER OR ALCOHOL SPILLED OR GOT OUT.

T: ALL RIGHT. WHAT DID THESE QUESTIONS DO?

The teacher prompts the students to reflect on their understanding of the inquiry process.

S: THEY TOLD US ABOUT WHAT HAPPENED—ABOUT THE OBJECTS AND WHAT YOU DID WITH THEM.

T: RIGHT. SO FIRST, YOU SAW THE PROBLEM OR THE PUZZLE. THEN YOU ASKED QUESTIONS ABOUT THE OBJECTS USED: THE CUPS AND THE LIQUID. AND YOU ASKED ABOUT THE CONDITIONS OF THE OBJECTS: THE TEMPERATURE OF THE LIQUIDS AND THE KINDS OF MEASURING CUPS.

The teacher paraphrases and summarizes. Note her use of "inquiry language."

TAKING THEORY INTO ACTION

This section further defines the phases and elements of the inquiry process, which were identified briefly in the overview reading. Included in the following pages are short exercises that check your understanding of these components of Inquiry Training. This reading also describes characteristics of students' initial inquiry efforts—specifically their difficulty in working with and expressing theories, in distinguishing between theory and data and understanding the relationship between the two, and in generating experimentation questions. Finally, drawing on Suchman's recommendations, we suggest a sequence of direct instruction that you can use to further your students' understanding of the process of inquiry.

The skills you will accomplish by the end of this reading include:

1. understanding the role of theories in data gathering
2. distinguishing verification from experimentation
3. generating data gathering questions
4. recognizing four types of data
5. recognizing four levels of theory building

Our purpose in discussing the phases and processes of inquiry is to enable you to recognize and label students' questions when it seems appropriate to do so, or to suggest other types of questions to them. We have found that additional practice in recognizing and generating the questions students ask will sharpen your ability to analyze their inquiry processes. Student questions are very revealing!

An Overview of the Elements of Inquiry

Increasing students' awareness of the elements of inquiry is regarded as an essential part of developing their inquiry skill. The teacher increases this awareness through informal means, such as using the terminology of inquiry during Inquiry Training activities, and through formal means, by providing direct instruction on the nature of inquiry.

The concepts of the inquiry process that you will want to introduce and discuss at some point are:

I. Data Gathering (Phases Two and Three)
   A. Verification (Phase Two)
      1. Objects
      2. Properties
      3. Conditions
      4. Events

B. Experimentation (Phase Three)
    1. Objects
    2. Events
    3. Property
    4. Condition

II. Theorizing (implicit in Phases Two, Three, and Four)
    A. Explanations, Laws, Principles, and Rules

Data gathering and theorizing are the two major intellectual operations in any inquiry. During data gathering in this model of teaching, students verify and experiment with four types of information—information about objects, properties, conditions, and events. Although we describe verification and experimentation as separate phases of the model, the students' thinking and the types of questions they generate usually alternate between these two aspects of data gathering.

Students' inquiries during data gathering are usually guided by theories—or, more accurately, their hunches, since their theories at this point are not fully developed. Their reasoning is something like this: "I think heat has something to do with it." Thus, informal theories play a part in both the verification and experimentation aspects of data gathering. Suchman reminds us that in the process of problem solving, the mind shifts back and forth between data gathering and theorizing. Data are used both to suggest theories and to validate them:

> One cannot say that data lead to theories or that theories lead to data. The process is cyclical and both relationships exist. . .the data suggest a theory and the theory suggests what other data should be gathered. The course of inquiry goes back and forth between the two. Without theories, data gathering would be a random and meaningless process. . .data are unlikely to prove useful unless [one] is purposefully collecting them to test some theory.[7]

Theorizing also stands on its own as the final, though tentative, result of the inquiry. In the Inquiry Training Model of teaching, we refer to theorizing in this sense as formulating an explanation (Phase Four of the model). Although the theories generated in Phase Two and especially Phase Three are used to guide inquiry, the purpose of theorizing in Phase Four is to combine the findings from the inquiry into a more formal explanation, statement, or principle.

Figure 3 shows the relationship between data gathering and theorizing as they occur in Phases Two, Three, and Four of the model.

Phase Two	Phase Three	Phase Four
Data Gathering: Verification	Data Gathering: Experimentation	Formulating an Explanation
Theorizing serves as a guide to data gathering.		Theorizing as formal statements.

Figure 3. *Relationship Between Data Gathering and Theorizing.*

[7]J. Richard Suchman, *Inquiry Development Program* (Chicago: Science Research Associates, 1966), p. 26.

The Process of Data Gathering

Suchman divides data gathering into two categories: verification and experimentation. "Verification is the process of gathering data pertinent to a single event."[8] Students gather data about what happened in an event they saw or experienced. In experimentation, on the other hand, we introduce new elements into the situation in order to see if the event would happen differently. Usually, this is done to isolate the variables essential to the original event or to test for causal relationships. Experimentation is usually guided by some theory or hypothesis, whereas verification is an attempt to pin down "what is." For instance, if in verification we find out that a certain liquid is water, and from our background knowledge we know that water boils at 212°F and interacts in predictable ways with certain chemicals, we might hypothesize that the interaction of the boiling water and the chemical creates the energy to move the cylinder. Using this hypothesis as a guide, we can design experiments to test it.

Experiments serve two functions. Suchman calls the first *exploration* and the second *direct testing*. Exploration—changing things just to see what will happen—is random in that it is not guided by a theory, but sometimes it may suggest ideas for a theory. Direct testing occurs when students utilize a theory, hypothesis, or hunch. The process of converting a hypothesis into an experiment is not easy, especially for students. It takes practice. It takes many verification and experimentation questions just to investigate one theory. We have found that even with adults, it is easier to say, "I think it has something to do with. . ." than to think of a series of questions that will test the theory. Also, few theories can be discarded on the basis of one experiment. It is tempting to "throw away" a variable if one "experiment" does not support it. It can be very misleading to do so. One of your roles is to restrain students whenever they assume that a variable has been "disproven" when it has not.

Exercise 1 contains several examples of verification (V) and experimentation (E). See if you can identify them correctly.

EXERCISE 1: DISTINGUISHING VERIFICATION FROM EXPERIMENTATION

_____ 1. Was the civilization English-speaking?

_____ 2. Did the women have to ask permission before they initiated discussion?

_____ 3. If *you* were to approach the oldest member of the group, would he respond?

_____ 4. When the wheels are removed, will the box still remain standing?

_____ 5. Did he speak to anyone before the murder?

_____ 6. Substitute salt for sugar.

_____ 7. Suppose she does not go to college until the following year; will the scholarship continue?

Answers

1.	V	5.	V
2.	V	6.	E
3.	E	7.	E
4.	E		

[8]Ibid., p. 28.

Note that experimentation can be *verbal*—that is, we can ask a question that rearranges the situation ("If this were not fresh water but salt water, would the cylinder still turn?")—or *manipulative*—that is, we can overtly rearrange actual objects or events (pouring in salt water for fresh water). Verbal experimentation, where we verbally substitute new elements and conditions through the use of if-then questions, is particularly important when we work with a non-physical-science problem such as a social problem ("What happened to this civilization?" "How was he murdered?"), where we cannot re-create the actual event or objects.

Reread the definitions of verification and experimentation, look over the examples in Exercise 1, and then see if you can generate your own examples. Use the following problem situation, or, if you prefer, make up one of your own. Generate both verbal and manipulative experimentation questions, and distinguish the ones whose purpose is to isolate variables from the ones that test causal relationships. Notice when you have a theory, and be aware of any difficulties you have in converting your theory into a series of investigative questions!

EXERCISE 2: GENERATING DATA-GATHERING QUESTIONS

Problem Situation: Some time ago at a murder trial in a medium-sized Midwest city, the defendant was found guilty of murder in the first degree by all the members of the jury. The trial occurred in a state that had an automatic death penalty for that charge. However, the jury recommended that the defendant be allowed to go free. Why?

Instructions: Write a list of questions based on the problem situation. Label the experimentation questions V (verbal) or M (manipulative) *and* IV (isolate variable) or TR (test relationship).

If you had difficulty with these exercises, try to identify the source of your confusion and ask your instructor or colleagues for further explanations. Also, note whether converting hypotheses to experimentation questions presented any difficulty for you.

Four Types of Data:
Objects, Conditions, Events, and Properties

Students need to gather information about aspects of the problem situation that may contribute to a discrepancy. Four types of data are important: objects, events, conditions, and properties. Each type of data is amenable to both verification and experimentation. Generally, questions verifying properties or conditions give a powerful thrust to the solution of the inquiry. It would be an unusual problem situation that could be resolved merely by determining the nature or identity of the objects! If we know something of the property of a substance or object, we are able to predict its behavior and formulate experiments that might give us further data.[9] Study the following definitions and examples of the four types of data, and then see if you can complete Exercise 3.

Objects refers to determining (verification) or changing (experimentation) the nature or identity of objects. Questions such as: "Is the knife made of steel?" "Is

[9]Ibid., pp. 56-57.

the liquid water?" and "Was that a compass?" are used to determine the nature and identity of objects.

Events refers to verifying the occurrence or nature of an action: "Did the knife bend upward the second time?" "Did the intruder enter through the window?"

Conditions refers to the state of objects or systems at a particular point in time. If students want to verify conditions, they must be specific about the time, since conditions vary with time: "Was the blade hotter than room temperature when he held it up and showed that it was bent?" "Was he holding the blade perfectly horizontal in the flame?" "Did the color change when the liquid was added?"

Properties refers to verifying the behavior of objects under certain conditions as a way of gaining new information to help build a theory: "Does copper always bend when it is heated?" "Did other tribes move when the water supply was low?"

EXERCISE 3: RECOGNIZING TYPES OF DATA

Check your knowledge of the four types of data. Indicate whether each of the following questions attempts to verify or experiment with objects (O), events (E), conditions (C), or properties (P).

———— 1.   Was the speed of the car greater than 50 mph just before the crash?

———— 2.   Was the city the state capital?

———— 3.   Was he angry during the conversation?

———— 4.   Does the fabric fade when it is washed?

———— 5.   Did the garage door close when the switch was pressed?

———— 6.   Did any of the people on the expedition stay behind?

———— 7.   Was he carrying a bag of sand?

———— 8.   Did the man have back trouble before the accident?

Answers

1.	C	5.	E
2.	O	6.	E
3.	C	7.	O
4.	P	8.	C

In your role of inquiry leader, you can gradually introduce students to these terms and cue them to focus on different types of data as may be necessary in the particular inquiry situations. In Phase Four (the analysis of inquiry), you can ask the students what questions were the most productive or helpful to them in their search. As students recall the questions, the group can identify the type of data that was represented in the question.

Theories

The first role of theories or theorizing in the Inquiry Training Model is to guide the students in their data-gathering operations. One of the things for teachers to be alert for in data gathering is being asked to verify a theory. Students frequently ask "yes" or "no" questions that are actually theories: "Did the heat cause the metal to bend?" "Did a change in the law have something to do with why the defendant was allowed to go free?" "Did it have anything to do with amnesty?" What you must do is recognize when you are being confronted with a "theory" question and inform the student that he or she is suggesting a theory. Tell the students you cannot respond to that question directly, but invite them to ask further questions that might verify or test the theory.

The second function of theorizing in this model of teaching is to present a more formal statement or explanation of the problem after the data-gathering operation; this type of theorizing takes place in Phase Four. In our explorations of this model, we have found two things to be true. First, even after exhaustive and apparently resolved inquiry, several explanations are possible. Students are frequently surprised to realize that the same set of data still suggests different explanations to different individuals. This is one of the best ways, we believe, of conveying the tentativeness of all knowledge. It is easy to assume that Phase Four is just a perfunctory step, a simple matter of putting into words what everyone now knows. This is not the case at all! Phase Four can be a rich experience involving searching discussion and reflection.

Our second finding is that any theory can be expressed at several levels of completeness. (One of the teacher's tasks is to pull students toward greater sophistication in their explanations.) Suchman describes four levels:

1. simple linear causation
2. theories of properties
3. analogies
4. application of a generalization or principle[10]

Simple linear theories assume that X causes Y—for example, heat causes bending. As Suchman points out, one can never prove a linear theory, but one can try to disprove it by manipulating X in different ways. Some teachers respond "yes" to simple linear theories, rather than pushing students to test the theory. Remember, there is always more data gathering and experimentation that can be done.

A more sophisticated level would result from questions aimed at determining the properties of the objects in question and postulating a theory based on the behavior of these properties. Consider this theory: "Different metals expand and contract at different rates, and differences in the rate of expansion produce the bending of the blade." Notice here that the notion of expansion has been added to the simple linear theory that heat causes bending.

"A third level of theory building, still more abstract, is by making analogies or 'the borrowing models from other phenomena.'"[11]

In the fourth level of theory building, students can apply generalizations or concepts from other events. "For example, a student might have developed the concept of equilibrium while observing the motions of certain objects; he theorizes that the blade bends because equilibrium has been disturbed and the blade is not subject to unbalanced forces."[12] Or in explaining a person's behavior, he might use concepts such as "cognitive dissonance" and "stereotyping."

[10]Ibid., pp. 26-27.
[11]Ibid., p. 27.
[12]Ibid., p. 27.

Resource books that describe fields of study and their theories, principles, or concepts are ideal support material for inquiry. Ideally, students alternate between the particulars of the problem situation before them and more general descriptions of areas of investigation, until they begin to make connections. In other words, the support materials are not constructed as solutions to any one problem situation; rather, they present knowledge that can be brought to bear on the problem. It is not a matter of finding "the answer," but of locating and applying information.

EXERCISE 4: LEVELS OF THEORY BUILDING

Read the problem situation about the disappearance of the islanders in the demonstration transcript in Component II. The following are some possible student responses. They include data verification, data experimentation and explanation responses. Each one implies or directly states a theory about causation. In some cases the theory serves as a guide for data gathering, and in other cases for verification or explanation. Identify whether the theory is (SL) simple linear, (P) properties, (A) analogies, (c) generalization or principle.

_____ 1. Was there a terrible earthquake?

_____ 2. Did the islanders practice a religion that required them to make pilgrimages?

_____ 3. Did the islanders practice any method of birth control?

_____ 4. Did the islanders move because there were no longer enough resources to sustain the community on that plot of land (overpopulation)?

_____ 5. Were they all killed by an enemy?

_____ 6. Did they get along with people in neighboring communities?

_____ 7. Did the introduction of Western technology cause them to change their life style?

Answers

1.	SL	5.	SL
2.	A	6.	P
3.	P	7.	C
4.	C		

Characteristics of Beginning Student Inquiry

Students are unaware of the formal elements of inquiry, and most of them do not automatically pursue the most effective strategies of inquiry. For example, one characteristic of beginning inquirers is that they theorize readily; however, they do not make a distinction between theory and data, nor do they see how data and theories relate to one another. Commenting on student inquiry, Suchman declares that beginning inquirers "do not think of theories or explanations as statements that are carefully constructed in the light of data. More typically, they feel that causation is directly obvious in the event itself."[13]

A second characteristic of beginning inquirers is their "tendency to grasp all the most obvious events associated with the phenomenon and to identify that as the cause of the phenomena."[14] The results of this are usually simple linear theories, such as: "The blade expands because of heat."

[13]Ibid., p. 25.
[14]Ibid., p. 25.

Finally, most students do not fully understand the role of experimentation in relation to theories, and they are not skilled at designing experiments. "They need many examples and many opportunities to try designing experiments. At first they will tend to use experimentation chiefly in random, exploratory fashion. As they become more skilled at inquiry, they will begin to design experiments carefully, to test theories."[15]

When the Inquiry Training Model is used over a long period of time, these initial habits and attitudes change. We describe them here to alert you to their possible presence and to suggest ways of counteracting them.

As we discussed in the overview to this model, there are several informal means by which the teacher can socialize students to inquiry. These include labeling, using the vocabulary of inquiry, modeling questions, and providing more structure in the beginning sessions by using verification questions and then suggesting moving on to experimentation.

A Sequence for Direct Instruction

In addition to these informal means by which teachers can socialize students to inquiry, Suchman recommends direct instruction. He alerts us that students are not intrinsically interested in the process of inquiry; rather, they want to explain the puzzling situation. Direct instruction should occur only after many inquiry experiences in which informal means of socialization are used. Once the decision is made to have formal sessions on the nature of inquiry apart from problem situations, the following sequence might be followed.

First to be discussed is the *idea of a theory*. Students can reflect on questions such as these: What is a theory? Where do theories come from? How do new theories arise? When should we modify or discard theories? Are there different types of theories? They can draw upon examples in previous Inquiry Training sessions in thinking about these questions.

The second topic concerns the process of data gathering. The teacher must first help students distinguish between data and theory, and then understand their contributions to each other. The third stage of "inquiry into inquiry" should be to help students distinguish properties from conditions. Finally, the students should see the greater power in verifying conditions and properties as opposed to objects and events. In other words, you should first discuss the major operations of inquiry, theorizing, and data gathering and then move on to the different types of data.

Summary

This reading described the two data-gathering processes of experimentation and verification and the four types of data used in these processes—objects, events, conditions, and properties. The role of theories in the data-gathering process was explored, and different levels of theorizing were identified. Common characteristics of initial student inquiry were discussed, and formal and informal means of socializing students to the attitudes, knowledge, and skills of inquiry were described.

[15]Ibid., p. 30.

Optional Task

The purpose of this reading was to provide information that would help you teach the inquiry process and analyze students' inquiry skills. To check your ability to apply these ideas in this reading to the analysis of student inquiry, read the transcript lesson in Component II and categorize the students' questions, using the following scheme:

	1	2	3	4	5	6	7	8	9	10	11	12	13	14
VERIFICATION														
1. Objects														
2. Events														
3. Properties														
4. Conditions														

	1	2	3	4	5	6	7	8	9	10	11	12	13	14
EXPERIMENTATION														
1. Objects														
2. Events														
3. Properties														
4. Conditions														

	1	2	3	4	5	6	7	8	9	10	11	12	13	14
THEORIZING														
1. Simple Linear Causation														
2. Theories of Properties														
3. Analogies														
4. Application of a Principle, Law, or Generalization														

THEORY CHECKUP FOR THE INQUIRY TRAINING MODEL

Instructions: Circle the response that best answers the question or completes the statement. Check your answers with the key that follows the exercise.

1. While observing an experiment during an Inquiry Training lesson, a student asked the teacher if the speed of the wind had any effect on the shape of the cloud. The teacher answered, "Yes." Given the rules of the inquiry procedure, the teacher should not have responded "Yes." Why was "Yes" not the appropriate response?

   a. The teacher lied. The speed of the wind has nothing to do with the shape of the cloud.
   b. The student was verifying a property.
   c. The student was isolating relevant variables.
   d. The student did not formulate his question so that it could be answered with a "yes" or a "no."

2. What would have been a better response for the teacher to make?

   a. Tell the student what a good guess he made.
   b. Inform the student he has a theory.
   c. Inform the student he is hypothesizing a theory and invite him to test the theory by setting up an experiment.
   d. Say "Maybe" and ask him to ask more questions.

3. If the student says exactly how the wind affects the shape of the clouds, he is

   a. experimenting.
   b. gathering data.
   c. formulating an explanation.
   d. summarizing.

4. List the phases of the Inquiry Training Model.

   a.
   b.
   c.
   d.
   e.

5. A student asks the following question: "Were the people of Indian origin?" She is

   a. experimenting with a property.
   b. verifying an event.
   c. theorizing.
   d. verifying a condition or property.

6. If a student states, "Young people always rebel against their parents," he is

   a. verifying a condition.
   b. theorizing.
   c. hypothesizing.
   d. isolating a relevant variable.

7. Which of the following is not a goal of Inquiry Training?

   a. development of problem-solving skills
   b. understanding of the scientific methodology

    c. resolution of social issues

    d. development of autonomy as a learner

8. Gathering data about a single event is called

    a. testing conditions.

    b. experimenting.

    c. verifying.

    d. exploring.

9. During inquiry sessions, the content of students' questions will alternate between Phases Two and Three. This is because problem solving

    a. is not easy.

    b. shifts between obtaining data and making judgments.

    c. shifts between data gathering and theory building.

    d. is difficult for them at first.

10. When, during inquiry, a student introduces new conditions and events and either verbally or experimentally determines the effects of these changes, she is

    a. theorizing.

    b. experimenting.

    c. verifying.

    d. exploring.

Theory Checkup Key

1. c

2. c

3. d

4. Phase One: Encounter with the Problem
   Phase Two: Data Gathering: Verification
   Phase Three: Data Gathering: Experimentation
   Phase Four: Formulation of an Explanation
   Phase Five: Analysis of the Inquiry Process

5. d

6. b

7. c

8. c

9. c

10. b

Component II

VIEWING

THE MODEL

One of the purposes of Component II is to provide examples of actual sessions in which the Inquiry Training Model is the strategy being used. Reading the two demonstration transcripts that follow, hearing a tape of a teacher and students, or viewing a live demonstration of class activity are alternate means of illustrating the "model in action."

As you study any of these alternatives, you will be introduced to the Teaching Analysis Guide for analyzing the model. This same Guide will also be used in Component III to analyze the peer teaching and microteaching lessons. We want you to become familiar with the Guide now, however, as it will sharpen your perception of the demonstration lesson.

The two activities in this component are (1) reading the Teaching Analysis Guide and (2) viewing (reading) the lesson. Before going on to them, you may wish to reread the material in the Introduction to this book that discusses the purposes and philosophy of the Teaching Analysis Guide.

Analyzing Teaching: Activity 1

The Teaching Analysis Guide for the Inquiry Training Model consists of twenty questions divided among three categories. Most of the questions concern implementation of the five phases of the model. The other areas of analysis are the teacher's role and specific teaching skills. If you review the Summary Chart of the model at the end of the Theory and Overview, you will notice that the questions in the Guide about the teacher's role are drawn from the principles of reaction in that chart.

Section III of the Guide (Teaching Skills) refers to particular teacher moves that are best thought of as general communication skills. They facilitate teaching effectiveness in many models, not just Inquiry Training. On the other hand, these communication skills are not appropriate for some models. The use of any particular teaching skill depends very much on the teacher role that is called for in the model.

The three teaching skills we feel are helpful in Inquiry Training, especially at the initial stages of inquiry, are:

1. paraphrasing students' ideas
2. summarizing, or inviting summaries
3. focusing

Paraphrasing restates students' ideas in another, perhaps more concise form. It reflects back to the inquirer and other students the substantive meaning of the probe or explanation, thereby increasing awareness and clarifying the explanation.

Summarizing, or inviting summaries, pulls together several ideas or discussion sequences and organizes them into a verbal list or central point. The teacher can summarize at different times during the discussion, or invite summaries from the students. Notice how the teacher in the transcript lesson did this (see annotations 3, 17, and 9 in the transcript).

Because the inquiry often proceeds in many directions at one time, it is important to establish and maintain some focus. Summarizing is one way of doing this. Focusing is another. In *focusing*, the teacher tries to pull the students back to particular points or areas of investigation, thereby confining the nature of the probe. The teacher may refer to a previous idea or suggest that the students stay with the point in question and explore it further. Cuing serves as a focusing move. Notice the cuing in the transcript (see annotation 9). There are many different moves that help the students establish and maintain a focus. We refer to all these as focusing moves.

In Inquiry Training, the teacher has the role of preserving an open intellectual climate that encourages mutual inquiry and colleagueship, and of maintaining the procedures and spirit of inquiry. Some of the means for maintaining this role include accepting all student inquiry, rejecting the role of evaluator, encouraging students to interact with one another by inviting their comments, structuring procedures, suggesting that students confer with one another, and using the terminology of inquiry when the opportunity arises.

Examine the Teaching Analysis Guide that follows. Discuss any unclear items with your group or instructor. The Guide can assist you as you study the demonstration, but at this point you do not need to learn to use it precisely.

TEACHING ANALYSIS GUIDE FOR THE INQUIRY TRAINING MODEL

This Guide is designed to help you analyze the process of teaching as you practice the Inquiry Training Model. The analysis focuses on aspects of teaching that are important to the syntax of the model, the teacher's role, and specific teaching skills.

The Guide consists of a series of questions and phrases. As you observe a practice session (whether peer teaching or microteaching), analyze the teaching using the rating scale that appears opposite each question and statement. This scale uses the following items:

Thoroughly. This item signifies that the teacher engaged in the behavior to the point where students were responding comfortably and fluently. Appropriateness varies from situation to situation. For example, discrepant events need to be presented differently to learners of different ages.

Partially. This item signifies that the teacher engaged in appropriate behavior, but not as thoroughly as possible. There is some doubt about whether the students are responding fully.

Missing. The teacher did not engage in the behavior; there appears to be a loss in student response or probably will be one.

Not Needed. The teacher did not explicitly manifest the behavior, but there is no loss. Either the behavior was included in others or the students began to respond appropriately without being led to.

For each question or statement in the Guide, circle the term that best describes the teacher's behavior.

I. SYNTAX

A. Phase One: Encounter with the Problem

1. Did the teacher present a discrepant event?	Thoroughly	Partially	Missing	Not Needed
2. Were the inquiry procedures explained to the students?	Thoroughly	Partially	Missing	Not Needed
3. Was the problem (discrepancy) clear to the students?	Thoroughly	Partially	Missing	Not Needed

B. Phase Two: Data Gathering: Verification

4. Was the inquiry directed toward verification of conditions, events, objects, and property?	Thoroughly	Partially	Missing	Not Needed
5. Did the teacher insure that students ask only "yes" or "no" questions by asking students to reformulate their questions, by pointing out invalid questions, and by refusing to answer open-ended questions?	Thoroughly	Partially	Missing	Not Needed

TEACHING ANALYSIS GUIDE FOR THE INQUIRY TRAINING MODEL

6. Did the teacher press students to clarify the terms and conditions of their questions?	Thoroughly	Partially	Missing	Not Needed
7. If necessary, was there a summary of the inquiry up to this point?	Thoroughly	Partially	Missing	Not Needed
8. Was there a formulation or redefinition of the problem?	Thoroughly	Partially	Missing	Not Needed

C. **Phase Three: Data Gathering: Experimentation**

9. Did the teacher invite testing (experimenting) of relationships and/or isolation of relevant variables?	Thoroughly	Partially	Missing	Not Needed
10. Where appropriate, did the teacher use the language of the inquiry process—for instance, identifying student questions as "theories" and inviting "experimentation" or "testing"?	Thoroughly	Partially	Missing	Not Needed

D. **Phase Four: Formulation of an Explanation**

11. If necessary, did the teacher induce students to formulate a rule or explanation of the discrepant event?	Thoroughly	Partially	Missing	Not Needed
12. Did the teacher press for clearer statement of theories and support for generalizations?	Thoroughly	Partially	Missing	Not Needed

E. **Phase Five: Analysis of Inquiry**

13. Was there a recapitulation of the steps of the inquiry?	Thoroughly	Partially	Missing	Not Needed
14. Was there a discussion of the elements of inquiry, such as data gathering, testing, hypothesizing?	Thoroughly	Partially	Missing	Not Needed

II. THE TEACHER'S ROLE

15. Were all inquiries accepted in a non-evaluative manner?	Thoroughly	Partially	Missing	Not Needed
16. Were interactions among students encouraged?	Thoroughly	Partially	Missing	Not Needed

TEACHING ANALYSIS GUIDE FOR THE INQUIRY TRAINING MODEL

17. Was the language of inquiry introduced? Thoroughly Partially Missing Not Needed

III. TEACHING SKILLS

18. Paraphrasing students' ideas Thoroughly Partially Missing Not Needed

19. Summarizing, or inviting summaries Thoroughly Partially Missing Not Needed

20. Focusing Thoroughly Partially Missing Not Needed

Viewing the Lesson: Activity 2

We would like you now to read the demonstration transcript that follows, identifying the phases of the model and commenting on the lesson as an illustration of the model. In the space below, record the occurrence of the phases. You may want to focus on the adequacy of each phase, the quality of the inquiry, the nature of the puzzling situation, or the skillful moves the teacher made (or did not make).

Phase One	Adequate	Minimal	Not at All
Phase Two	Adequate	Minimal	Not at All
Phase Three	Adequate	Minimal	Not at All
Phase Four	Adequate	Minimal	Not at All
Phase Five	Adequate	Minimal	Not at All

Analyzing the Lesson: Activity 3 (Optional)

View a taped or live demonstration and analyze it by completing the Teaching Analysis Guide. You can do this in two ways: complete the form as the lesson is viewed, or complete it afterwards. If you are working in a group, you may want to divide the task of analysis with one or more of the others, each person taking a particular phase or aspect of analysis. Duplicate as many copies of the Guide as are needed.

DEMONSTRATION TRANSCRIPT

This demonstration was made by Michael McKibbin with a group of students in Palo Alto, California. It employs the map and fact sheet that follow.

Problem Statement. This map shows an island in the middle of a lake. The island is connected to the shore by a causeway made of stones piled on the bottom of the lake until the pile reached the surface. Then smoothed stones were laid down to make a road. The lake is surrounded by mountains,

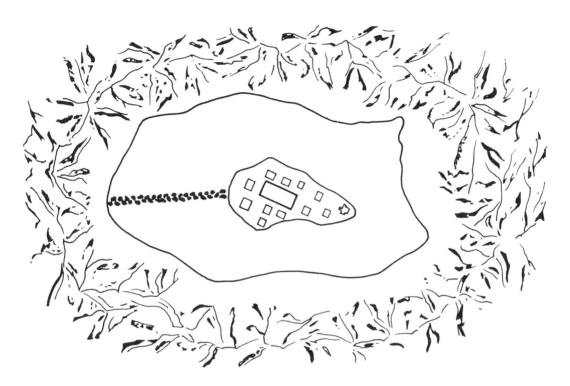

and the only flat land is near the lake. The island is covered with buildings whose walls are still standing although the roofs are now gone. It is completely uninhabited.

Your task is to discover what happened to the people who lived there. What caused the place to be empty of human beings?

Instructor Fact Sheet

1. The lake is 500 feet deep, 600 feet across.
2. The lake is 6,500 feet above sea level. The mountains rise to 11,000 feet.
3. The causeway is made of dumped rocks.
4. The houses are close together. Each one is about 20 by 25 feet and has more than one room. They are made of limestone blocks.
5. Some broken tools and pottery have been found in the homes.
6. The edifice in the center is made of marble and has three levels. At the bottom it is six times larger than the houses. At the top level of the edifice, you can sight the planets and stars through a hole slit in a stone. You can sight Venus at its lowest rise, which occurs on December 21.
7. There is evidence that the islanders fished with traps. They also had livestock such as sheep, cows and chickens.
8. Apparently, there was no art, but evidence of graphic writing has been found.
9. Cisterns have been found under limestone streets.

10. There is no habitation within 80 miles.

11. The island has been uninhabited for about 300 years.

12. The area was discovered in 1900.

13. It is located in a subtropical area of South America where there is plenty of drinking water and where every available area was farmed. There is evidence of irrigation but no evidence of crop rotation. In general, the land is marginal for farming.

14. There is a thin layer of topsoil over a limestone shelf.

15. About 1,000 to 1,500 people lived on the island.

16. The mountains around the island can be crossed with difficulty.

17. There is a stone quarry in nearby mountains and a burial ground across the lake.

18. Dead bodies with hands folded have been found.

19. There is no evidence of plague, massive disease, or war.

T: WE'RE GOING TO DO A STRATEGY CALLED INQUIRY TRAINING. THAT IS, WE WILL TRY TO FIGURE OUT AN EVENT—A DESTRUCTIVE EVENT—SOMETHING THAT WE CAN'T EXPLAIN EASILY. YOU WILL ASK ME A SERIES OF QUESTIONS TO GET INFORMATION IN ORDER TO TRY TO VERIFY WHAT HAPPENED. I USED THE WORD "VERIFY." DOES ANYONE KNOW WHAT THE WORD "VERIFY" MEANS?

Phase I: Encounter with the Problem

S: TO PROVE?

T: EXACTLY. TO PROVE—TO ATTEMPT TO FIGURE OUT WHAT HAPPENED. THEN WE'RE GOING TO TRY TO DEVELOP THEORIES ABOUT THE EVENT. WHAT I'M GOING TO DO IS TELL YOU ABOUT THE EVENTS. AND THEN YOU'VE GOT TO SUPPLY ANY FURTHER INFORMATION BY ASKING QUESTIONS. I'LL ONLY ANSWER "YES" OR "NO" TO EACH OF YOUR QUESTIONS. I'M GOING TO TELL YOU ABOUT THE EVENT NOW; THEN I'M GOING TO EXPLAIN THE RULES OF OUR PROCEDURE.

IN SOUTH AMERICA THERE IS A VERY DEEP LAKE AND IT'S FAIRLY WIDE ACROSS. YOU COULD SWIM IT, BUT IT WOULD BE DIFFICULT. IN THE MIDDLE OF THE LAKE THERE IS AN ISLAND, AND SURROUNDING THE LAKE ARE SEVERAL VERY RUGGED MOUNTAINS WHICH RISE TO ABOUT 11,000 FEET. THE LAKE IS 6,500 FEET ABOVE SEA LEVEL. SOMEHOW THE PEOPLE DUMPED A LOT OF ROCKS INTO THE WATER TO MAKE A CAUSEWAY; THESE ROCKS MAKE IT POSSIBLE TO WALK BACK AND FORTH TO THE ISLAND.

THE PROBLEM IS, THERE'S NOBODY THERE. THE ISLAND IS UNINHABITED. PEOPLE LEFT IT ABOUT THREE HUNDRED YEARS AGO. ARCHAEOLOGISTS WITH OTHER METHODS HAVE USED CARBON-14 DATING IN ORDER TO FIND OUT WHAT HAD HAPPENED. THESE LITTLE THINGS

THAT YOU SEE HERE ARE REPRESENTATIVE OF SEVERAL HOUSES MADE OUT OF SANDSTONE AND LIMESTONE. THEY ALSO HAD VERY SOPHISTICATED CISTERN AND STREET SYSTEMS, AS WELL AS FAIRLY SOPHISTICATED ARCHITECTURE. EXCEPT FOR THE HOUSES AND THE STREETS, EVERY AVAILABLE SPACE WAS USED FOR PRODUCING CROPS AND RAISING LIVESTOCK. AND THERE IS SOME EVIDENCE OF FISHING.

IN THE MIDDLE OF THE ISLAND WAS A BIG MARBLE SQUARE WITH SEVERAL SMALLER LEVELS ON TOP OF IT. IF YOU GO TO THE VERY TOP OF THIS MARBLE EDIFICE, YOU CAN SIGHT THE PLANETS AND STARS, AND ACTUALLY SEE VENUS AT ITS WINTER SOLSTICE, WHICH IS DECEMBER 21; IN OTHER WORDS, WHERE IT IS AT ITS LOWEST RISE IN THE SKY. ACROSS THE LAKE THERE ARE LIMESTONE QUARRIES AND A BURIAL GROUND. HERE THE PEOPLE HAVE BEEN BURIED WITH THEIR HANDS FOLDED.

THAT'S ALL THE INFORMATION THAT I'M GOING TO GIVE YOU RIGHT NOW. IF I NEED TO GIVE YOU SOME MORE LATER ON, I WILL. WE KNOW THIS HAPPENED ABOUT THREE HUNDRED YEARS AGO AND WE DON'T KNOW WHY. WE CAN ONLY GUESS WHY, AND WE'D LIKE YOU TO HELP US TRY TO FIGURE OUT WHAT HAPPENED.

NOW THE RULES OF OUR GAME. YOU MAY ASK "YES" OR "NO" QUESTIONS; IF THEY'RE NOT "YES" OR "NO" QUESTIONS OR I CAN'T ANSWER THEM "YES" OR "NO," I'M GOING TO ASK YOU TO REPHRASE THEM, BECAUSE I CAN'T ANSWER THEM OTHERWISE.

S: DO YOU KNOW THE ANSWER?

T: WE THINK WE KNOW THE ANSWER.

S: OH, WE'RE SUPPOSED TO TRY TO GET IT OUT OF YOU.

T: YEAH. THE POINT IS THAT ALL SCIENTIFIC INFORMATION IS REALLY TENTATIVE—WE CAN ONLY GUESS. AND THAT'S THE CASE WITH THIS. NOBODY REALLY KNOWS BECAUSE IT WAS THREE HUNDRED YEARS AGO. ALL WE CAN DO IS PUT THINGS TOGETHER. THAT'S YOUR JOB. I THINK I HAVE AN ANSWER. I WANT TO SEE IF YOU COME UP WITH THE SAME ONE. ONCE YOU'VE ASKED A QUESTION, YOU CAN CONTINUE TO ASK AS MANY QUESTIONS AS YOU WANT.

S: IT'S LIKE WHAT'S MY LINE?

T: IT'S A LITTLE BIT LIKE THAT. IT'S BASED UPON THE OLD GAME TWENTY QUESTIONS. BUT WE'RE GOING TO BE A LITTLE MORE SOPHISTICATED THAN THAT. ONE OF THE THINGS THAT YOU CAN DO IS CALL FOR A CONFERENCE AND THEN YOU CAN TALK AMONG YOURSELVES ABOUT

Teacher explains the rules.

THE INFORMATION THAT YOU ARE GETTING. I'LL KIND OF PULL OUT AND YOU CAN WORK TOGETHER TO FORM YOUR HYPOTHESIS. I WON'T MISLEAD YOU INTENTIONALLY. IF A QUESTION CAN'T BE ANSWERED "YES" OR "NO," I'LL TELL YOU "YES, BUT THAT'S GOING TO BE MISLEAD-ING," AND I'LL ASK YOU TO SHARPEN YOUR QUESTION—OK? I WON'T MISLEAD YOU PUR-POSELY. ANY TIME THAT YOU WANT TO ASK A THEORY QUESTION, I HOPE YOU'LL DO IT, BECAUSE ALL OF OUR SCIENTIFIC EVIDENCE IS GOING TO BE BASED UPON THE THEORIES THAT WE'RE GOING TO FORM. THEN WE'RE GOING TO TEST OUR THEORIES. YOU CAN FORM A THEORY EVERY TIME YOU WANT; BUT WHEN YOU DO, I WANT TO MAKE SURE THAT YOU KNOW THAT YOU'VE ASKED A THEORY QUES-TION. IF YOU'RE GOING TO ASK ME A THEORY QUESTION, I WON'T ANSWER YOU. YOU'LL HAVE TO FIND OUT THE ANSWERS FOR YOURSELVES. UNDERSTAND THAT RULE?

NOW, WHAT I WANT YOU TO DO IS TO GATHER DATA; IN OTHER WORDS, I WANT YOU TO ASK QUESTIONS IN ORDER TO VERIFY THE EVENTS. FOR EXAMPLE, YOU CAN ASK QUESTIONS ABOUT THE OBJECTS, SUCH AS THE PIECES OF LIME-STONE. YOU CAN ASK ABOUT THE EVENTS THAT HAPPENED OR ASK ABOUT THE CONDITIONS. THESE ARE DATA QUESTIONS AND I CAN ANSWER THESE "YES" OR "NO." ONCE YOU HAVE FORMED A THEORY, WE'LL BE ASKING YOU TO EXPERI-MENT WITH "IF/THEN" SORT OF QUESTIONS LIKE, "IF SOMETHING HAPPENED, THEN SOME-THING ELSE HAPPENED," BUT WE'LL GET INTO THOSE LATER. WHO WANTS TO ASK ME THE FIRST QUESTIONS IN ORDER TO GET MORE INFORMATION?

S: WERE THEY PRIMITIVE?

T: YOU'LL HAVE TO DEFINE WHAT YOU MEAN.

S: WELL, THEIR MATERIAL WAS NOT MADE OUT OF STEEL OR IRON. I'M ASKING IF THEY WERE PRIMITIVE, AND WHAT I MEAN BY THAT IS, ARE THE THINGS THAT THEY USED—WERE THEY LIKE ARROWHEADS—WERE THEY CARVED?

T: ARE YOU ASKING ME, "WERE THERE ARROW-HEADS?"

S: WERE THERE ARROWHEADS?

T: YES, THERE WERE. OK, YOU WANT TO GO ON?

S: THERE WAS?

T: YES, NOT A LOT, BUT SOME.

S: COULD YOU GET THROUGH THE MOUNTAINS?

T: YOU COULD GET THROUGH THE MOUNTAINS.

Phase II: Data Gathering (Verification)

THERE WERE SOME PASSAGEWAYS, BUT IT WAS VERY DIFFICULT.

S: WELL, MAYBE SOME TOOK A CHANCE. DID THEY TAKE A CHANCE AND GO THROUGH THESE MOUNTAIN PASSES?

T: THEY DISAPPEARED.

S: WAS THERE ANY EVIDENCE OF REALLY BAD OR STRANGE WEATHER?

T: NO EVIDENCE OF THAT.

S: OTHER THAN THE BURIAL PLACE, WAS THERE THE REMAINS OF HUMAN BONES?

T: YES.

S: JUST AROUND IN DIFFERENT PLACES? BESIDES THE BURIAL GROUNDS?

T: NO, THERE WAS NO OTHER EVIDENCE. ALL OF THE HUMAN BONES WERE IN THE BURIAL GROUND.

S: WERE THERE A LOT OF PEOPLE IN THE BURIAL GROUND?

T: NO.

S: WERE THERE ANY WILD ANIMALS?

T: NO.

S: NATURAL PREDATORS?

T: NOT ON THE ISLAND.

S: WERE THERE ANY PERSONAL BELONGINGS ON THE ISLAND, LIKE PEOPLE WERE LIVING THERE?

S: HAD THEY TAKEN EVERYTHING WITH THEM?

T: NO, BUT I DON'T WANT TO MISLEAD YOU; MOST OF THE THINGS THAT WERE LEFT THERE WERE BROKEN.

S: SO IT SEEMS AS IF THEY LEFT AND TOOK MOST OF THE USEABLE THINGS WITH THEM?

T: YES.

S: WERE THEY THE ONLY PEOPLE IN THAT AREA? WAS THERE ANYBODY ELSE AROUND THEM?

T: YOU HAVE TO SHARPEN YOUR QUESTION.

S: WAS THERE ANYONE ELSE IN THAT PARTICULAR PLACE?

T: WHAT DO YOU MEAN BY AREA? ON THE ISLAND?

S: ON THE ISLAND.

T: NO, THEY WERE THE ONLY PEOPLE ON THE ISLAND.

S: WERE THERE PEOPLE IN THE MOUNTAINS AROUND THE ISLAND?

T: WHAT DO YOU MEAN BY THE AREA?

S: OH, A HUNDRED-MILE RADIUS?

T: NO.

S: WERE THE MAJORITY OF THEM WOMEN AND CHILDREN?

T: NO.

S: WAS THERE ANY EVIDENCE OF DISEASE?

T: YOU'LL HAVE TO EXPLAIN SOME.

S: WHEN THEY DID THE CARBON DATING OF THE BONES, DID THE ARCHAEOLOGISTS CHECK FOR OTHER THINGS?

T: YES, THERE WAS EVIDENCE OF DISEASE.

S: DO YOU KNOW THAT DISEASE WAS THE CAUSE OF DEATH?

T: WELL, DISEASE WOULD HAVE BEEN A CAUSE OF DEATH.

S: WAS THERE EVIDENCE THAT THERE WAS A REALLY WIDESPREAD EPIDEMIC OR SOMETHING?

T: NO.

S: DO YOU THINK THAT ALL THE PEOPLE THAT DIED WERE DISEASED?

T: NO.

S: YOU DID AT FIRST.

S: HE WAS TRYING TO TRICK ME.

T: I DON'T WANT TO MISLEAD YOU; THAT'S THE POINT. BUT I WANT YOU TO SHARPEN YOUR QUESTION. DO YOU NEED MORE INFORMATION?

S: WAS THERE EVIDENCE OF A DROUGHT? WAS THERE EVIDENCE OF IRRIGATING?

T: THERE IS SOME EVIDENCE OF IRRIGATION.

S: DID YOU SAY WHEN YOU THOUGHT THOSE PEOPLE LIVED? WAS IT THREE THOUSAND YEARS AGO?

T: THREE HUNDRED.

S: DID YOU SAY HOW THE ROCKS FORMED THE CAUSEWAY? WAS IT FROM A LANDSLIDE?

T: NO. THEY WERE DUMPED THERE.

S: THE CAUSEWAY WAS NOT MAN-MADE?

T: THE CAUSEWAY WAS MAN-MADE.

S: DO THEY KNOW WHEN THE CAUSEWAY WAS MADE, LIKE FROM THE EROSION IN THE ROCKS?

T: NO.

S: THREE HUNDRED YEARS IS WHEN THE INDIANS— AMERICAN . . .

T: IT'S IN THE MOUNTAINS OF SOUTH AMERICA AND THEY'RE ABOUT 11,000 FEET HIGH.

S: DID SOMEONE COME AND TAKE THEM AWAY— FROM OTHER PARTS OF THE COUNTRY, PEOPLE THAT WERE MORE MODERN THAN THEY MIGHT HAVE BEEN?

T: I CAN'T ANSWER THAT QUESTION. WHAT IS IT?

S: DID SOMEONE FROM ANOTHER PART OF THE WORLD WHO HAD MODERN TRANSPORTATION COME OVER THE MOUNTAINS AND TAKE THE PEOPLE AWAY?

T: IS THAT A THEORY QUESTION?

S: I WANT A "YES" OR "NO" . . .

T: ARE YOU TRYING TO VERIFY IT?

S: IT WAS THREE HUNDRED YEARS AGO, SO WHAT WAS MODERN THEN?

S: SOME PEOPLE HAD NEVER HEARD OF HORSES— I'M QUITE SURE THEY DIDN'T HAVE HORSES—BUT IN OTHER PARTS OF THE WORLD THERE WERE PEOPLE WHO WE KNOW HAD MORE MODERN SKILLS; THEY WERE MORE DEVELOPED. SO I WANT TO KNOW IF THEY DISCOVERED OR CAME UPON THIS ISLAND AND WENT ACROSS THE CAUSEWAY AND GOT THE PEOPLE OFF OF IT.

T: I'M SUGGESTING TO YOU THAT THAT'S A THEORY QUESTION, IF YOU'D LIKE TO TEST IT. YOU ARE SUGGESTING THAT A GROUP MORE MODERN THAN THEY CAME AND TOOK THEM OFF THE ISLAND. IS THAT WHAT YOU'RE SUGGESTING?

Phase III: First Hypothesis

S: ANYONE WHO IS LIVING IN A PLACE WHERE THERE ARE MOUNTAINS IS LIKELY TO BE NOT QUITE AS CIVILIZED OR ADVANCED. MAYBE SOMEONE ELSE WAS.

T: IT'S A GOOD THEORY. THAT'S FINE. NOW OUR JOB IS TO ASK QUESTIONS THAT EXPLORE THAT POSSIBILITY. REMEMBER THAT ALL EVIDENCE IS TENTATIVE. THERE ARE TWO KINDS OF QUESTIONS THAT YOU CAN ASK TO EXPERIMENT WITH YOUR THEORY. THE FIRST ARE EXPLORATION QUESTIONS. IN OTHER WORDS, YOU WOULD SAY, "WOULD IT MAKE A DIFFERENCE IF THIS HAPPENED?" AND I COULD ANSWER THAT, "YES" OR "NO." OR YOU CAN ASK, "WOULD THE SAME THING HAPPEN IF . . . ?" AND I CAN ANSWER THAT, "YES" OR "NO." OR IF YOU WERE TESTING A SCIENTIFIC THEORY, "IF I HELD IT NEAR A FIRE, WOULD THE SAME THING HAPPEN?" IN OTHER WORDS, I'M TRYING TO FIND OUT WHAT THE VARIABLES ARE. DO YOU UNDERSTAND WHAT WE'RE GETTING AT HERE? I'M GOING TO FOCUS ON HER THEORY UNTIL YOU GIVE IT UP OR GO TO ANOTHER ONE. REMEMBER, ALL KNOWLEDGE IS TENTATIVE. OKAY, HER THEORY IS THAT SOMEBODY HAS COME AND TAKEN THEM AWAY.

Phase II: Data Gathering (Experimentation)

S: I HEARD A STORY ONCE THAT A SMALL GROUP OF INDIANS WERE LIVING TOGETHER AND ANOTHER GROUP OF PEOPLE CAME OVER THE MOUNTAIN AND TOOK SOME OF THEM AWAY.

T: OKAY, LET'S TEST IT NOW. WHAT EVIDENCE DO YOU HAVE TO TEST YOUR THEORY?

S: DID YOU SAY WHERE THE PEOPLE HAD COME FROM BEFORE THEY WENT TO THE ISLAND?

T: WE DON'T KNOW.

S: DID THEY GET THE LIMESTONE ROCKS FROM QUARRIES?

T: YES, IN THE MOUNTAINS AROUND THEM.

S: THEY DUG OUT QUARRIES, SO THEY MUST HAVE HAD SOME TECHNOLOGY.

T: YES.

S: WERE THEY AS ADVANCED AS PEOPLE IN THE FLATLANDS?

T: I DON'T THINK WE HAVE EVIDENCE THAT THERE WERE PEOPLE IN THE FLATLANDS.

S: WAS THERE ANY EVIDENCE OF THOSE PEOPLE WHO LIVED QUITE FAR AWAY?

T: YES, THERE WERE SOME PEOPLE, QUITE A DISTANCE AWAY.

S: WERE THE PEOPLE ON THE ISLAND STRANGE? IS THAT WHY THEY LIVED THERE, BECAUSE THEY COULDN'T BE WITH OTHER PEOPLE?

T: NO.

S: THEY WERE THE SAME RACE, THEN?

T: YES. IF YOU TAKE RACE IN ITS BROADEST SENSE.

S: SO THERE WASN'T ANYTHING THE MATTER WITH THEM THAT WOULD MAKE IT NECESSARY FOR THEM TO STAY ON THE LITTLE ISLAND?

T: WE HAVE NO EVIDENCE OF THAT. YOU SHOULD EXPLAIN WHAT YOU MEAN BY "SOMETHING WRONG WITH THEM."

S: WELL, WERE THEY CRAZY?

T: NO, THERE'S NO EVIDENCE OF THAT.

S: DID YOU SAY SOMETHING ABOUT WHEN THEY LEFT, THAT EVERYTHING WAS BROKEN?

T: WHAT I SAID WAS THAT THE ONLY THINGS THAT WERE LEFT WERE THINGS THAT WERE BROKEN.

S: WAS THERE EVIDENCE OF A FIGHT?

T: NO. BUT REMEMBER WE'RE STILL ON HER THEORY. LET'S FOCUS. DO YOU WANT TO DROP THE THEORY AND GO ON TO ANOTHER ONE?

S: NO, BECAUSE IT'S THE ONLY POSSIBLE REASON, UNLESS THEY ALL DIED OFF.

S: THE THINGS THAT WERE LEFT WERE BROKEN OR PROBABLY THINGS THAT WERE NOT NECESSARY TO TAKE ALONG, IF THEY WERE GOING ON A LONG JOURNEY.

T: WHAT'S YOUR QUESTION?

S: WAS THERE EVIDENCE OF CHILDREN?

T: YES.

S: WELL, MAYBE THESE PEOPLE DID DECIDE THAT THERE WERE OTHER PARTS OF THE WORLD THEY WANTED TO SEE.

Evidence doesn't support hypothesis.

Teacher refocuses students.

T: WHY DON'T YOU GET SOME QUESTIONS? YOU'VE GOT SOME GOOD POINTS; LET'S FIND OUT IF THEY'RE TRUE OR NOT.

S: DO YOU KNOW WHAT KINDS OF ANIMALS WERE THERE?

T: DOMESTIC.

S: COWS?

T: YES.

S: WERE THERE REMAINS OF HORSES, BURROS, DONKEYS, OR SOMETHING LIKE THAT?

T: I DON'T KNOW IF THERE WERE HORSES OR NOT. THERE WERE SOME BURROS, YES.

S: WERE THERE REMAINS OF ANIMAL BONES ON THE ISLAND?

T: YES, SOME.

S: ALL DOMESTIC?

T: GENERALLY, YES.

S: DID YOU TELL US WHAT'S ON THIS SIDE?

T: MOUNTAINS. THERE IS A TREACHEROUS PATH-WAY TO THE LEFT. THE BURIAL GROUND AND THE STONE QUARRIES ARE IN THESE MOUN-TAINS.

S: HOW LONG WAS THE CAUSEWAY. DID YOU SAY THAT?

T: ABOUT A HALF-MILE.

S: ARE THE ROCKS STILL THERE?

T: YES.

S: WERE THERE REMAINS OF BONES AROUND THE LAKE?

T: SOME, BUT NOTHING OUT OF THE ORDINARY.

S: WHAT IS THE ORDINARY?

T: NOTHING THAT WOULD INDICATE FOUL PLAY.

S: WHAT WAS THE GRADE ON THE CAUSEWAY? HOW WAS IT, FLAT? HOW FAR APART WERE THE ROCKS AND THINGS?

T: IT WAS EASY TO DRIVE A CART ACROSS IT.

S: YOU COULD WALK?

T: THEY COULD HAVE USED THE ANIMALS AND TRAVELLED.

S: IT SEEMS AS IF THEY HAD LEFT?

T: YES.

S: WAS THERE ANY EVIDENCE OF TRAVEL?

T: YES, THEY LEFT. NOW YOU'VE GOT TO FIGURE OUT WHY THEY LEFT.

S: WAS THERE AN EARTHQUAKE?

T: NO EVIDENCE OF AN EARTHQUAKE.

S: WAS THERE EVIDENCE OF OVERPOPULATION ON THE ISLAND?

T: WE'VE GOT A LOT OF STUFF NOW. YOU MIGHT WANT TO GET IT TOGETHER AND FORMULATE A THEORY.

S: WELL, MAYBE WHEN IT SNOWED AND RAINED, THE LEVEL OF THE LAKE ROSE AND THE PEOPLE THOUGHT THAT THEY HAD TO SPLIT.

T: OK, YOUR THEORY IS THAT THE LAKE ROSE. HOW CAN WE EXPLORE THAT?

S: IF THE LAKE ROSE, WOULDN'T THE CAUSEWAY HAVE BEEN SUBMERGED?

T: IT WAS THE SAME HEIGHT AS THE ISLAND.

S: WERE THE BROKEN PARTS THAT YOU FOUND MOSTLY IN THE MIDDLE OF THE ISLAND?

T: NO.

S: THEY WERE AT THE EDGES TOO?

T: YES.

S: SO LIKE IT COULDN'T BE THAT THE WATER CAME OVER THE ISLAND?

T: THERE'S NO EVIDENCE OF THAT.

S: WAS THERE EVIDENCE OF FURNITURE IN THE LAKE?

T: NO.

S: DO YOU KNOW HOW LONG THEY WERE LIVING THERE?

T: I CAN'T ANSWER THAT QUESTION.

S: WHY?

T: BECAUSE IT'S NOT A "YES" OR "NO" QUESTION.

S: DO YOU KNOW?

T: WE KNOW THAT THEY LEFT ABOUT THREE HUNDRED YEARS AGO.

S: SO THEY MUST HAVE LIVED THERE A LONG TIME. IT WAS A SMALL CIVILIZATION.

S: LOOK AT ALL THE ROCKS THAT THEY MOVED.

S: I'M SURE THERE WERE SMART PEOPLE THERE. COULD THEY HAVE FIGURED OUT THAT THE WATER WAS RISING? AND THEY SAID IN SO MANY YEARS THE WATER IS GOING TO RISE.

T: SO ASK ME A QUESTION TO GET AT THAT—AN IF-THEN QUESTION. THAT'S WHAT YOU NEED TO DO; YOU NEED TO EXPLORE AND EXPERIMENT NOW.

S: IF THE WATER HAD RISEN, THEN WOULD THE ISLAND HAVE GONE UNDER?

T: NO.

S: WOULD THE ROCKS CAVE IN OR SOMETHING? WAS IT SOLID?

T: THERE'S NO EVIDENCE OF IT CAVING IN.

S: IS THERE ANY EVIDENCE OF ANY RELIGION THEY HAD, LIKE THEY WORSHIPPED A CERTAIN GOD?

Relevant experimentation question.

T: YES.

S: WHAT GOD?

S: IS IT SOMETHING THAT WE'VE HEARD OF BE-FORE? DID THEY WORSHIP SOMETHING THAT WE'VE HEARD A LOT OF PEOPLE WORSHIPPING?

T: YES.

S: WAS IT CHRISTIAN?

T: NOT THAT WE KNOW OF. THERE WAS NO EVI-DENCE OF CHRISTIANITY.

S: WAS THERE EVIDENCE OF FLOATING MATERIALS LIKE GRASS BOATS?

T: NO. WE'RE ON HIS THEORY—FOCUS.

S: WHAT WAS IT AGAIN?

T: WATER RISING.

S: WITH THE WATER RISING, COULDN'T THEY HAVE MADE RAFTS?

Evidence doesn't support hypothesis.

T: NO EVIDENCE OF IT. BOBBY, DO YOU WANT TO GIVE UP ON YOUR THEORY AND GO ON TO ANOTHER ONE?

S: WAS THERE ANY EVIDENCE OF EXTRATERRES-TRIAL LIFE?

T: THERE'S NO EVIDENCE OF LIFE FROM ANOTHER PLANET.

S: WERE THERE ANY CALENDARS ON THE ISLAND?

T: YES. I SHOULD TELL YOU THAT THERE WERE CALENDARS, BUT NOT LIKE THE ONES WE HANG ON THE WALL.

S: WERE THE CALENDARS LIKE THOSE AT EASTER ISLAND?

T: YOU HAVE TO TELL ME WHAT EASTER ISLAND IS.

S: ALL THOSE ROCKS LINED UP IN A CERTAIN WAY.

T: WHAT DID I SAY IN THE BEGINNING?

S: YOU SAID THAT THEY HAD TWO ROCKS THAT LINED UP WITH VENUS.

T: RIGHT, YES.

S: WAS VENUS THEIR GOD?

T: WE DON'T KNOW THAT. WE KNOW THAT VENUS CAN BE SEEN ON DECEMBER 21.

S: COULD THAT HAVE BEEN—IF THERE WERE OTHER PEOPLE LIVING AROUND THE ISLAND— COULD THEY HAVE GOTTEN THOSE PEOPLE, PUT THEM ON A BOAT, PUT THEM ON THE ISLAND, AND COME BACK. THEY WERE LIKE PRISONERS. SO THEY GOT ALL THOSE ROCKS AND PUT THEM IN THE WATER SO THAT THEY COULD GET OFF. SO WOULD IT BE LIKE A PRISON?

T: YOU'RE THEORIZING. YOU HAVE A COUPLE OF THEORIES THERE AND I'M NOT SURE THAT YOU'VE ASKED AN INFORMATION QUESTION. IS THERE ANY EVIDENCE OF IT BEING A JAIL? IS THAT YOUR QUESTION?

Teacher helps by refocusing.

S: YES.

T: NO.

S: IS THERE ANY EVIDENCE OF THEM BEING DRIVEN OFF?

T: NO.

S: DID THEY LEAVE ANY WRITING BEHIND?

T: NO.

S: FOR ALL PRACTICAL PURPOSES, THEY JUST LEFT OF THEIR OWN FREE WILL?

T: AS FAR AS WE KNOW—YES.

S: YOU SAID THEY DID IRRIGATE, BUT YOU DIDN'T SAY WHETHER THERE'D BEEN A DROUGHT OR SOMETHING, OR WHETHER THEIR IRRIGATION SYSTEM HADN'T WORKED.

T: THERE'S NO EVIDENCE THAT WATER FAILED.

S: HOW ABOUT A FAMINE?

T: YOU'LL HAVE TO EXPLAIN YOURSELF.

S: WERE THEY IN NEED OF FOOD, SO THEY LEFT?

T: IS THAT A THEORY QUESTION? STATE IT IN THE FORM OF A THEORY.

S: IF SOMETHING HAD GONE WRONG WITH THE PLANTS—THE PLANTS DIED—SO THEY DECIDED TO GO SOME PLACE ELSE. THEY TOOK WHAT ANIMALS THEY COULD, BUT THEY COULDN'T GET THEM ALL.

T: SO GIVE ME A THEORY.   Teacher prompts for a theory.

S: MY THEORY IS THEY WERE RUNNING OUT OF   Significant hypothesis
FOOD AND THEY ALL DECIDED TO LEAVE. A
FEW STAYED BEHIND, BUT THEY LEFT BECAUSE
OF LACK OF FOOD.

T: FINE. THAT'S OUR THEORY. WE'RE GOING TO   "If/Then" questions
FOCUS ON THAT. WHAT EVIDENCE DO WE HAVE
THAT WILL PROVE OR DISPROVE THAT? ASK
YOUR "IF-THEN" QUESTIONS. BOBBY?

S: IF THEY RAN OUT OF FOOD, COULD THEY HAVE EATEN THEIR CATTLE?

T: YES, THEY COULD HAVE.

S: IF THEY RAN OUT OF FOOD AND THEN RAN OUT OF CATTLE, COULD THEY HAVE STARTED EATING EACH OTHER?

T: THERE'S NO EVIDENCE OF CANNIBALISM.

S: IS THERE ANY EVIDENCE THAT THE SUPPLY OF FISH IN THE LAKE WAS GOING DOWN?

T: NO.

S: THERE WASN'T A LOT OF STUFF ON THE ISLAND LIKE THERE WAS ON THE MOUNTAIN. THERE WERE MORE TREES AND THINGS THAT THEY COULD EAT. BERRIES . . .

T: TO ANSWER YOUR QUESTION, "DID IT MAKE A   Would it make a difference?
DIFFERENCE WHERE THEY WERE?" THE ANSWER
IS, "YES, IT DID."

S: WAS IT JUST A NATURAL DIFFERENCE? THINGS GREW ON THE ISLAND, BUT DIFFERENT THINGS GREW IN THE MOUNTAINS. BECAUSE THEY DIDN'T HAVE THE SEEDS.

T: YES, I THINK SO.

S: WAS THERE ANY EVIDENCE OF THE VEGETATION DYING?

Seeking evidence to support hypothesis.

T: YES, THERE WAS.

S: IT WAS DYING AT A FASTER RATE THAN WHAT WE CONSIDER NORMAL?

More support for hypothesis.

T: YES.

S: DO THEY HAVE A REASON FOR IT DYING?

T: I THINK I KNOW IT.

S: BECAUSE OF BLIGHT—A DISEASE OF THE VEGE-TATION.

T: YOU HAVE TO DEFINE DISEASE.

S: LIKE BUGS?

T: BUGS, NO.

S: ANY KIND OF BACTERIA?

T: WHAT DO YOU MEAN BY BACTERIA?

S: DID THE SOIL HAVE A DISEASE?

T: THERE IS SOME EVIDENCE OF THAT.

S: WAS IT HARD TO GROW THINGS ON THAT ISLAND?

T: YES.

S: WAS VERY MUCH SUN HITTING THE ISLAND?

T: YES, A LOT OF SUN.

S: IT WAS SOMETHING IN THE SOIL, THEN?

T: YES.

S: WAS IT THE SOIL—THE MINERALS? THE SOIL WAS WORN OUT, FROM REUSE, BEING USED OVER AND OVER AGAIN?

T: YES.

S: SO THERE WAS LACK OF MINERAL CONTENT IN THE SOIL. NOT ENOUGH OF THE MINERALS THE PLANTS NEED, LIKE NITROGEN.

T: YES. OK, YOU GOT IT. NOW ONE MORE QUICK ONE I WANT YOU TO FIGURE OUT, IF YOU CAN. YOU TALKED A LITTLE BIT AGO ABOUT WHY THEY LEFT. BUT NOW I WANT YOU TO GO BACK. YOU'VE GOT THE EVIDENCE ALREADY—ABOUT HOW THE DECISION WAS MADE TO LEAVE.

Phase IV: Refocusing to Extend the Problem

S: DID THAT SIGHTING OF THE TWO ROCKS WITH VENUS HAVE ANYTHING TO DO WITH IT?

T: YES.

S: THEY WERE VERY SUPERSTITIOUS, WEREN'T THEY?

T: WHAT DO YOU MEAN?

S: VENUS, WE ALL KNOW, ISN'T A GOD. IT'S JUST

A PLANET. AND SO PERHAPS THEY WORSHIPPED IT AS A GOD. IT TOLD THEM TO LEAVE . . .

S: SOME TYPE OF OMEN.

S: YEAH, SO I'M ASKING, DID VENUS HAVE SOMETHING TO DO WITH IT?

T: YOU'RE THEORIZING THAT VENUS HAD SOMETHING TO DO WITH IT, AND IT WAS SOME SORT OF OMEN?

S: YES.

T: OK—TESTABLE—THAT'S TESTABLE. GOOD.

S: LIKE WE USE ALMANACS—IN THE FARMER'S ALMANAC, THEY SIGHT THE MOON AND THEY CAN TELL CROP SUCCESS AND THINGS LIKE THAT.

S: WERE THEY LOOKING FOR SOMETHING SPECIFIC? WERE THEY LOOKING FOR RELIEF? WAS THERE SUPPOSEDLY SOMETHING COMING THAT THEY WERE LOOKING FOR? THAT WOULD HAVE RELIEVED THEM IF IT HAD COME?

T: I DON'T KNOW HOW TO ANSWER YOUR QUESTION. DID SOMETHING COME—OR WOULD SOMETHING COME? I DON'T KNOW. WERE THEY LOOKING FOR SOMETHING?

S: DID THEY BELIEVE THIS?

T: YES. THAT'S A LITTLE BIT MISLEADING, BUT I DON'T THINK IT'S TOO MUCH.

S: WERE THEY TOLD TO LEAVE?

T: YES.

S: WELL, THEIR VENUS TOLD THEM.

T: VENUS TOLD THEM TO LEAVE? ONLY IN THE BROADEST SENSE.

S: WOULD IT BE POSSIBLE FOR THEM TO HAVE A LEADER THAT WOULD SAY HE COULD TALK TO VENUS? DID THEY HAVE A MAIN MAN?

T: YES, THERE'S SOME EVIDENCE OF THAT.

S: WAS THERE A THRONE OR A PALACE OF SOME KIND—SOMETHING THAT A KING . . .

S: WHERE THE ROCKS WERE FACING VENUS.

S: WAS THERE A PALACE ON THE ISLAND THAT LOOKED LIKE A PLACE WHERE A KING MIGHT HAVE LIVED?

T: WAS THERE?

S: AN OBSERVATORY.

S: THE CENTER.

T: YES, THE CENTER. THE ROCKS THAT FACED VENUS ARE THE ONES IN THE MIDDLE.

S: AND SO THE TEMPLE WAS THERE TOO?

S: WAS THERE A METEORITE?

T: NO, THERE'S NO EVIDENCE OF METEORITES.

S: IS THERE EVIDENCE THAT THERE WERE FARMERS AND AGRICULTURE?

T: YES.

S: WERE THERE FISHERMEN?

T: SOME, BUT YOU'VE KIND OF ESTABLISHED THAT IN YOUR LAST THEORY THAT YOU DEMONSTRATED. WE'VE MOVED ON TO ANOTHER ONE. WE'RE FOCUSING ON WHETHER THERE WAS AN OMEN DECIDED BY SOME—WHAT WAS IT?   Teacher is refocusing students.

S: DEITY?

T: OK, IT SOUNDS LIKE YOU PEOPLE HAVE ALL THE INFORMATION YOU NEED. SOUNDS LIKE YOU NEED A CONFERENCE THAT I WON'T PARTICIPATE IN.

S: OK. LET'S HAVE A CONFERENCE.

S: WHAT DO YOU THINK, GANG?   Conference

S: I THINK IT WAS STARVATION.

S: YEAH, THAT WAS ONE OF THE THEORIES, BECAUSE ALL THE MINERALS IN THE LAND WERE BEING USED UP. THEY HAD TO SPLIT BECAUSE THE FOOD WAS RUNNING OUT.

S: WE KNOW THAT ALREADY.

S: SOMEBODY TOLD THEM TO LEAVE.

S: THAT TIME WOULD ONLY COME ON DECEMBER 21.

S: THE WINTER SOLSTICE IS THE SHORTEST DAY OF THE YEAR. THEY MUST HAVE THOUGHT SOMETHING WAS GOING TO HAPPEN ON THE WINTER SOLSTICE.

T: OK, READY? GOT SOME QUESTIONS YOU WANT TO ASK?   Further questioning

S: DO YOU KNOW IF THE REASON WHY THEY LEFT HAD ANYTHING TO DO WITH THE WINTER SOLSTICE?

T. YES.

S: WAS SOMETHING SUPPOSED TO HAPPEN ON THE 21ST?

S: THE SUN WENT DOWN OR SOMETHING?

S: AN ECLIPSE!

S: VENUS CROSSED IN FRONT OF THE SUN AND ECLIPSED!

T: YOU'RE ON THE RIGHT TRACK. THAT'S NOT, IN FACT, WHAT HAPPENED. YOU'RE REALLY SO CLOSE, I'M GOING TO TELL YOU WHAT HAPPENED.

LET ME HELP YOU WITH THIS ONE. APPROXIMATELY EVERY EIGHT HUNDRED YEARS THERE ARE CROSSINGS OF VENUS AND SEVERAL OTHER PLANETS. NOW LET'S FIGURE BACK EIGHT HUNDRED YEARS. WHAT HAPPENED ABOUT SIXTEEN HUNDRED YEARS BEFORE THIS HAPPENED? IS   **Phase IV: Formulating an Explanation**

ANYBODY SCIENTIFIC ENOUGH TO EXPLAIN THE STAR OF BETHLEHEM? WHAT IS THE SCIENTIFIC EXPLANATION OF THE STAR OF BETHLEHEM?

S: THERE WAS A FLUKE. SOMETHING HAPPENED AT THAT TIME.

T: WHAT HAPPENED? VENUS AND WHAT CROSSED? I CAN'T REMEMBER WHICH STAR, BUT THAT'S WHAT MADE IT BRIGHTER THAN EVERY OTHER. SO SIX HUNDRED YEARS LATER, WHAT HAP-PENED?

S: SAME THING.

T: AND WHAT HAPPENED?

S: IT WAS AN OMEN.

T: BASICALLY THEY CONSIDERED IT AS AN OMEN AGAIN, SO THEY FOLLOWED THE STAR. THEY WENT ABOUT THREE HUNDRED MILES AWAY, AND INTERESTINGLY ENOUGH, ABOUT THREE HUNDRED MILES AWAY YOU FIND A LARGE MARBLE THING IN THE MIDDLE OF A CITY MADE OUT OF LIMESTONE HOUSES.

NOW, LAST PHASE AND WE'RE DONE. WHICH QUESTIONS THAT YOU ASKED GOT YOU THE MOST INFORMATION?

S: THE SOIL.

S: VENUS, THE STAR.

S: FOOD.

T: WHAT ABOUT THE "YES" "NO" QUESTIONS? DID THE "YES" QUESTIONS GET YOU MORE INFORMATION OR THE "NO" QUESTIONS?

S: "NO."

S: THE "YES" QUESTIONS.

T: BUT SOME "NO" QUESTIONS, WERE THEY VALUABLE?

S: YES.

T: WHAT QUESTIONS DID YOU ASK FIRST?

S: ABOUT PEOPLE—LIFESTYLE.

S: ANIMALS.

S: THE GRAVES.

T: RIGHT—THE QUESTIONS ABOUT SOME OF THE OBJECTS. AND WHAT ABOUT THE EVENTS QUES-TIONS?

S: ABOUT THE MOUNTAINS.

T: RIGHT, THE RUGGEDNESS.

S: SO THAT'S WHY SCIENTISTS THINK THAT THEY LEFT.

T: YES.

S: THEY MUST HAVE BEEN THERE A LONG TIME.

T: REMEMBER YOU SAID SOMETHING ABOUT THEM HAVING A LEADER, A RELIGIOUS LEADER. THE LEADER SAID, "WE'RE GOING."

S: THEY LEFT BECAUSE OF THAT STAR, RIGHT? THEN THEY DIDN'T LEAVE BECAUSE OF SOIL DEPLETION; THE SOIL WAS DEPLETED SO THAT TOLD THEM TO GO.

S: EXACTLY. ALL RIGHT.

T: WHAT DO YOU THINK ABOUT THE PROCESS?   **Phase V: Analysis of the Inquiry Process**

S: YOU LEARN A LOT.

T: HOW ABOUT YOUR QUESTION-ASKING SKILLS? NOW WHAT DO YOU THINK ABOUT THE WAY YOU ASK QUESTIONS?

S: IT WAS ALL RIGHT THAT NOBODY STUCK TO ONE THING. IF IT WASN'T RIGHT, THEY'D MOVE ON TO A TOTALLY DIFFERENT QUESTION.

T: WELL, REMEMBER THAT'S WHAT WE THINK HAPPENED! WE DON'T KNOW FOR SURE, BUT THAT'S WHAT WE THINK.

S: SOME OF US COULD BE RIGHT.

Component III

PLANNING
AND
PEER TEACHING

To plan an Inquiry Training lesson, you must formulate a discrepant event and have enough knowledge of the problem situation to respond accurately to the students' inquiry. Remember, there does not have to be one definite answer; all knowledge is tentative, and your judgment about the most likely hypothesis will be sufficient.

We encourage you to formulate problems in areas other than the physical sciences—areas such as literature, music, psychology, and art. Although these areas may present some difficulty in the construction of experimentation and other aspects of inquiry, they are very amenable to this model.

The steps in planning and teaching the model include:

1. selecting and formulating a discrepant event
2. determining educational objectives
3. completing the Planning Guide
4. peer teaching
5. analyzing the peer teaching lesson
6. after peer teaching: microteaching (audio taping is recommended)

The following section contains examples of how to formulate a discrepant event; these events may also be used for peer teaching or microteaching. But we do recommend that you try to select or identify at least one discrepant event of your own.

SELECTING AND FORMULATING A DISCREPANT EVENT

Anything that is mysterious, unexpected, or unknown is grist for a discrepant event. A simple puzzle, riddle, or magic trick can be used as a puzzling situation. Of course, the ultimate goal is to have the students, especially the older ones, experience the creation of new knowledge much as scholars do. However, beginning inquiries can be based on very simple ideas.

Ideas for problem situations can come from the sources already available to us. One source of puzzling situations is the texts and resource books that teachers and students use. (These may require some adaptation to remove the "solutions.") One English teacher we knew used a story from Kurt Vonnegut's *Venus on the Half Shell* as a basis for a puzzling situation, eliminating the ending.

After you have identified a puzzling situation, you need to "shape it into form" so that (1) the precise problem is clear to the student (for example, "How did the murderer get into the house?" or "Why wasn't he allowed to join the organization?") and (2) the students have enough context for the problem situation to begin the inquiry.

If the problem is one that can be demonstrated with equipment or objects, such as the problem of the bimetallic strip discussed in Component I, then providing the context entails a live or filmed demonstration. If the problem involves human behavior, we must construct a Problem Statement that gives the context and the issue or question. Problem Statements can be read aloud by teacher or students, or copies can be given to students.

The second step in constructing the problem situation is to identify the factual information that backs up the inquiry. It is important to remember that as a teacher, you don't have to know everything. You cannot anticipate all of the students' questions, and at times you must simply state, "I don't know," "I'm not sure," "We don't have clear evidence on that point," or "Scientists aren't sure," depending on the question. At the same time, you can project several lines of inquiry that students might take, and gather the data for them.

Problem statements and fact sheets that were developed for three sample problems are offered below:

Problem 1: The Latrine Project

Problem Statement

All of us, at some time in our lives, have tried to do something that failed, and we didn't know why. When that did happen, we probably tried to figure out why. The following problem involves a failure. I have come up with an explanation that I am satisfied with. I'd like to see if, through the process of inquiry, you come up with the same explanation.

In the mid-'60s in India, the U.S. government accumulated a large quantity of rupees (Indian currency) through the sale of PL480 wheat. In order to get the money back into circulation, they were willing to fund nearly any reasonable development proposal. A number of Peace Corps volunteers submitted proposals that were funded. One of these was a latrine project in a village in Rajasthau.

A Peace Corps volunteer had noticed that the villagers used the fields adjacent to the village for elimination. In fact, the women went a considerable distance away for their morning "constitutional." The volunteer decided that, for reasons of both convenience and sanitation, a sanitary latrine complex would meet one of the needs of the village and worked up the plan that is illustrated in the following diagram.

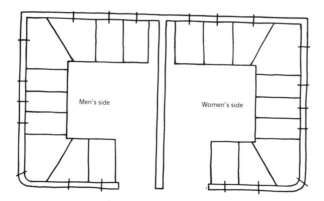

The latrine complex was divided into men's and women's areas, with covered entrances and an opening where the waste material could be removed from the outside by a latrine cleaner.

The volunteer took the plan to the *pauchayet* (elected village council of prominent men in the community) and they agreed, without exception, that the idea was a good one for three reasons. First, it was an example to other communities that their village was progressive. Second, they liked the idea of receiving American development money. Third, the volunteer was well liked by the pauchayet and a good number of the villagers.

The pauchayet used the grant to provide for the labor force and buy the materials. The project was well constructed. The first month after completion, the latrines were well used by both men and women villagers, but by the second month, the latrines were used by considerably fewer people. By the third month, they were virtually unused. The villagers, particularly the women, had gone back to the fields for their constitutional. Why did this happen?

Fact Sheet

1. The feces were not used as fertilizer.
2. The latrines were quite sanitary, with little odor.
3. The latrine cleaners could perform their caste-designated function without causing any caste problems.

Explanation

Building individual stalls had eliminated the only opportunity the women had to communicate with one another. The rest of the time, the women were inside their homes serving the needs of their family.

Problem 2: The Japanese Internment

Problem Statement

During the spring of 1942, the United States government began the removal and internment of 110,000 Americans (two thirds of them native-born) of Japanese ancestry. These Japanese-Americans were not charged individually with any crime, but were collectively ordered to report for internment under Executive Order 9066. California, Oregon, and Washington were the prime strategic areas from which people of Japanese descent were removed.

Much hardship followed, since these orders were enacted faster than adequate facilities could be completed. Evacuees went to Idaho, Wyoming, Utah, and Arizona, where they suffered blistering summers and freezing winters in squalid, inadequate facilities.

The Japanese also suffered incalculable financial losses because they were forced to sell personal as well as real property in a matter of days; they fell victim to financial opportunists who bought their property far below market value. The government "acquired" much of the evacuees' farmland.

During World War II, Japanese-Americans fought bravely in Europe and the Pacific, despite the injustice being imposed on their families.

How do you explain the loss of Japanese-American liberty during World War II when:

the United States was fighting a war against the "internment" of another ethnic group, at the same time that they were interning the Japanese?

German-Americans were not interned during World Wars I or II?

the act of internment violated the basic American right of "due process," especially the presumption of innocence and the right to a hearing?

Fact Sheet

Anti-Oriental sentiment in the United States began in the 1850s; it was directed against the Chinese railroad-construction workers. When this labor was over, the Chinese tried to become assimilated into the citizenry. Denis Kearney's slogan "The Chinese must go!" was later transformed by him into "The Japs must go!" By 1900, San Francisco mayor J. D. Phelan was saying, "Chinese and Japanese are not bona fide citizens, not stuff of which Americans are made; their culture is different; let them keep their distance."

The government passed legislation to prevent immigration of Orientals. The Japanese counter-demonstrated against these tactics, but the Chinese never did. Most of this legislation did not survive the courts, but it did incite prejudice. There were three important actions: the Gentlemen's Agreement of 1908, the Alien Land Law of 1913, and the Japanese Exclusion Act of 1924.

Gradually, the Japanese, who were restricted from working in urban areas by strong labor unions, gravitated to agricultural labor and became prosperous. The

Alien Land Law was passed in 1913, preventing alien-born Japanese from buying or leasing land for more than three years.

During the 1920s and 1930s, growing Japanese military strength fanned anti-Japanese sentiment, particularly in California, and an immigration act was passed that specifically excluded Japanese. During this time, literary and cinematic stereotypes depicted the Japanese as sly, ruthless Oriental villains.

After the catastrophe of Pearl Harbor, the evacuation of Japanese-Americans from the Pacific Coast began (1942). President Roosevelt gave the Western Defense Commander authority to designate "military areas" and exclude "any and all persons" from them (Executive Order 9066).

Some Speculation on Causes of Internment

1. Americans were under the delusion that they were without guilt as a nation during World War II, and thought of themselves as guardians of freedom and justice the world over.

2. Complete lack of understanding, respect, and regard by the communities where the Japanese-Americans were born, reared, and worked.

3. Racial hatred.

4. Economic and political opportunism.

5. Fear.

6. Saturation of the job market by Oriental groups.

Problem 3: The Health Worker's Rejection

Problem Statement and Fact Sheet

A neighborhood health worker and registered nurse had spent about six months in a Denver housing project encouraging residents to utilize the neighborhood health facilities provided by a federal health center. The area of the housing project contained about one hundred families and some local shopping. Just when she felt she had achieved rapport with the residents and acceptance in the neighborhood, a strange thing happened.

For the two previous weeks she had been visiting door to door to talk about health care services with reasonable receptivity. On Thursday, June 14, she began visiting homes as before, but no one would answer the door. She heard sounds of activity in the homes, but was unable to get anyone to answer her knock. Rather puzzled, she went to the neighborhood grocery store and tried to find out what was wrong. The woman running the store told her she was no longer welcome in her store, but gave her no reason. Confounded by the situation, the health worker returned to the health center to involve the staff in figuring out what had happened.

Explanation

During the past two weeks, the health worker had been talking about family planning and distributing information about how to get free birth control pills. The neighborhood included Black, Chicano, and Anglo families. The birth control information had been well received by Black families that were matriarchal in organization. On the day before her "shut out" experience, the health worker had visited a Chicano mother in a home that was patriarchal in organization and against birth control measures of any kind. This Chicano mother was beaten severely by her husband when he came home and found the birth control information.[1]

Summary

After you have outlined a problem situation, constructed the problem statement or demonstration, identified the backup data, and developed a fact sheet, it is useful to locate resource materials that bear on the problem. These materials can be made available to the students, or they can be used by the teacher.

To repeat, the stages in selecting and organizing a puzzling situation are roughly as follows:

1. Identify and outline the problem.
2. Construct a problem statement or demonstration that makes the problem or issue clear.
3. Determine the facts and develop a fact sheet.
4. Select and organize additional resource material.

EXERCISE 1

Identify a potential puzzling situation, preferably from your subject area. Develop a problem statement or demonstration. Describe the discrepant event by completing Part I of the Planning Guide.

DETERMINING EDUCATIONAL OBJECTIVES

The major focus of the Inquiry Training Model is on the development of inquiry skills, rather than on the acquisition of specific content or the mastery of particular concepts. That is, we are more interested in students applying the skills and operations of inquiry than that they master a particular body of information. However, because Inquiry Training taps students' curiosity and motivation, they can (and should), in the course of an investigation, seek out and acquire much content, both facts and concepts. Inquiry Training is also a natural test of students' ability to apply concepts, principles, and facts they may have acquired in previous instruction.

When first introducing Inquiry Training, the teacher may be chiefly interested in getting students to ask data questions (or possibly to simply formulate pertinent questions). With practice, the objective may be to get students to ask data questions using all four types of data: events, conditions, properties, and objects. Eventually, the teacher will want students to demonstrate all the inquiry operations and carry out inquiry successfully with progressively more complex problems.

Inquiry Training can also promote attitudes, such as a willingness to be

[1]We are grateful to our colleague, Roger Pankratz of Western Kentucky University, for contributing this problem situation.

tentative, to pursue a line of thinking to its conclusion, and to drop an unproductive line of thinking. Still other objectives are the development of the ability to listen and to contribute to or question another student's ideas.

EXERCISE 2

Below are a list of objectives for Inquiry Training lessons. For your peer teaching, select or formulate at least two objectives. Record these on the Planning Guide. Specify what strategies you will concentrate on to ensure that these objectives are met.

Acquiring new factual information (specified or unspecified)

Applying previously acquired principles and concepts

Asking data questions

Asking data questions related to objects, events, properties, and conditions

Asking "If-Then" (experimentation) questions

Developing hunches (hypotheses) to guide inquiry

Converting hypotheses into experimentation

Using concepts to guide inquiry

Stating formal explanations, statements, or principles

Increasing the level of theory-building by using theories of properties, analogues, and generalizations

Consulting resource books

Applying information gained in resource books

Using theories to guide experimentation

Recognizing someone else's theory

Using the terminology of inquiry: verification, experimentation, object, event, property, theory, hypothesis

Experimenting to isolate variables

Experimenting to test relationships

Experimenting to explore

Experimenting to directly test a theory

Summarizing the status of data gathering

COMPLETING THE PLANNING GUIDE

We have developed a Planning Guide to help you organize your Inquiry Training lesson. We have tried to anticipate situations that arise during a session. The Guide is especially useful the first few occasions you use the model. After that, such extensive planning is probably not necessary.

In the following pages, a completed Planning Guide is provided as a sample. The lesson here was based on Chapter 6 in Kurt Vonnegut's *Venus on the Half-Shell* (published under the pen name of Kilgore Trout). This lesson was prepared by Della Chestnut of Carrollton, Georgia. We are grateful for her skilled participation in planning and teaching this Inquiry Training lesson.

The portion read to the class by the teacher in Step VI, Phase One is:

"I'm going back to the ship. So long, Goobnatz."

"I'm not Goobnatz," she said. I'm Dunnernickel."

Simon was so shaken up that he didn't ask her what she meant by that. He assumed that he had had a slip of memory. The next day, however, he apologized to her.

"Wrong again," she said. "My name is Pussyloo."

There was a tendency for all aliens of the same race to look alike to Earthmen. But he had been here long enough to distinguish individuals easily.

"Do you Shaltoonians have a different name for every day?"

"No," she said. "My name has always been Pussyloo. But it was Dunnernickel you were talking to yesterday and Goobnatz the day before. Tomorrow, it'll be Quimquat."

This was the undefinable thing that had been making him uneasy.[2]

SAMPLE PLANNING GUIDE FOR THE INQUIRY TRAINING MODEL

I. Discrepant Event
   1. Describe the discrepant event. Attach any material you have prepared for your students.

   Simon, a space traveler from Earth, visited the planet Shaltoon. He was disconcerted to find that the Shaltoonians had different voices and personalities every day. Apparently they were different people every day, except for their physical appearance, which remained unchanged.

   2. What is the discrepancy that has to be accounted for?

   Personality changes from day to day.

II. Educational Objectives
   3. List at least two educational (behavioral) objectives you will teach for in this lesson.

   a. To give participants experience in deductive problem solving.
   b. To develop skills in asking verification questions.

   4. How will you ensure that these objectives are met?

   a. Introduce class to Inquiry Training model.
   b. Provide examples of verification questions and label them as they arise.
   c. Use the "language" of the Inquiry Training model (hypothesis, experimental question).

[2]Kilgore Trout, *Venus on the Half-Shell* (New York: Dell Publishing Co., Inc., 1974), pp. 54-55.

SAMPLE PLANNING GUIDE FOR THE INQUIRY TRAINING MODEL

III. Theory

5. Describe several alternative theories or explanations that might be considered in relation to this problem.

    a. Reincarnation.
    b. External agent responsible for assigning spirits to bodies (government, God, computer).

6. What is the theory or explanation that does account for the discrepant event? Are there satisfactory alternatives?

    Ancestor rotation. Each Shaltoonian carried memory cells representing an almost infinite number of ancestors, at the onset of puberty, each memory cell was allowed one day to manifest itself. Every seventh day the living Shaltoonian was allowed to be himself.

IV. Data Gathering

Generate two questions appropriate to this event that ignore items irrelevant to this problem.

7. Verify objects

    Were the Shaltoonians human beings? (yes)

8. Verify events

    Did Simon's personality change from day to day? (no)
    Did the Shaltoonian's physical appearance change daily? (no)

9. Verify properties

    Did the Shaltoonians have abnormally long life spans? (yes)
    Did the Shaltoonians have siblings? (no)
    Did the Shaltoonians ever have the same name? (yes)

10. Verify conditions

    Did individuals choose which personality they would have each day? (no)
    Did any two living Shaltoonians ever have the same personality? (no)

182

SAMPLE PLANNING GUIDE FOR THE INQUIRY TRAINING MODEL

V. Experimentation
11. How could students experiment with various explanations or theories?

> If a Shaltoonian were ten years old, would he have a different personality every day? (no)
> If the memory of a Shaltoonian could be destroyed, would the same phenomenon occur? (no)

VI. Phases of the Model: Generating Opening Moves
Describe the moves you will use to initiate each phase of the model.

Phase One: Encounter with the problem

> I'm going to read you a description of an unusual situation and I'd like you to figure out what is going on here. You'll see what I mean in just a minute.

Phase Two: Data Gathering: Verification

> Before you start guessing what the causes are, let's spend the first few minutes finding out more about the people and events. Ask me questions that give you more information. One thing you might want to find out is if the Shaltoonians practice a religion.

Phase Three: Data Gathering: Experimentation

> You've probably got a few ideas or theories in mind by now. Ask me questions that might test your ideas. Let me show you how to do this with "if-then" questions. Suppose you believe there was a terrible accident that caused all the Shaltoonians to lose their identities. Then you could partially test this by asking, "If I were a Shaltoonian several hundred years ago, would I behave in the same way that Shaltoonians do today?"

Phase Four: Formulating an Explanation

> "We've gathered a lot of information and probed some theories. Let's see if we can come up with a clear explanation of exactly what's causing this strange occurrence."

Phase Five: Analysis of Inquiry

> I'd like us to think back over the questions we asked and identify the lines of inquiry that we explored to see what happened to them. Also you may be able to tell me what questions were most helpful to you.

PLANNING GUIDE FOR THE INQUIRY TRAINING MODEL

I. Discrepant Event
    1. Describe the discrepant event. Attach any material you have prepared for your students.

    2. What is the discrepancy that has to be accounted for?

II. Educational Objectives
    3. List at least two educational (behavioral) objectives you will teach for in this lesson.

    4. How will you ensure that these objectives are met?

III. Theory
    5. Describe several alternative theories or explanations that might be considered in relation to this problem.

    6. What is the theory or explanation that does account for the discrepant event? Are there satisfactory alternatives?

IV. Data Gathering
    Generate two questions appropriate to this event that ignore items irrelevant to this problem.
    7. Verify objects

PLANNING GUIDE FOR THE INQUIRY TRAINING MODEL

8. Verify events

9. Verify properties

10. Verify conditions

V. Experimentation
    11. How could students experiment with various explanations or theories?

VI. Phases of the Model: Generating Opening Moves
    Describe the moves you will use to initiate each phase of the model.
        Phase One: Encounter With the Problem

        Phase Two: Data Gathering: Verification

        Phase Three: Data Gathering: Experimentation

PLANNING GUIDE FOR THE INQUIRY TRAINING MODEL

Phase Four: Formulating an Explanation

Phase Five: Analysis of Inquiry

Analyzing the Peer Teaching Lesson

After you have peer taught the Inquiry Training lesson, analyze your teaching by completing the Teaching Analysis Guide on the following pages. Duplicate as many copies of the Guide as you may need to analyze the peer teaching and microteaching of all group members.

TEACHING ANALYSIS GUIDE FOR THE INQUIRY TRAINING MODEL

This Guide is designed to help you analyze the process of teaching as you practice the Inquiry Training Model. The analysis focuses on aspects of teaching that are important to the syntax of the model, the teacher's role, and specific teaching skills.

The Guide consists of a series of questions and phrases. As you observe a practice session (whether peer teaching or microteaching), analyze the teaching using the rating scale that appears opposite each question and statement. This scale uses the following items:

Thoroughly. This item signifies that the teacher engaged in the behavior to the point where students were responding comfortably and fluently. Appropriateness varies from situation to situation. For example, discrepant events need to be presented differently to learners of different ages.

Partially. This item signifies that the teacher engaged in appropriate behavior, but not as thoroughly as possible. There is some doubt about whether the students are responding fully.

Missing. The teacher did not engage in the behavior; there appears to be a loss in student response or probably will be one.

Not Needed. The teacher did not explicitly manifest the behavior, but there is no loss. Either the behavior was included in others or the students began to respond appropriately without being led to.

For each question or statement in the Guide, circle the term that best describes the teacher's behavior.

I. SYNTAX

A. Phase One: Encounter with the Problem

1. Did the teacher present a discrepant event?	Thoroughly	Partially	Missing	Not Needed
2. Were the inquiry procedures explained to the students?	Thoroughly	Partially	Missing	Not Needed
3. Was the problem (discrepancy) clear to the students?	Thoroughly	Partially	Missing	Not Needed

B. Phase Two: Data Gathering: Verification

4. Was the inquiry directed toward verification of conditions, events, objects, and property?	Thoroughly	Partially	Missing	Not Needed
5. Did the teacher insure that students ask only "yes" or "no" questions by asking students to reformulate their questions, by pointing out invalid questions, and by refusing to answer open-ended questions?	Thoroughly	Partially	Missing	Not Needed

TEACHING ANALYSIS GUIDE FOR THE INQUIRY TRAINING MODEL

6. Did the teacher press students to clarify the terms and conditions of their questions?	Thoroughly	Partially	Missing	Not Needed
7. If necessary, was there a summary of the inquiry up to this point?	Thoroughly	Partially	Missing	Not Needed
8. Was there a formulation or redefinition of the problem?	Thoroughly	Partially	Missing	Not Needed

C. **Phase Three: Data Gathering: Experimentation**

9. Did the teacher invite testing (experimenting) of relationships and/or isolation of relevant variables?	Thoroughly	Partially	Missing	Not Needed
10. Where appropriate, did the teacher use the language of the inquiry process—for instance, identifying student questions as "theories" and inviting "experimentation" or "testing"?				

D. **Phase Four: Formulation of an Explanation**

11. If necessary, did the teacher induce students to formulate a rule or explanation of the discrepant event?	Thoroughly	Partially	Missing	Not Needed
12. Did the teacher press for clearer statement of theories and support for generalizations?	Thoroughly	Partially	Missing	Not Needed

E. **Phase Five: Analysis of Inquiry**

13. Was there a recapitulation of the steps of the inquiry?	Thoroughly	Partially	Missing	Not Needed
14. Was there a discussion of the elements of inquiry, such as data gathering, testing, and hypothesizing?	Thoroughly	Partially	Missing	Not Needed

II. THE TEACHER'S ROLE

15. Were all inquiries accepted in a non-evaluative manner?	Thoroughly	Partially	Missing	Not Needed
16. Were interactions among students encouraged?	Thoroughly	Partially	Missing	Not Needed

17. Was the language of inquiry introduced?	Thoroughly	Partially	Missing	Not Needed

III. TEACHING SKILLS

18. Paraphrasing students' ideas	Thoroughly	Partially	Missing	Not Needed
19. Summarizing, or inviting summaries	Thoroughly	Partially	Missing	Not Needed
20. Focusing	Thoroughly	Partially	Missing	Not Needed

AFTER PEER TEACHING: MICROTEACHING

Peer teaching was an opportunity to "walk through" the pattern of activities of the model you are using. It should have helped you identify areas of understanding or performance that were amiss for you!

Aside from the specifics of the Teaching Analysis Guide, we would like you to reflect intuitively on your peer teaching experience. Did you feel that the essence of Inquiry Training was incorporated into the learning activity? Were you able to maintain the teacher's role as you had anticipated?

As you prepare to teach your first lesson to a small group of students, identify aspects of the inquiry activity that you want to improve upon or include. Usually, these aspects are such things as being more precise in your directions, cuing students, and giving them examples of inquiry probes. We suggest walking yourself mentally through the microteaching.

It is natural in microteaching to wonder, "Am I doing this right?" Except for any glaring omissions or commissions that may have emerged in your peer teaching, the "pursuit of excellence" in a model is more a matter of refinement, style, and personal goals for the teaching situation. If you have been operating in the "Did I get this right?" frame of mind, now is the time to change to "What do *I* want to get across or elicit in this first teaching situation? How will I go about doing that?" If you have internalized the *basic* goals, principles, and procedures of the model, now is the time to shift from an external way of thinking to an internal one. Build the variations that seem appropriate to you.

We suggest audio-taping the first microteaching session, so that you can reflect on the lesson afterwards. Students will respond differently from your peers. It is a good idea to use the Teaching Analysis Guide with the microteaching lesson. You may also want to share the experience with your colleagues and receive their comments and suggestions.

The fourth and last component (Application of the Inquiry Training Model) suggests how to use the model over a long-term period and how to adapt curriculum materials. The emphasis of your training in this model will gradually shift now from mastery of the basic elements of teaching to curriculum design and application.

Component IV

ADAPTING
THE MODEL

In this component we discuss (1) possible curriculum transformations, (2) the development of a long-term plan for pupil skill development and independence in using the model, and (3) ways of combining Inquiry Training with other models of teaching.

TRANSFORMING CURRICULUMS

Except perhaps in the area of the sciences, most curriculum materials do not readily identify or lend themselves to puzzling problem situations. Even in the sciences, the familiar laboratory demonstration is not necessarily shaped as a puzzling situation. Sometimes it is more like a cooking task and a recipe! There are two steps, then, in transforming curriculums for Inquiry Training. The first is to determine some of the puzzlements in your subject area. The second step is to "shape" the puzzlement and develop the materials, much as we did in Component III when we constructed problem statements and fact sheets.

Every subject area has puzzlements. That is one of the interesting aspects about scientific knowledge! Sources of potential puzzlements are the major principles and generalizations in a field. Think about it for a minute. Most of these principles, laws, or generalizations came about in order to explain something unusual. If we work backwards from the generalization (or principle) and create a situation that is explained (or partially explained) by these sources, we then have the makings of a puzzling situation. Often, the specifics or incidents that reflect these principles are found in the curriculum materials, but too often potential puzzlements or contradictions are explained by these materials or they are not treated as puzzlements at all. Mathematical principles, for example, are not approached as puzzlements. Anthropological or historical curiosities, such as the Japanese internment question in Component III, are not seen as events to be explained. However, some of the newer curriculum projects, such as the Amherst History Project, do just that. Imagine developing a problem situation around the Watergate incident. Woodward and Bernstein perceived a puzzling situation and inquired! In the social studies, students might be asked to inquire into the vast differences between the Bedouin culture and the nearby Israeli culture. Social studies texts probably discuss both of these cultures in sections on the Middle East. The teacher's job is to perceive the puzzlement in the situation and develop it into an object of inquiry.[1]

The lesson in the Sample Planning Guide in Component III was developed from Kurt Vonnegut's book, *Venus on the Half-Shell*. It was based on Chapter 6, "Shaltoon, the Equal Time Planet." If you have time, read the entire chapter. Notice how the teacher extrapolated the puzzling situation and used portions of the story as part of the problem statement. Reread the Sample Planning Guide based on this book.

The newspaper is another good source of problem situations. Journalists are always reporting the unusual! The puzzling situation about the defendant who was found guilty but permitted to go free, which was made into an exercise in Component I, was based on a newspaper account.

In the physical and biological sciences, both the principles and the puzzlements appear to be readily available and easily locatable in existing curriculum materials. The major work is in transforming the puzzling situation so that it can be used to initiate the inquiry process. The materials on the following pages are from Wong and Dolmatz's series, *Ideas and Investigations in Science*. Investigation 5 presents us with a problem to explain: What caused the differences in the two test tubes? The student is asked to collect data and develop experiments. The model in these materials does not exactly follow the Inquiry Training Model we have been working with. A perceptive teacher can recognize Investigation 5 as a ready-made puzzling situation and can easily develop an Inquiry Training lesson. Study these materials. Locate the puzzling situation. Imagine how you might shape the puzzling event (Phase One). What changes or use would you make of the remaining materials?

---

[1] A good source of generalizations from the social sciences can be found in the appendix of Clinton Boutwell's *Getting It All Together* (San Rafael, Calif.: Leswing Press, 1972).

Investigation 5

Bubble, Bubble, Toil–No Trouble

You have been experimenting with plants in the last four investigations. From these experiments, you have been developing a model which tells you how plants interact with their environment. Your model tells you that many things in the environment, such as light, carbon dioxide, water, and chlorophyll, are needed by plants. Your model may look like the diagram shown.

Your model shows the process by which plants make starch and sugar. This process is called *photosynthesis*. Photo means "light" and synthesis means "to make." Therefore, photosynthesis refers to a plant's ability to make starch and sugar in the presence of light. What does a plant do with the starch and sugar that it makes?

A. CAN YOU PREDICT?

You will be shown two test tubes. Each has sugar, water, and yeast in it. Each container is closed and a tubing leads from it into some water. What do you think is the cause of the differences between the two test tubes?

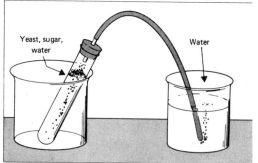

Harry K. Wong and Marvin Dolmatz, *Biology Idea 5: Ecology; Ideas and Investigations in Science Series* (Englewood Cliffs: Prentice-Hall, Inc., 1971), pp. 237-39. Reprinted by permission.

1. Remember, a scientist is a good observer. What do you see?

2. What do you predict is the reason for the differences? List your predictions. (To help you get started, one prediction is given.)

Your list of predictions represents possible solutions to the problem.

3. Would you test all your predictions at once? Explain.

Scientists often make predictions about an experiment. This helps them to find the answer.

4. How can you find which of your predictions is the cause of the differences?

B. LET'S TEST YOUR PREDICTION

Before we begin, let's make sure that we know what we are looking for. Remember, your predictions will guide the experiment.

5. Which one of your predictions will you test in this experiment?

6. How will you set up your control?

The photograph is an illustration of the setup you were looking at earlier.

7. Explain how you will prepare and run your experiment.

Obtain the necessary materials from your teacher and assemble your experiment.

C. LOOKING FOR SOMETHING?

What will you be looking for in your experiment?

8. What data will you collect?

Organize your data by constructing a table in your data sheet (Table 1). Draw a graph of your results in Graph 1.

9. What conclusion(s) can you draw from your data?

10. What are some possible sources of error in this experiment?

D. IT NEVER ENDS

Just when you think you've drawn a conclusion, you find out there is more to learn. Science can certainly keep you thinking. For instance, some of you may be wondering about the bubbles. You may be asking:

a. What kind of gas is making the bubbles?

b. Where does the gas come from?

To help you answer the first question, you will be given some limewater. Allow some of the bubbles from your experiment to bubble into the limewater.

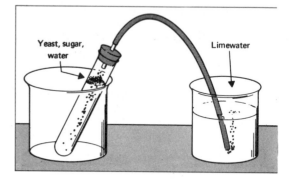

11. What happens to the color or condition of the limewater?

12. What gas is bubbling into the limewater? (If you have forgotten the purpose of the limewater, check your results in Idea 1, Investigation 4.)

Where is the gas coming from? It can't be from the water in the tube, because water is made of hydrogen and oxygen (H_2O). That leaves either the yeast or the sugar. Could it be possible that the gas comes from the yeast?

Study Graph 2.

13. According to the data in Graph 2, why do the yeast die?

14. Why is the sugar important?

15. What is the yeast able to obtain from the sugar?

16. In order to obtain energy, what must the yeast do to the sugar?

17. Where do you think the gas is coming from?

GRAPH NO. 2

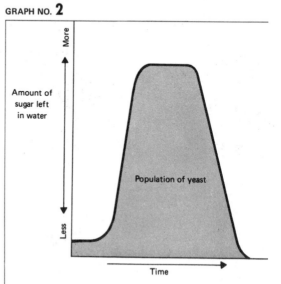

194

A LONG-TERM PLAN

Pupil skill development has been conceptualized in the Inquiry Training Model in terms of three stages:

1. mastery of the basic inquiry skills
2. process awareness
3. internalization

These levels have their parallel in the degree of structure of the learning situation. That is, mastery of the basic inquiry skills occurs primarily in the highly structured inquiry setting. Process awareness involves some autonomy and initiation on the pupils' part, and the setting for these process skills is less formalized. Finally, at the level of internalization, students are fully independent in carrying out the skills and activities of the model. The skills involved in each of these three stages are listed in Figure 1. Keep in mind that this scheme and these skills are meant to be heuristic. They are not a definitive or exhaustive list of inquiry skills, nor are they scaled in absolute order of difficulty. The order of difficulty makes intuitive sense to us, but has not been empirically tested.

Stage One: Mastery of Basic Inquiry Skills	Stage Two: Process Awareness	Stage Three: Internalization
Asking Questions: a) Formulating a "yes"-"no" question b) Formulating increasingly precise questions c) Formulating verification questions d) Formulating experimentation ("if"-"then") questions e) Eliminating theory questions Explanations: a) Formulating explanations b) Formulating a more complex explanation	Reflecting on thinking process during inquiry Using language and terminology of inquiry Searching for and incorporating outside data sources into the inquiry activities	Conducting Inquiry Training activities on one's own or with peers Generating or recognizing discrepancies and problems for inquiry Using principles and practices of inquiry on one's own in various learning situations

Figure 1. *Progression of Inquiry Skills.*

COMBINING INQUIRY TRAINING
WITH OTHER MODELS OF TEACHING

We have identified four functions of Inquiry Training, which juxtapose with other models of teaching or instructional sequences. These are: (1) the "kickoff" function, (2) the training function, (3) the setting function, and (4) the evaluation function.

The kickoff function perceives Inquiry Training activities as stimuli to a larger unit of study. In this case, Inquiry Training kicks off, or periodically boosts, a sequence of information processing activities that could involve models such as Concept Attainment, Concept Formation, Advance Organizer, and the Jurisprudential Model. The expectation is that Inquiry Training will stimulate students to acquire additional knowledge about a general problem, topic, or subject area. Thus, it is used to introduce areas of inquiry to students in such a way that they will be prompted to ask questions or become interested in learning more about them.

The training function assumes that this model trains students in basic inquiry skills and orientation, which will facilitate other, perhaps more complex problem-solving activities. For example, Inquiry Training will prepare students to use the Group Investigation Model (see Chapter 2, *Models of Teaching*), or to pursue less structured inquiry models, such as the Biological Science Inquiry Model (see Chapter 9, *Models of Teaching*). It can also be helpful in teaching some of the skills underlying the Social Inquiry Model (see Chapter 4, *Models of Teaching*).[2]

Inquiry Training can certainly facilitate the kinds of learning expected of students in open education environments. Once students have internalized the attitudes and skills of this model, we can expect them to inquire with more assurance and richness into the spectrum of topics and activities available in an open education setting.

The third function of Inquiry Training is as a context for other models. If we conceive of the phases of inquiry stretching over days or weeks, other models can be interspersed as a basis for generating and gathering new data pertinent to the inquiry. For example, Role Playing and Simulation models generate data about human behavior and social processes. Concept Attainment, Concept Formation, and the Advance Organizer models can provide additional information or concepts that might be useful. Thus, these other models can be used to provide students with additional knowledge at critical points in their inquiry.

Finally, Inquiry Training, like Concept Attainment, can function as an informal evaluation tool for knowledge of subject matter. Of course, both models require intellectual processing skills far beyond the retention of information or concept. Students may have acquired important knowledge quite adequately but be unable to apply it, because they were not trained to do so or because they lack the skills of inquiry.

[2] Bruce Joyce and Marsha Weil, *Models of Teaching* (Englewood Cliffs, N.J.: Prentice-Hall, 1972).

ADVANCE ORGANIZER MODEL

SCENARIO FOR THE ADVANCE ORGANIZER

A docent (teacher-guide) beginning a tour of an art museum with a group of children says, "I want to give you an idea that will help you better understand the pictures and sculpture we are about to see. The idea is simply that art, although it is a personal expression, reflects the culture and times in which it was produced in many ways. This may seem obvious to you at first when you look at Oriental and Western art, and to be sure, the differences between the Orient and the West are reflected in their art. However, it is also true that as cultures change, so the art will change, and that is why we can speak of *periods* of art. The changes are often reflected in the artist's techniques, subject matter, color, and style. Major changes are often reflected in the forms of art that are produced." The guide then points out examples of one or two changes in these characteristics. She also asks the students to recall their elementary school days and the differences in their drawings when they were five and six and when they were older. She likens the different periods of growing up to different cultures.

In the tour that follows, as the students look at pictures and sculpture, the teacher points out to them the differences that are due to changing times. "Do you see here," she says, "how in this picture the body of the person is almost completely covered by his robes, and there is no hint of a human being inside his clothes? In medieval times, the church taught that the body was unimportant and that the soul was everything." Later on she remarks, "You see in this picture how the muscularity of the man stands out through his clothing and how he stands firmly on the earth. This represents the Renaissance view that man was at the center of the universe and that his body, his mind, and his power were very important indeed."

This teacher of art is using an *advance organizer*—in this case, a powerful proposition used by art historians. This idea has many subideas that can be linked to the particular characteristics of the arts. By providing such an organizer, the teacher hoped to provide what David Ausubel calls an "intellectual scaffolding," a structure on which the students could hang the ideas and facts to which they would be exposed during their lesson.

The art teacher used the Advance Organizer on an idea the students were already familiar with. They had recently completed a ten-week anthropology unit that introduced the concept of culture. During the unit, the students had read case studies of both simple and complex societies, and of Western and non-Western cultures. They compared and contrasted the manifestations of culture in the different cases. The teacher capitalized on this background by presenting an idea that would link art to its cultural matrix.

OUTLINE OF ACTIVITIES FOR THE ADVANCE ORGANIZER MODEL

Objective	Materials	Activity

COMPONENT I: DESCRIBING AND UNDERSTANDING THE MODEL

Objective	Materials	Activity
1. To recognize the goals, assumptions, and procedures of the Advance Organizer Model.	Theory and Overview	Reading
2. To gain a sense of the model in action.	Theory in Practice	Reading
3. To recognize and generate four skills of the Advance Organizer Model: formulating an organizer, strengthening cognitive structure, promoting active reception learning, and promoting a critical approach to information.	Taking Theory Into Action	Reading/Writing
4. To evaluate your understanding of the Advance Organizer theory.	Theory Checkup	Writing

COMPONENT II: VIEWING THE MODEL

Objective	Materials	Activity
1. To become familiar with the Teaching Analysis Guide and identify items you do not understand.	Teaching Analysis Guide	Reading
2. To identify phases of the model and comment on the lesson.	Demonstration Transcript	Reading/Writing/Discussion
3. **Option:** To analyze alternative demonstration using the Teaching Analysis Guide.	Video tape or live demonstration/ Teaching Analysis Guide	Viewing/Group discussion or individual analysis

COMPONENT III: PLANNING AND PEER TEACHING

Objective	Materials	Activity
1. To create a knowledge hierarchy.	Creating a Knowledge Hierarchy	Reading/Writing
2. To select an appropriate organizer.	Diagnosing the Learner, Determining the Learning Task, and Identifying the Advance Organizer	Reading/Writing
3. To develop an Advance Organizer presentation.	Formulating the Advance Organizer Presentation	Reading/Writing
4. To develop behavioral objectives related to the Advance Organizer Model.	Determining Educational Objectives	Reading/Writing
5. To plan an Advance Organizer lesson using the Planning Guide.	The Planning Guide	Writing

OUTLINE OF ACTIVITIES FOR THE ADVANCE ORGANIZER MODEL

Objective	Materials	Activity

COMPONENT III: PLANNING AND PEER TEACHING (continued)

Objective	Materials	Activity
6. To peer teach the Advance Organizer Model.	3 to 4 peers, teaching materials	Teaching
7. To analyze the Advance Organizer Model.	Teaching Analysis Guide	Group discussion/Writing

Optional

8. To teach the Advance Organizer Model to a small group of students.	6 to 8 students, teaching materials, audio-cassette recorder and tape	Teaching/Taping
9. To analyze the microteaching lesson.	Teaching Analysis Guide and tape recorder	Individual or group listening to audio tape/Writing

COMPONENT IV: ADAPTING THE MODEL

1. To recognize potential Advance Organizer presentations in existing curriculum materials and make the necessary adaptations.	Curricular Adaptations and Transformations	Reading
2. To plan the use of the Advance Organizer Model for long-term development of pupil and teacher skills.	Long-Term Plans	Reading
3. To be aware of the possibilities for combining the Advance Organizer Model with other models of teaching.	Combining the Advance Organizer With Other Models of Teaching	Reading

Component I

DESCRIBING
AND UNDERSTANDING
THE MODEL

THEORY AND OVERVIEW

David Ausubel is unusual among educational theorists. First of all, he addresses himself to the goal of learning subject matter. Second, he advocates the improvement of *presentational* methods of teaching (lectures and reading) at a time when other educational theorists and social critics are challenging the validity of these methods and stressing the passiveness of expository learning. Ausubel stands in contrast with those who advocate discovery methods of teaching, open education, and experience-based learning. He stands unabashedly for the mastery of academic material.

Ausubel is also unusual because he is one of the few educational psychologists to address themselves simultaneously to learning, teaching, and curriculum. His Theory of Meaningful Verbal Learning deals with three concerns:

1. how knowledge (curriculum content) is organized

2. how the mind works to process new information (learning)

3. how these ideas about curriculum and learning can be applied by teachers when they present new material to students (instruction)

Many of us have been frustrated by theorists who can explain how learning occurs but do not help us teach and organize a curriculum. The Theory of Meaningful Verbal Learning and its derivative, the Advance Organizer Model of teaching, provide recommendations to teachers for selecting, ordering, *and* presenting new information.

Goals and Assumptions

Ausubel's primary concern is to help teachers convey large amounts of information as meaningfully and efficiently as possible. He believes that the acquisition of information is a valid, indeed an essential goal of schooling, and that there are theories that can guide teachers in their job of transmitting bodies of knowledge to their students. His own ideas of how this learning takes place is embodied in his Theory of Meaningful Verbal Learning.

This theory applies to situations where the teacher plays the role of lecturer or explainer. The major purpose is to help students acquire subject matter. Characteristically, the teacher presents the entire content of what is to be learned directly to the learner. The learner's primary role is that of recipient of ideas and information. Unlike other types of learning, such as problem solving, the Advance Organizer does not expect the learner to have to "do anything with" the material except to internalize it.

The Advance Organizer Model is designed to strengthen students' cognitive structures. By cognitive structure, Ausubel means a person's knowledge of a particular subject matter at any given time and how well organized, clear, and stable it is.[1] In other words, cognitive structure has to do with what kind of prior knowledge of a field is in our minds, how much of it there is, and how well organized it is.

Ausubel maintains that a person's existing cognitive structure is the foremost factor governing whether new material is potentially meaningful and how well it can be acquired and retained. Before we can present new material effectively, we must increase the stability and clarity of our students' prior knowledge. Strengthening students' cognitive structure in this way facilitates their acquisition and retention of new information and is one of the model's primary goals.

Is Expository Learning Rote Learning?

Meaningful learning is not an easy task, either for the student, who must internalize the new material, or the teacher, who must select, arrange, and present the content. In recent years there has been much criticism (wrongly, in Ausubel's view) of this type of learning. Reception (or expository) learning has been accused of leading to rote memorization, fostering intellectual passivity rather than curiosity, and inherently lacking meaning for the student. Ausubel rejects the notion that expository teaching (or learning) is necessarily rote, passive, or nonmeaningful. He maintains that problem-solving approaches to instruction can lead to rote learning as well as expository instruction, as is the case where students memorize the steps of mathematics or physics problems and apply them mechanically to similar problems without understanding why they are performing the operations. Expository or reception teaching does not inherently lead to rote learning; this is a

[1]David Ausubel, *The Psychology of Meaningful Verbal Learning* (New York: Grune and Stratton, 1963), p. 27.

function of how it is conducted. Unfortunately, reception teaching is often conducted in a preponderantly rote fashion.

Meaningful learning implies that what we have learned is intellectually linked and understood in the context of what we previously knew. It also implies that we can transform this knowledge and apply it creatively in new and rather novel situations. Rote learning, in contrast, typically lacks conceptual and critical approaches to the information we acquire. It usually does not prepare us to transform this knowledge or apply it in new contexts. Furthermore, rotely learned material is highly subject to forgetting.

Researchers and practitioners often fail to distinguish among various types of learning. There is a need for many types of learning processes, since they promote different educational objectives. Discovery learning procedures, for example, are useful for some objectives and not others. Similarly, rote learning is absolutely essential for certain tasks. For example, rote learning is crucial to the medical student who must memorize the names and labels of the various parts of the body, and discrimination learning is an essential part of learning the letters of the alphabet. It is important to remember, then, that there are many types of learning, each drawing on different mental processes, each serving different educational objectives, and each requiring its own method of teaching. They are all necessary to the process of education. Problems arise not so much because a particular instructional method is inherently bad, but because it is used for the wrong purposes.[2]

What is Meaningful?

Another widely held belief that Ausubel disagrees with is the assumption that anything meaningful cannot be "presented" but must come through independent problem-solving and manipulative experience. According to Ausubel, whether material is meaningful depends on the learner and the material, not the method of presentation. If the learner employs a meaningful learning set, and if the material is potentially meaningful for the student, then meaningful learning can occur. In both of these conditions, the key to meaning involves solidly connecting the new learning material with existing ideas in the learner's cognitive structure. In other words, *we must relate and reconcile what we know with what we are learning*. A meaningful learning set implies that the learner must be ready to comprehend and relate what is being presented, rather than to memorize it verbatim. Material is potentially meaningful if the learner has, in his or her storehouse of knowledge and experience, ideas to relate the new material to.

Is Reception Learning Passive?

Finally, and not unrelated to the question of meaningfulness, is the assumption that the learner's role in reception learning is a passive one. On the contrary, during a lecture or other form of expository teaching, learners can be quite active. To be so, however, they must relate the new material to existing knowledge, judging which concept or proposition to catalogue the new knowledge under. Ausubel talks about the learner struggling with the material—looking at it from different angles, reconciling it with similar or perhaps contradictory information, and finally trans-

[2]David Ausubel, *Educational Psychology: A Cognitive View* (New York: Holt, Rinehart & Winston, 1968), pp. 83-84.

lating it into his own frame of reference and terminology. Each of these mental activities increases the meaning and internalization of new information. Learners who passively receive new material or organize themselves to memorize information do not engage in these particular activities. Ausubel assumes that for meaningful verbal learning to occur, the learner plays an active role, whether covert or overt. However, this does not happen automatically. The teaching model for reception learning must be designed in such a way that it facilitates these types of active mental operations.

Organizing Information: The "Structure of the Discipline" and Cognitive Structure

Ausubel believes there is a parallel between the way subject matter is organized and the way people organize knowledge in their minds (their cognitive structure). He firmly expresses the view that each of the academic disciplines has a structure of concepts (and/or propositions) that are organized hierarchically.[3] That is, at the top of each discipline are a number of very broad concepts that include or subsume the inclusive concepts at lower stages of organization. Ausubel conceptualizes a discipline as levels of these hierarchically organized concepts that begin with perceptual data at the bottom and proceed through increasing levels of abstraction to the most abstract concepts at the top. Thus, we may imagine a discipline as being composed of a pyramid of concepts all linked together, with the most concrete concepts at the bottom and more abstract concepts at the top (see Figure 1).

Like Jerome Bruner, Ausubel believes that the structural concepts of each discipline can be identified and taught to students, which then become an information processing system for them; that is, they become an intellectual map that students can use to analyze particular domains and to solve problems within those domains. For example, students can use economic concepts to analyze events from an economic point of view. Suppose we present filmed case studies depicting activities on a farm, in a grocery store, in a suburban household, and in a brokerage house. Each case contains many pieces of information; the students see people engaged in various activities, observe many behaviors, and listen to several conversations. If the students were then to make an economic analysis of these cases, they would catalog the behaviors and activities of the people in terms of such concepts as: supply and demand, wants and needs, goods and services, consumers and producers. These concepts help in several ways. They enable students to make sense of large amounts of data and to compare and contrast the four case studies, discovering the underlying commonalities in the apparent differences.

Ausubel describes the mind as an information-processing and information-storing system that is analogous to the conceptual structure of an academic discipline. That is, it is a hierarchically organized set of ideas that provide anchors for new information and ideas as these are received, and that serves as a storehouse for them. In Figure 2 we see the hierarchy of an individual's cognitive structure in the discipline of economics. We find that it is similar to the hierarchy of economic subject matter presented earlier. The shaded concepts are the most inclusive: they have been "learned" and exist presently in the learner's cognitive structure. The unshaded concepts are potentially meaningful because they can be *linked* to the existing con-

[3]Ausubel, *Psychology of Meaningful Verbal Learning*, p. 18.

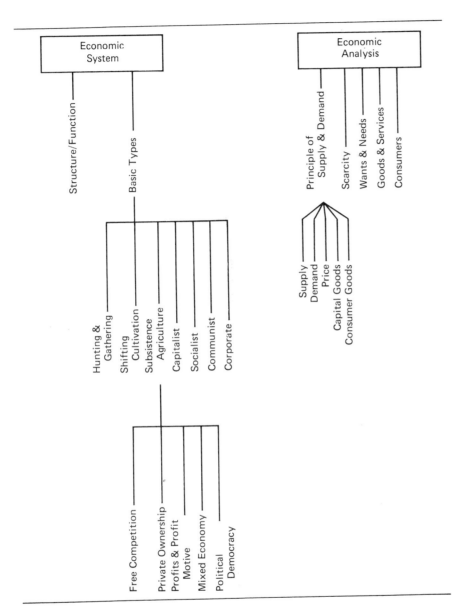

Figure 1. *Major Economic Concepts (based on Clinton Boutwell,* Getting It All Together, *San Rafael, Cal.: Leswing Press, 1972).*

cepts. The black circles are not yet potentially meaningful concepts because suitable anchors for them are not yet incorporated in the cognitive structure.

As this information processing system acquires new information and new ideas, it reorganizes itself to accommodate those ideas. Thus, the system is in a continuous state of change. However, Ausubel maintains that new ideas can be use-

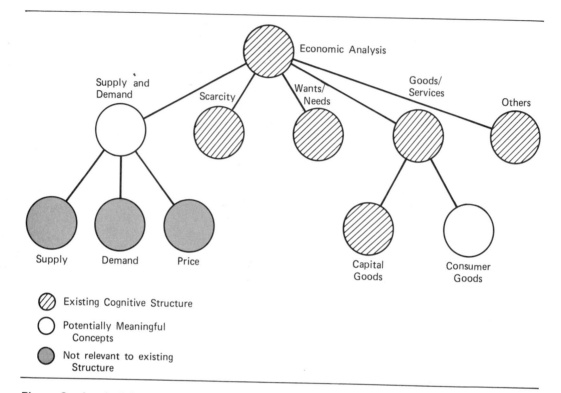

Figure 2. *An Individual's Cognitive Structure with Respect to Economics (based on Clinton Boutwell,* Getting It All Together, *San Rafael, Cal.: Leswing Press, 1972, pp. 180-280).*

fully learned and retained only to the extent that they can be related to already available concepts or propositions that provide ideational anchors. Although a new set of ideas can be incorporated into an existing cognitive structure, and in fact must be so incorporated for learning to persist, if the new material conflicts too strongly with the existing cognitive structure *or* is so unrelated that no linkage is provided, the information or ideas may not be incorporated or retained. To prevent this from occurring, the teacher must organize a sequence of knowledge and present it in such a way that the ideational anchors are provided. In addition, the learner must actively reflect on the new material, thinking through these linkages, reconciling differences or discrepancies with existing information, and noting similarities.

Implications for Curriculum

Two principles are suggested for programming content in the subject fields in such a way that the concepts become a stable part of a student's cognitive structure and that the material has psychological meaning. The first is progressive differentiation and the second is integrative reconciliation.

Progressive differentiation means that the most general ideas of the discipline are presented first, and then are progressively differentiated in terms of detail and specificity. *Integrative reconciliation* simply means that new ideas should be consciously reconciled with and integrated with previously learned content. In other words, the sequence of the curriculum is organized so that each successive learning is carefully related to what has been presented before. If the entire learning material has been conceptualized and presented according to progressive differentiation, then integrative reconciliation follows naturally, though not without some intent on the teacher's part. Gradually, as a result of both of these principles, the discipline is built into the mind of the learner. It must be kept in mind that the discipline and the sequence of instruction are built from the top down, rather than the bottom up. The most inclusive concepts, principles, and/or propositions are presented first.

In the previous section, we explored the idea of a hierarchy of knowledge in terms of economics. In Figure 3 we present a knowledge or curriculum hierarchy in the area of psychiatry. In the knowledge hierarchy of psychiatric disorders, four levels of concepts are progressively differentiated. The most general idea, psychiatric disorder, is presented first, and eight major categories of disorder are specified next. Each category of disorders, in turn, has its subtypes, and some of these are divided further.

Psychiatry, much like biology, is a relatively easy area of knowledge on which to build a curriculum hierarchy because at least one of its functions has been as a classificatory system. Divisions and subdivisions flow nicely because that is what classification is all about! Other subject-area hierarchies are somewhat different. Literature is made up of several rather discrete but central concepts (character, mood, style, setting) and very few principles or generalizations. In general, there is no *one* right hierarchy for any subject area. Furthermore, the different areas of knowledge (the humanities, the social sciences, the physical sciences, and mathematics) present different problems in the construction of knowledge hierarchies.

From the learner's standpoint, the absolute accuracy of the hierarchy is probably less important to meaningful verbal learning than the fact that the teacher is operating on the basis of some reasonable hierarchy in presenting the sequence of learning tasks. If this is true, the ideas can be "integratively reconciled" with and probably less important to meaningful verbal learning than the fact that the teacher medical school introduces a unit on three types of psychotic disorders, the general concept of psychotic disorder should be distinguished from (and integrated with) the concept of organic brain syndrome, a previously introduced concept. That is, the learner should know how psychotic disorders differ from organic brain syndromes. (Organic brain syndromes are disturbances in psychic functioning that may be due to damage or destruction of the neurons. The major symptoms are reductions in the level of awareness and in the level of efficiency of cognitive functions such as judgment, orientation, and memory. Psychotic disorders are not primarily organic in origin. They are characterized by profound alterations in mood, disorganization in thinking, and withdrawal from the real world into personal preoccupations.)[4] This type of comparison and contrast is what Ausubel means by integrative reconciliation of existing knowledge with new learning material. However, in order to have integrative reconciliation, we must have some implicit hierarchy or progressively differentiated subject matter. We cannot integrate if we do not know which concepts are to be integrated and what basis is to be used for determining their similarities and differences.

[4] Definitions based on DSMII, *Diagnostic and Statistical Manual of Mental Disorders* (Washington, D.C.: American Psychiatric Association, 1968).

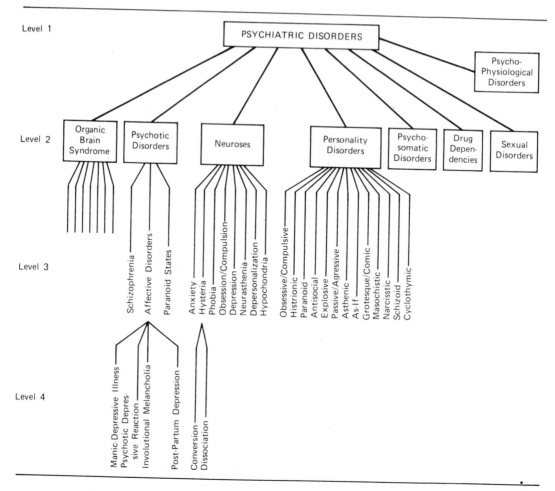

Figure 3. *A Knowledge Hierarchy for Psychiatric Disorders (based on* Diagnostic and Statistical Manual of Mental Disorders II, *Washington, D.C.: American Psychiatric Association, 1968).**

*Some definitions for Figure 3:

Psychotic Disorder: An illness that seriously interferes with the demands of everyday life. It may be caused by distortions in recognizing reality, as hallucinations and delusions, by profound alterations in mood, or by disorganization in thinking.

Neuroses: A condition characterized chiefly by anxiety and experienced as subjectively distressful by the patient. This condition may hinder a person's judgment and ability to relate effectively with others.

Personality Disorder: Longstanding patterns of behavior that are maladaptive.

Ausubel points out that the organization of most textbooks puts each topic into a separate chapter or subchapter, all at the same level of abstraction and generality. "Thus, in most instances students are required to learn the details of new and unfamiliar disciplines before they have acquired an adequate body of relevant subsumers at an appropriate level of inclusiveness."[5]

Just to get the feeling of what this means to the learner, look back over our subject area hierarchy for psychiatric disorders in Figure 3. Imagine spending ten weeks covering the details of thirteen different personality disorders before becoming aware that there are seven categories in major disorders, or before realizing the ways in which a personality disorder is different from a neurosis or psychotic disorder.

Implications for Teaching: Using Advance Organizers

In the actual teaching situation, the primary way of strengthening cognitive structure and enhancing retention of new information is through the use of advance organizers. Ausubel describes advance organizers in the following way: An Advance Organizer is introductory material that is presented ahead of the learning task and is at a higher level of abstraction and inclusiveness than the learning task itself. Its purpose is to explain, integrate, and interrelate the material in the learning task with previously learned material (also to help the learner discriminate the new material from previously learned material).[6] The most effective organizers are those that use concepts, terms, and propositions that are already familiar to the learner as well as appropriate illustrations and analogies.

Suppose, for example, you wanted students to acquire information about current energy problems. You would provide learning material containing data about possible power sources, general information about United States economic growth and technology, and alternative policy stances with respect to the energy crisis and future planning. The learning material would be in the form of newspaper articles, a lecture, or perhaps a film. The learning task for the students is to internalize the information—to remember the central ideas and perhaps the key facts. Before introducing students to the learning material, you would provide introductory material in the form of an advance organizer, a scaffolding on which the students can "hang" and relate the new data.

Advance organizers are generally based upon the major concepts, propositions, generalizations, principles, and laws of a discipline. For example, a lesson or text describing the caste system in India might be preceded by an organizer based on the concept of social stratification. The generalization, "Technological changes can produce major changes in society and culture," could be the *basis* for an organizer for the study of many historical periods and places.

Usually, the organizer is tied closely to the factual or less abstract material it precedes. That is, the organizer seems to emerge from, or is integrally related to, the teaching material. The organizer can also be used creatively, to provide a new perspective. For instance, the concept of balance or form, though generic to the arts, may be applied to literature, to mathematics, to the functioning of the branches of government, or even to our daily activities. Conversely, specific material (such as a study of churches) can be viewed under the rubric of many different organizers.

[5]Ausubel, *Educational Psychology*, p. 153.
[6]Ibid., p. 148.

Some organizers can generate the economic implications of the material, others the cultural implications; still others can introduce sociological perspectives, and yet others can cause the material to be viewed from an architectural perspective. In other words, the meaning and significance of the material can vary with the organizers or perspectives that are applied to it.

The organizer is important content in itself and needs to be taught. It may be a concept or a statement of relationship. In either case, time must be taken to explain and develop the organizer, for only when it is fully understood can it serve to organize the subsequent learning material. For example, the students must fully understand the concept of *culture* before it can be effectively used to organize factual information about different culture groups.

In the case of a lesson on the energy crisis, one concept you might use as the basis of the organizer is the concept of energy; you might also want to use related concepts, such as energy efficiency and energy conservation. Another potential organizer for this lesson would be the concept of ecology and its various subsystems, such as the environment, the economy, the political arena, social structures, and patterns of behavior. This second organizer would focus students' attention on the *impact* of old and new energy sources on the subsystems of our ecological system, whereas the first organizer would encourage them to process the data through a consideration of energy efficiency and/or energy conservation. Figure 4 illustrates the relationship between the introductory material and the learning task for this topic.

Advance Organizer	Learning Task
Review comments on the concepts of energy, efficiency, conservation, and energy laws (physics).	Statistics and information on alternative power sources, U.S. growth rate, and policy stances.

Figure 4. *Advance Organizer and Learning Tasks for a Study of Energy.*

There are two types of advance organizers—*expository* and *comparative*. Expository organizers provide a general model of class relationship as a general subsumer for a new class, subclasses, and species before more limited subsumers (classes) are provided for the particular subclass or species. Thus, varying kinds of forest are first distinguished from one another before the component subforests and trees are differentiated. Before discussing specific types of mechanical energy, such as potential and kinetic, an instructor would build an expository organizer around the concept of mechanical energy, describing what it is and how it functions and providing several examples. Expository organizers are especially helpful because they provide ideational scaffolding for *unfamiliar* material.

Comparative organizers, on the other hand, are used most with relatively familiar material. They are designed to integrate new concepts with basically similar concepts existing in the cognitive structure; yet they are also designed to discriminate between the old and new concepts in order to prevent confusion caused by their similarity. For example, when the learner is being introduced to long division, a comparative organizer might be used that would stress the similarity, and yet the differentness, of division facts and multiplication facts. Whereas in multiplication, the multiplier and multiplicand can be reversed without changing the product—that is, 3 times 4 can be changed to 4 times 3—the divisor and dividend cannot be reversed in division without affecting the quotient—that is, 6 divided by 2 is not the same as 2 divided by 6. The comparative organizer can help the learner see the relationship between multiplication and division, and therefore anchor the new material on division in the old material on multiplication. The implications of the Advance Organizer approach for a developing model of expository teaching are presented in the next section.

Syntax of the Advance Organizer Model of Teaching

There are three phases of activity in the Advance Organizer Model. *Phase One* is the presentation of the advance organizer, *Phase Two* is the presentation of the learning task or learning material, and *Phase Three* is the strengthening of cognitive organization. Phase Three tests the relationship of the learning material to existing cognitive organization and induces active reception learning. A summary of the syntax appears in Figure 5.

The syntax and activities found within the phases of the model are based on: (1) the principle of integrative reconciliation, (2) the principle of progressive differentiation, and (3) active reception learning. The two principles are intended to increase the discriminability, clarity, and stability of the new learning material so that fewer ideas are lost, confused with one another, or left vague. Active reception learning is intended to bring about learner involvement in expository teaching. The students should operate on the material as they receive it by relating the new learning material to personal experience and to their existing cognitive structure and by taking a critical stance toward knowledge. Thus, Ausubel's concept of active reception learning includes the basic skills of critical thinking (Phase Three of the model). These skills find their way into the model as principles of reaction that guide the teacher's responses to the students, and as activities that strengthen cognitive organization (Phase Three).

Phase One: Presentation of Advance Organizer	Phase Two: Presentation of Learning Task or Material	Phase Three: Strengthening Cognitive Organization
Clarify aims of lesson.	Make logical order of learning material explicit to student.	Use principles of integrative reconciliation.
Present organizer:	Maintain attention.	Promote active reception learning.
Identify defining attributes.	Make organization explicit.	
Give examples.		Elicit critical approach to subject matter.
Provide multicontext.		
Repeat terminology of subsumer.		Clarify.
Prompt awareness of relevant knowledge and experience in learner's background.		

Figure 5. *Syntax of the Advance Organizer Model.*

In addition, we have tried to incorporate some general principles of expository teaching that educational researchers studying the lecture method of teaching have found enhance learning. Steps such as clarifying the aims of the lesson (Phase One) and maintaining attention (Phase Two) are typical of the teaching skills found attendant to effective presentational teaching.[7]

Phase One: Presentation of the Advance Organizer

This phase consists of three activities: clarifying the aims of the lesson, presenting the advance organizer, and prompting awareness of relevant knowledge and experience. To illustrate the activities in this and other phases of the model, we are going to use the example of a group of first-year medical students taking an introductory course in clinical psychiatry. Part of each class is devoted to a lecture on a new type of mental illness and a discussion of its major symptoms and origins. The students then interview a patient they have not seen before, and on the basis of the live interview and all the information they have learned about possible types of mental illness, they attempt to make a diagnosis. The two-hour class is usually divided, then, into three parts: first, the introduction or review of new learning material or information; second, a live interview and recapitulation of the interview; and third, the diagnosis.

Assume that the new learning material in the medical-school class has to do with mood-affective disorders. There are four types of these disorders. (From Figure 3 we know that mood-affective disorders are a type of psychotic disorder, the other types being schizophrenia and paranoid states.) These were discussed in the last class. The instructor begins by clarifying the aims of the lesson. She can do this in a number of ways—giving the topic as a title, stating a generalization, making a statement, summarizing the main points, defining the objectives, asking students about related topics, or using a combination of these strategies. In this case, she states, "We talked about schizophrenia last week, and today we want to discuss mood-affective disorders. We want to be clear at the end of the session about the types of affective disorders, the major symptoms, and the chief differences between mood-affective disorders and schizophrenia."

The instructor has used a combination of techniques in clarifying the aims. Because of the aims of the lesson, the structure of the subject matter, and the medical approach of making a diagnosis by ruling out other possible illnesses, the instructor chooses to use a comparative organizer for the advance organizer: "Whereas schizophrenia is primarily a disorder of thinking processes, affective disorders are severe disorders of *mood*. Like affective disorders, schizophrenia is also marked by mood and behavior changes, but the really distinguishing features are the distortions of thought processes one finds in schizophrenia. These include such distortions as hallucinations and delusions. This type of thought distortion is not the predominant part of affective disorders."

The instructor next lists the major symptoms of schizophrenia and compares these to the major symptoms of affective disorders (identifies defining attributes). She then cites several cases of affective disorders (gives examples), drawing from different age and cultural groups and personality types (provides multicontext).

[7]Nathaniel Gage and David Berliner, *Educational Psychology* (Chicago: Rand McNally Publishing Co., 1975), pp. 500-527.

Finally, the instructor reminds the students that in their courses on genetics and the sociology of medicine, they learned that people of a certain socioeconomic background and sex are more susceptible to mood-affective disorders than other people. She also reminds them of a personal incident that one of the students shared with them last week, which involved a person who probably had a mood-affective disorder (prompts awareness of relevant knowledge and experience in the learners' backgrounds).

Phase Two: Presentation of the Learning Task or Material

The learning task in this case consists of diagnosing the patient being interviewed. It could also be a presentation of the four types of affective disorders, but the instructor chooses to save this for the following week. At this point in the semester, the instructor wants the students to make their diagnosis only in terms of (1) organic brain syndromes (2) psychotic disorders, either schizophrenia or mood-affective disorders, or (3) neuroses. She figures that at this point in the course, the students' cognitive structures look something like the framework shown in Figure 6.

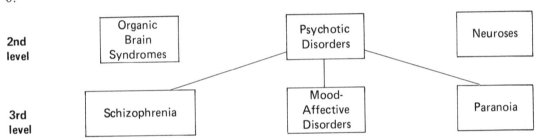

Figure 6. *Cognitive Structure for a Study of Mental Illness.*

There are several tasks to be accomplished in Phase Two. In addition to the presentation of the new learning material, some of these tasks are general teaching skills that enchance reception learning—providing a logical order to the learning material, maintaining attention, and making organization explicit.

The new learning material in the medical-school class is the material from the patient interview. Since the interview is spontaneous, the information (learning material) cannot be organized ahead of time. However, the students do know the major areas of information they need to ask patients about, although it is not always possible to cover all the areas. Therefore, after the interview is over, the instructor summarizes the major areas on the chalkboard as follows. The students discuss what they observed in terms of these areas. This procedure provides a logical organization for the descriptive material.

general appearance
kinetics
affect
formal thought
 content
 process

speech
    quantity
    quality
    organization
cognitive functioning
    judgment
    orientation
        time
        place
        person
    memory
    mood changes
    calculations

There are several procedures for making organization explicit. Among them are employing the rule-example-rule technique, using explaining links ("because"; "in order"; "if. . . . then"), making the organization explicit by means of an outline or diagram, using verbal markers of importance ("Now note this," "This is especially critical"), and repetition.

In our medical-school example, the instructor uses several of these techniques. She puts the organization scheme on the board and underlines the most significant characteristics of the patient that were observed in the interview. It is not difficult to keep her students' attention during the interview or during the debriefing afterwards. However, she does allow the students a quick break before discussing what they observed. Other techniques for maintaining attention are varying stimuli (movement, gesture, tone of voice), using other media to supplement the presentation, and inserting questions into the lecture. Some of these techniques will be more appropriate the following week, when the students will not be interviewing a patient. Instead, there will be a lecture (the learning task) on the five types of affective disorders.

Phase Three: *Strengthening of Cognitive Organization*

This last phase draws students into a more overt though not necessarily intellectually more active role. The teacher's task is to further strengthen the anchoring of the new learning material in the students' existing cognitive structure. In this phase, the teacher can also answer students' questions about discrepancies or ambiguities.

There are several ways to facilitate integrative reconciliation of the new material with material in the existing cognitive structure. The teacher can:

1. remind students of the whole cognitive organization (the larger picture)
2. ask for a summary of the major attributes of the new learning material
3. repeat precise definitions
4. ask for differences between parallel subsumers
5. ask students to describe how the learning material supports the concept or proposition that is being used as a subsumer

Active reception learning can be promoted by:

1. asking students to describe how the new material relates to a single aspect of their existing knowledge
2. asking students for additional examples of the concept or propositions in the learning material
3. asking students to verbalize the essence of the material, translating it into their own terminology and personal frame of reference
4. asking students to examine the material from alternative points of view
5. relating the material to contradictory material, experience, or knowledge

A critical approach to knowledge is fostered by asking students to recognize assumptions or inferences that may have been made in the learning material, to judge and challenge these assumptions and inferences, and to reconcile contradictions among them.

Finally, the students will probably have many questions about parts of the learning material or task (the observation, film, reading, or whatever) that are unclear to them. The teacher can clarify still further by giving additional new information, rephrasing previously given information, or applying the ideas to a new problem or example.

It is not possible or desirable to use all these techniques in one lesson. Constraints of time, topic, and relevance to the learning situation at hand will guide their use. However, it is important to keep in mind the four goals of this phase and to have in your teaching repertoire the techniques for implementing them. In the next section, further explanation of these techniques is provided and opportunities for practice are given.

Ideally, the initiation of Phase Three is shared by teachers and students. At first, however, the teacher will have to respond to the students' need for clarification of some area of the topic and for integration of the learning material with existing knowledge. Until students become socialized to the goals and procedures of meaningful verbal learning, the teacher will have to initiate questions or comments that promote active reception learning and a critical approach to the subject matter.

The Teacher's Role

The teacher has several functions to perform in the Advance Organizer Model in addition to presenting the learning material. He or she must decide under what concept, proposition, or issue to catalogue the new learning material and must, over the course of instruction, continually reorganize knowledge in relation to more inclusive concepts. The teacher, in other words, designs the hierarchy of knowledge in a subject area and also makes decisions about definitions and meanings. Based on these definitions, the teacher must point out discrepancies, conflicts, and similarities between existing knowledge and new knowledge. Finally, the teacher must translate the new material into a frame of reference that has personal meaning for the student. That is, the material must reflect the student's experiential and intellectual background.

The Social System

The social system of this model is one in which the teacher retains control of the intellectual structure, as it is necessary to continually relate the learning material to the organizers and to help students discern new material, differentiating it from previously learned material. During the presentation of the organizer and, to a lesser extent, the presentation of the learning material, the interaction is primarily oneway, teacher to student. In Phase Three, however, the learning situation is ideally much more interactive, with students initiating many questions and comments. The successful acquisition of the material will depend upon the learners' desire to integrate the meaning of the material with prior knowledge, upon their self-critical faculty, and upon the teacher's presentation and organization of the material.

Principles of Reaction

The teacher's solicited or unsolicited responses to the learners' reactions will be guided by the purposes of clarifying the meaning of the new learning material, differentiating it from and reconciling it with existing knowledge, making it personally relevant to the student, and helping to promote a critical approach to knowledge. Ideally, students will initiate their own questions in response to their own drive for meaning. If not, the teacher will elicit students' reactions through questions or will provide brief explanations.

The Support System

Well-organized material is the critical support requirement of this model. The effectiveness of the advance organizer depends upon an integral and appropriate relationship between the conceptual organizer and the content. This model provides guidelines for building (or reorganizing) instructional materials. However, the model was designed for use in face-to-face teaching in the form of lectures and explanations.

SUMMARY CHART: ADVANCE ORGANIZER MODEL

Syntax

> Phase One: Presentation of an Advance Organizer
> > Clarify aims of lesson.
> > Present Organizer
> > > Identify defining attributes.
> > > Give examples.
> > > Provide multicontext.
> > > Repeat terminology of subsumer.
> > Prompt awareness of relevant knowledge and experience in learner's background.

> Phase Two: Presentation of learning task or material
> > Make logical order of learning material explicit to students.
> > Maintain attention.
> > Make organizer explicit.

Phase Three: Strengthening cognitive organization
    Use principles of integrative reconciliation.
    Promote active reception learning.
    Elicit critical approach to subject matter.
    Clarify.

Social System
    Teacher controls the content (intellectual structure) and instructional process (social structure). The interaction is primarily from teacher to student.

Principles of Reaction
    1. Clarify meaning of the new material.
    2. Differentiate and reconcile new material with existing knowledge.
    3. Promote personal relevance of the material.
    4. Promote a critical approach to knowledge.

Support System
    Well-organized material.

THEORY IN PRACTICE

No amount of description can convey a sense of a model of teaching as well as an example of the model in practice. In fact, reading too much theory before gaining a rough "image" of the practice can be confusing and, for some people, frustrating and discouraging. So we encourage you, at this point of your study of the Advance Organizer Model, to read the following abbreviated transcript of an actual classroom session. We suggest that you first read only the teacher-student dialogue and then go back to note the annotations. Remember, the goal at this point in your training is to gain a sense of the model—its flow and feeling—not to master the techniques of implementation.

This lesson was taught at the Rogers School in the Alum Rock School District in California. The children are junior high school students and the teacher is Bruce Joyce. The children and teacher have not met prior to the lesson. The material of the lesson is a series of books about small towns representing several different cultures of the world. One is an Indian pueblo, the second is a small town in France, and the third is a middle-sized town in England.

The strategy here is to present the students with major ideas (organizers) that can help them as they read and try to understand the material. In this particular episode, two organizers are presented: a primary organizer based on the concept of culture and a secondary organizer based on the proposition that culture is a set of behavior patterns that are learned as one grows up in a culture.

T: WELL, TODAY WE'RE GOING TO WORK WITH SOME MATERIAL ABOUT DIFFERENT TOWNS IN DIFFERENT PLACES. WE'RE GOING TO LEARN A LITTLE BIT ABOUT A TOWN IN NEW MEXICO, A PUEBLO TOWN, A LITTLE BIT ABOUT A TOWN IN SOUTHERN FRANCE, AND A LITTLE BIT ABOUT A TOWN IN MEDIEVAL ENGLAND. WE'RE GOING TO READ A FEW PIECES ABOUT THESE TOWNS AND DISCUSS THEM. WHAT I WANT TO DO IS GIVE YOU SOME IDEAS THAT WILL HELP YOU, I THINK, READ THAT MATERIAL AND UNDERSTAND IT. I'M GOING TO GIVE YOU SOME IDEAS, THEN SOME

Orientation to the material and process.

STUFF TO READ, THEN WE'LL TALK ABOUT THE STUFF YOU'VE READ, AND THEN I'LL GIVE YOU SOME MORE IDEAS, AND THEN WE'LL TALK AGAIN.

TELL ME, WHAT ARE WE LIKE AROUND HERE? SUPPOSE YOU WERE TRYING TO DESCRIBE US TO SOME PEOPLE THAT HAD NEVER BEEN HERE AND CAME FROM A LONG WAY AWAY. SUPPOSE PEOPLE CAME FROM ASIA OR AFRICA. HOW WOULD YOU DESCRIBE US, LIZ?

S: WE'D BE A LITTLE BIT DIFFERENT BECAUSE WE HAVE TV AND RADIOS AND STUFF LIKE THAT AND CARS, AND, YOU KNOW. THEY WOULDN'T SEE THAT, IF THEY CAME FROM THERE.

T: OK.

S: THEY'D BE DRESSED DIFFERENTLY THAN US.

T: RIGHT. SO WE HAVE TELEVISION AND AUTO-MOBILES. WE HAVE DIFFERENT CLOTHES. JERRY?

S: THEY WOULDN'T UNDERSTAND OUR ENGLISH. THEY WOULDN'T UNDERSTAND ENGLISH.

T: OK, WE HAVE A DIFFERENT LANGUAGE. WHAT ARE SOME OF THE OTHER THINGS ABOUT US? LET'S IMAGINE THAT SOMEBODY JUST CAME IN FROM SOME OTHER PLACE, AND HE COULDN'T SEE US, AND HE WAS JUST SITTING HERE IN THE GROUP, AND WHAT WE WANTED TO DO WAS TELL HIM WHAT WE ARE LIKE. WOULD WE TALK ABOUT TELEVISION, CARS, OTHER STUFF? WHAT ARE SOME OF THE THINGS WE WOULD TALK ABOUT?

S: WHAT FOOD WE EAT.

T: YES.

S: BECAUSE THEY EAT DIFFERENT FOOD.

T: WE MIGHT TELL THEM ABOUT A DAY, MIGHTN'T WE? IN THE MORNING WE GET UP AND HAVE BREAKFAST, AND WE MIGHT TELL HIM WHAT WE HAVE FOR BREAKFAST; THEN WE COME TO SCHOOL. WE'D TELL HIM ABOUT THE THINGS WE DO ALL DAY, WOULDN'T WE?

NOW, THE THINGS WE DO WE CALL BEHAVIOR. WHAT WE HAVE IS A SET OF BEHAVIORS. WE WATCH TELEVISION, WE DRIVE AUTOMOBILES, WE COME TO SCHOOL, WE TALK TO EACH OTHER, WE SPEAK ENGLISH. ALL OF THESE ARE OUR BE-HAVIORS. WE SPEAK OF THE COLLECTION OF THOSE BEHAVIORS AS A CULTURE. YOU KNOW HOW WE HAVE A BANK ACCOUNT, WHERE YOU PUT PENNIES AND DOLLARS IN? WELL, IN A SENSE, A CULTURE IS THE BANK OF THINGS WE ARE, THE WAY WE ARE, THE WAY WE GET AROUND, THE WAY WE TALK TO EACH OTHER, AND ALL THAT. AND SO A CULTURE IS A BE-HAVIOR, WHAT WE CALL A BEHAVIOR PATTERN.

Phase One: Advance Organizer is introduced.

Teacher presents many examples of the concept of culture in multiple context. He is also pro-moting Active Reception Learning by associat-ing the Organizer (subsumer) to the students' own experience.

WE HAVE A BEHAVIOR PATTERN, AND IN ORDER TO UNDERSTAND A PERSON FROM ANOTHER CULTURE, WHAT WE TRY TO DO IS UNDERSTAND THEIR PATTERN OF BEHAVIOR. LANGUAGE DIFFICULTY IS PART OF IT, BUT WE UNDERSTAND OTHER KINDS OF BEHAVIOR TOO. FOR EXAMPLE, IF YOU WERE IN A FRENCH SCHOOL AND YOU DID SOMETHING WRONG, DO YOU KNOW WHAT THE TEACHER WOULD DO? THE TEACHER WOULD MAKE YOU STAND UP—IN THIS PARTICULAR FRENCH TOWN PARTICULARLY—YOU'D HAVE TO STAND UP AND THEY PUT A DUNCE CAP ON YOU OR THEY PUT A SIGN ON YOU, AND YOU'D HAVE TO STAND THERE AND THEY'D MAKE FUN OF YOU. NOW IF THE TEACHER DID THAT HERE, ALL OF YOU WOULD RESENT THE TEACHER, WOULDN'T YOU?

The method of school discipline is presented as one example of culture.

S: YES.

S: YOU BET.

T: YOU'D ALL GET MAD. IN FRANCE THEY WOULDN'T GET MAD. THEY WOULD ACTUALLY MAKE FUN OF THE PERSON. AND IF SOMEBODY DID SOMETHING REALLY SERIOUS, THEY'D GET HIM TO STAND UP IN THE TOWN SQUARE FOR ABOUT A HALF AN HOUR WITH A SIGN ON HIM, AND THEN EVERYBODY WHO CAME BY WOULD MAKE FUN OF HIM. YOU SEE THE DIFFERENCE? WHEREAS HERE WE BEHAVE A LITTLE DIFFERENTLY WHEN WE HAVE A PROBLEM WITH EACH OTHER. WELL, THAT'S ONE PIECE OF BEHAVIOR PATTERN THAT BELONGS TO THE FRENCH CULTURE THAT IS DIFFERENT FROM OURS. I'M GOING TO GIVE YOU SOME MATERIAL TO READ, AND WHAT I WANT YOU TO THINK ABOUT WHEN YOU READ IT IS THAT A CULTURE IS A PATTERN OF BEHAVIORS.

Note that by this time the teacher has repeated the term culture *five* times and behavior *eleven* times. (Culture and behavior are the two most important terms of the subsumer)

Phase Two:
Presentation of Learning Task or material.

Phase Three:
Strengthening Cognitive Organization

Time out for reading

T: LET'S TALK ABOUT WHAT YOU'VE READ. WHAT WAS IT ABOUT?

S: PEOPLE WERE OUT OF FOOD. THE LAND WAS DRY. THEY COULDN'T GET ANY ANIMALS FOR MEAT.

S: THEY NEEDED FOOD AND THEY NEEDED CLOTHING.

S: THEY NEEDED A NEW PLACE TO GO SO THE ENEMIES WOULDN'T GET THEM.

T: SO THAT WHAT WOULDN'T GET THEM?

S: ENEMIES.

S: THEIR GODS.

T: WHAT ARE THEY LIKE AS PEOPLE? TELL ME ABOUT THEM.

S: THEY'RE POOR.

S: STARVING.

T: DO THEY HAVE A RELIGION?

S: YEAH, THEY HAVE A GOD.

T: IS THAT A STRONG RELIGION? DO THEY REALLY CARE ABOUT HIM A LOT?

S: YES.

T: DO THEY HAVE A GOVERNMENT?

S: NO.

S: THEY HAVE A MEDICINE MAN.

T: CAN THE MEDICINE MAN LEAD THE PEOPLE?

S: NO.

S: THEY HAVE TRIBES.

T: OK. ALL RIGHT. DO YOU THINK YOU WOULD LIKE TO LIVE THERE?

S: NO.

T: WHY NOT?

S: NO WATER.

S: NO CLOTHING.

T: OK. DO YOU THINK THAT THEIR PATTERN OF BEHAVIOR IS A LOT DIFFERENT FROM OURS?

S: YES.

T: YOU'D HAVE TO LEARN A LOT OF NEW BEHAVIORS IF YOU LIVED THERE.

S: YES.

T: WOULD YOU SAY THEIR CULTURE IS CLOSE TO OURS? OR FAR AWAY IN TERMS OF THE NEW KINDS OF BEHAVIOR YOU'D HAVE TO LEARN IF YOU WENT THERE?

S: FAR AWAY.

S: FAR AWAY.

T: OK. SO IT'S A CULTURE THAT HAS A LOT OF DIFFERENT BEHAVIOR PATTERNS. IS THAT RIGHT?

S: YES.

T: OK. NOW WE'RE GOING TO READ ABOUT ONE OF THE OTHER PLACES. I'M GOING TO GIVE YOU ANOTHER IDEA, AND THE IDEA IS THAT IF CULTURE IS A BEHAVIOR PATTERN, AND IF DIFFERENT GROUPS OF PEOPLE HAVE DIFFERENT CULTURES, WHAT HAPPENS IF YOU GROW UP IN A DIFFERENT CULTURE THAN THE ONE YOU'RE IN? IF YOU WERE TO MOVE TO ANOTHER CULTURE WHAT WOULD HAPPEN? WOULD IT MEAN THAT WHEN YOU WERE FINISHED YOUR PATTERN OF BEHAVIORS WOULD BE PARTLY THE ONE YOU ALREADY HAVE AND PARTLY THE ONE YOU TOOK ON?

S: YES.

T: AND A NEW LANGUAGE AND SOME NEW OTHER KINDS OF THINGS? OK. WELL, THE IDEA RELATED TO THAT IS THAT BEHAVIOR IS LEARNED.

Here the teacher directs the discussion by asking about a cultural trait the students have not yet brought up.

Again the teacher directs the discussion.

Promoting Active Reception Learning.

A principle of integrative reconciliation—relating the learning material to the subsumer—is being used. The teacher is also asking students to develop a critical approach to the material.

Phase One: A second organizer is presented.

The teacher provides an example of the new subsumer—*behavior is learned*—which will be labeled shortly.
(Note the process of progressive differentiation through which the teacher has led the lesson. The first culture is introduced, then the less inclusive concept that *behavior is learned* is introduced.)

A new subsumer—Behavior is learned—is introduced.

TAKING THEORY INTO ACTION

In this section we provide discussion and training in four critical areas:

1. formulating an advance organizer
2. promoting active reception learning
3. strengthening cognitive organization
4. promoting critical thinking

Formulating the advance organizer is the central skill of Phase One of the model; the other skills occur primarily in Phase Three. We shall describe each of these areas and provide short exercises so that you may check your understanding of them and begin to develop ease in applying them.

Formulating an Advance Organizer

The notion of an advance organizer makes such good intuitive sense that we can easily forget to inquire about the *form* of an organizer. Which introductory remarks are organizers and which ones are not? Many of us, when we teach, begin our instruction by asking students to recall what we did last week or last year or telling them what we're going to do tomorrow. In this way, we give them a context or orientation for our presentation. We may also do this by asking the students to recall a personal experience and then acknowledging that what we are about to say resembles that situation or will help the students understand a previous experience. We may also tell them the objectives of the session—what we hope they will get out of the presentation or discussion. None of these techniques are advance organizers. However, all of them are useful and are part of a well-organized presentation, and some of them reflect principles that are central to Ausubel's Theory of Meaningful Verbal Learning and part of the Advance Organizer Model of teaching.

The actual organizer is built around the major concepts and/or propositions of a discipline or area of study. However, the presentation of an organizer must include more than a simple statement, or even a simple definition, of the concept being used as the organizer. First, the organizer has to be constructed so that the learner can perceive it for what it is—an idea distinct from and more inclusive than the material in the learning task itself. The chief feature of an organizer is that it is an idea that is at a much higher level of abstraction and generality than the learning material itself. This higher level of abstraction is what distinguishes organizers from introductory overviews, which are written (or spoken) at the same level of abstraction as the learning material because they are, in fact, previews of the learning material.

Second, whether the organizer is expository or comparative, the essential features of the concept or proposition must be pointed out and carefully explained. (Definitional statements do not always point out the essential features of the term being defined.) Thus, the teacher and students must explore the organizer as well as the learning task. To us, this means citing the essential features, explaining them, and providing examples. The presentation of an organizer need not be lengthy, but it must be perceived (the learner must be aware of it), clearly understood, and continually related to the material it is organizing. This means the learner must be already familiar with the language and ideas in the organizer.

To illustrate, we now provide two potential advance organizers from elementary curriculum materials. Imagine that they were previously learned material being used to anchor new material. These materials need to be augmented in order to meet all the criteria for a well-formulated organizer presentation; however, they are heuristic. The first is an expository organizer and the second is a comparative organizer. It's helpful if you imagine these written organizers as being spoken.

An Expository Organizer on Landscapes

In this geography unit we shall learn about several different rural landscapes. But first we need to know what a landscape is.

Look out of the window. How far can you see? Two miles? One mile? A half mile? Not very far. A person can see only a tiny part of the earth at one time.

You see a landscape through a window. *A landscape* is that part of the earth you can see and look over. When you drive along the highway, you see many different landscapes.
a. What is a landscape?
b. How large is the landscape of an ant?
c. How large is the landscape of an astronaut orbiting the earth?
d. Can we say that landscapes vary in size?[8]

A Comparative Organizer on Landscapes

There are two types of landscapes. They are urban landscapes and rural landscapes. An *urban landscape* is what we see in a city. Urban means city. An urban landscape has tall buildings, crowded sidewalks, expressways, factories, and many different types of houses. We see many different urban landscapes when we drive in a city.

Rural refers to open country and farming. Every landscape that is not in a city is a rural landscape. Some rural landscapes are made up of farms and farm villages. Other rural landscapes are forests.
a. How does a rural landscape differ from an urban landscape?
b. Which type of landscape do you see through the classroom window?[9]

The following material on culture change is another example of an expository organizer. The organizer precedes the learning task, which is an explanation of acculturation in Kenya.

---

[8] John E. Steinbrink, *Comparative Rural Landscapes: A Conceptual Geographic Model*, Geography Curriculum Project (Athens, Ga.: University of Georgia, 1970), p. M2.
[9] Ibid., p. M2.

Acculturation: The British in Kenya[10]

Organizer

Acculturation takes place when the people of one culture acquire the traits of another culture as a result of contact over a long period of time. The British governed Kenya for about 80 years. During this period, the direction of cultural change was largely one way—African traits were replaced or modified by European traits. Almost all African traits have been influenced by European culture, especially in the cities. The people in the cities have been most affected by modernization in Kenya.

In 1886, Kenya came under the control of the British. Kenya was ruled by the British for almost 80 years. British laws became the laws of Kenya. English became the official language. The schools that were started were taught in English.

Contact with the British brought many changes to African culture. This contact with the British is an example of innovations coming from outside the culture. Look at the Cultural Change Model in Chapter 2, Figure 5. This kind of innovation is called acculturation, because Africans and British came into direct contact. Acculturation is the change that takes place in a culture over a period of time as a result of contact between different cultures.

In Kenya there were European settlers and British officials. Kenyans came into contact with Europeans in government work, in factories, and on the farms. Many new traits came to Kenya through acculturation.

Why have Africans wanted to change? If you can ride in a car to work, would you want to walk? If you can have a refrigerator, would you want to cool meat in a spring? If you can have a pair of shoes, would you want to always go barefooted? People everywhere want to live better. Living better is related to making and having more things. People all over the world want to have enough food to eat, enough clothes to wear, and more time to have fun. Africans are no different from other people. They want many of the same things other people want.

The direction of acculturation was largely one way. European traits replaced or changed African traits, but African traits had little impact on European traits. The new traits have helped in the modernization of Kenya. Modernization in Kenya has resulted in the replacement of African traits by European traits. Table 1 summarizes some of these changes. On the left of this table is the "Cultural Universal" column. A cultural universal is a trait that is found in all cultures. The second column shows the "African Trait," and the third column shows the "European Trait" that is replacing or changing the African Trait. Acculturation has been strongest in the urban areas. Here the three major forces, nationalism, urbanization, and industrialization, have affected more people for the longest length of time.

---

[10] Elmer U. Clauson and Marion J. Rice, *The Changing World Today*, Anthropology Curriculum Project (Athens, Ga.: University of Georgia, 1972), Publication 72-1, pp. 56-59.

Trait Changes: A Result of Acculturation

Cultural Universal	African Trait	Replaced by or Changing to European Trait
Social Organization	Tribe and smaller kin groups	National government
Family	Extended. Man has more than one wife	Nuclear. Man has only one wife
Children	Many	Fewer
Dress	Unfitted dress	Cut and fitted pants, shirts, coats, dresses
Housing	Round and square huts with thatched roofs; no water and electricity	Shantytowns and modern housing with water and electricity
Settlement	Small family groups; kinship, clan, village	Villages, town, cities; pull of urbanization
Making a Living	Subsistence agriculture and nomadic herding	Crops to export for foreign exchange
Cultivation of Soil	Hoe, hand tools	Plows, pulled by animal or tractor
Work	For self or in exchange for work	Day laborers for wages
Power	Man and animal	Steam, diesel, gasoline, electricity (machine)
Manufacturing	Handcrafts and hand tools	Light and heavy industries with assembly lines
Material goods	Few material goods	Related to income; wealthier government workers and businessmen have many modern goods
Exchange system	Barter in weekly markets	Money and banks; importers and exporters
Language	Tribal language and Swahili	In government business, schools, the national language is English; Swahili
Education	Learning the customs of the tribe	Primary, secondary, university education
Medicine	Magic, herbs	Doctors, nurses, hospitals
Population Growth	Low: high infant death rates; short life expectancy	High, decreased infant death rate; longer life expectancy
Transportation	Safari, caravan, man and animals	Railroads, roads, airplanes
Communication	Messenger, drums	Newspapers, radio, television, telephone, telegraph, post office
Cultural Stability	Few innovations; highly stable culture	Many innovations; many cultural changes

The organizers we have considered so far have been based on single concepts. Generalizations, principles, and propositions also serve as organizers. A unit of study called "Life Cycle" from the Anthropology Curriculum Project at the University of Georgia is built around a set of propositions:

> Some of the major ideas of anthropology emphasized in the unit on the life cycle include: (1) life as a biological continuum that begins at birth and ends with death; (2) biological life cycle; (3) universals in the life cycle growing out of the limits imposed by adjusting to the universals in the life cycle; (4) childhood as a period of slow biological development which facilitates enculturation or the learning of basic culture traits; (5) achieving self-identify and personal responsibility during adolescence or the transition from childhood to adulthood; (6) work and family obligations as a continuing responsibility of adulthood; (7) decline in physical ability and shift in social position with advancing years or at old age; and (8) how changes in the patterning of the total culture bring about changes in the life cycle. [11]

The eight major ideas that form the life cycle are what we call *expository organizers*. Each organizer is presented to the learner prior to the study of four cultures: 1) Middle class U.S.A., 2) Balkans, 3) Chinese, and 4) Tiv. For example. the first organizer (life as a biological continuum that begins at birth and ends with death) is presented to the learner with necessary clarifying information. The student is subsequently presented with specific information about how life begins and ends in the four subcultures. Each of the eight organizers mentioned above is presented in sequence for each of the four subcultures.

EXERCISE 1

Below is a description of the concept of culture and the two subconcepts of material and nonmaterial culture. We'd like you to read this description and then construct expository and comparative advance organizers that you can use with your students. (Assume that the students have been introduced briefly to the concept of culture.) Each organizer can be based on all or part of the explanation of culture, and it can be a concept or a proposition. In addition, provide a two- or three-sentence description of the learning material that might accompany the organizer. This concept should lend itself to a wide variety of subject matter—not just anthropology, but literature, history, and of course all the social sciences. It can also be used to analyze students' immediate environment— the school culture, peer culture, and family culture. The purpose of this exercise is not to test your knowledge of anthropology but to help you develop Advance Organizer presentations from conceptual material.

> *Culture:* Culture is the most important concept in anthropology. Its corollary in sociology is "society." Culture is the life style and material objects acquired by man as a member of a social group and which are transmitted from one generation to another. Culture is learned behavior not biologically inherited, even though man's physical development did make it possible for

[11] Pauline Persing, Wilfred C. Bailey, Milton Kleg, *Life Cycle*, Anthropology Curriculum Project Publication 49 (Athens, Ga.: University of Georgia, 1969), p. v.

man to develop cultures. A culture is made up of the interrelationship and interdependence of religion, art, economics, politics, technology, customs, traditions, and values of a given people in a given time and given place. Cultural values are the organizers and cohesive factors of human societies. Cultures are different in different places and times due to different reactions man had to different environments, different values assigned to certain behavioral patterns, isolation, and the passage of time.

Mankind represents diversity. Men have developed hundreds of different cultures. An individual in one culture can easily see the differences between his own and others. Culture is not associated with political boundaries or race. Cultures existed long before political boundaries. Cultures change only slowly. Cultures form a whole in the sense that there is an inextricable link and relationship between values, institutions, and behavior. Since the various subcomponents that make up a culture interact and interrelate, culture may be thought of as a system.

Cultures should not be judged "good," "bad," "primitive," or "advanced" since none of those terms helps us to understand cultures as systems, but does help to emphasize attitudes which are pejorative. So-called primitive cultures, for example, are as complex in value systems and behaviors as are so-called advanced cultures. The study of culture should emphasize the humanity of man as expressed through his culture and cultures as systems.[12]

If you prefer another content area beside the anthropological concept of culture, you may use the material from a high school textbook in American History on the following pages. There is a great quantity of factual material in these pages related to the concept of nationalism; however, the meaningfulness of the material can be enhanced by an Advanced Organizer presentation.

[12]Clinton Boutwell, *Getting It All Together* (San Rafael, Calif.: Leswing Press, 1972), p. 296.

SECTION 1. NEW FEELINGS OF NATIONALISM

Nationalism. Nationalism is the feeling in a person that his first loyalty is owed to his nation. This feeling has many causes. For some people it comes from a love of their land and the things their country has done for them. For others it is a sense of belonging to the same group as other people who speak the same language and share the same history. For most people, it comes as well from the feeling that they and others of that nation have the same goals for their future. Nationalism can be all of these things. In the last 200 years it has been one of the most important forces in the world. It has become perhaps the greatest single driving force for many peoples.

Nationalism grew greatly in the United States in the years immediately following the War of 1812. This war had ended in a draw, with neither side making any great gains. Still, Americans had fought together and had sometimes fought well. At the Battle of New Orleans, Jackson had won a victory which most Americans thought of as a national triumph over Great Britain. The United States had won a victory over a major power. Now Europe would let it alone. The country could give its attention to its own needs. The prospects for the future of the nation seemed promising. More and more Americans became nationally minded and gave their support to the interests of the nation. More and more became nationalistic.

Madison's Nationalism. The new feelings of nationalism were important to our people. Many of them never forgot how the Federalists in New England had opposed the war. A few of the Federalists at the Hartford Convention had even proposed that New England break away from the Union. It was the Republican party which saw the war through. Under President Madison, it had saved the nation. In the presidential election of 1816, Rufus King, the Federalist candidate, spoke of his campaign as "a fruitless struggle." He was right. James Monroe, the Republican candidate, won an easy victory in this election; he won a second easy victory four years later in 1820.

James Madison sent his last annual message to Congress late in 1815. In it he showed his concern with the needs of the whole nation. He spoke of the importance of strong national defenses. He urged protection for manufacturers. He asked for the building of roads and canals—what were then called "internal improvements." A. J. Dallas, his Secretary of the Treasury, favored chartering a second Bank of the United States to make the country's finances stronger. Many people believed that the Republicans were trying to get the government into more new activities than the Federalists had ever planned.

National Defense Laws. Republican Congressmen approved of Madison's views. They passed laws which would carry them into effect. The War of 1812 had led to increased demands for larger armed forces. The Republicans had long feared that a large standing army would be a threat to liberty. But the war was hardly over before Congress passed laws to establish an army of 10,000 men. It approved $8,000,000 to build new ships. It improved the Military Academy at West Point which had been begun in 1802.

The Tariff Act, 1816. Trade with Europe had almost ended during the long years of trouble with England and the War of 1812. Some men had begun factories in this country, and had been able to supply needed manufactured goods to other Americans. When the war ended, British merchants began to sell their products at very low prices as they tried to win back their American customers. New industries asked Congress and the President for help. Otherwise, they would be badly hurt.

Madison had asked for protection for American industry. Congress passed a protective tariff law. It was supported by people in every part of the country, although some merchants, shipowners, and importers were against it. These men were more interested in building trade than in promoting the growth of industry. Daniel Webster spoke for the New England groups who wanted no protective tariff. He was a great speaker and would be a leader in

Boyd C. Shafer, Richard A. McLemore, Everett Augspurger, and Milton Finkelstein, *A High School History of Modern America* (River Forest, Ill.: Laidlaw Brothers, 1966), pp. 166, 167. Reprinted by permission.

national politics, alongside Clay and Calhoun, for the next thirty-five years. However, his efforts, and those of his followers, could not stop the passage of the law.

Many other American leaders believed that industry in America should be helped and protected. They had seen how people had suffered during the war because of the shortage of products from Europe. They decided to pass laws that would make the United States better able to supply its own needs in times of both war and peace. In 1816 President Madison signed the new tariff law. It placed higher import duties on many products and gave special protection to cottons, woolens, iron, and other goods which had become more widely manufactured during the war. The Tariff of 1816 was the first really protective tariff in the country's history.

A New National Bank, 1816. Congress also took steps to strengthen the nation's money system. In 1811 it had refused to recharter the first Bank of the United States. During the War of 1812 Congress saw that a national bank was needed to keep the country's currency sound. State legislatures had chartered state banks. These had often issued more paper money than they could support with gold and silver. People then refused to give full value to such bills. Madison asked Congress to approve a second national bank. It did so. Men who had felt that the first national bank was unconstitutional now voted to give a charter to the second Bank of the United States.

The new bank would be allowed to operate for twenty years. It would begin with $35,000,-000 in capital, a very large amount for any bank at that time. The government would supply one fifth of this money; private investors would raise the rest of the capital. The bank would have twenty-five directors; the President would appoint five of them. In return for the charter, the bank would give the government a bonus of $1,500,000. Otherwise the new bank was much like the first bank that had been set up under Hamilton's plan in 1791. It carried on the regular business of banking, such as holding money at interest for its customers and making loans. But it was bigger and richer than other banks.. It also seemed to have the backing of the United States government. This second Bank of the United States (people called it the BUS) began to operate in 1817. The money it issued replaced most of the state bank notes that were not backed by gold or silver. The country's money problem was solved.

Internal Improvements. John C. Calhoun, Henry Clay, and their followers asked that Congress set aside money for internal improvements throughout the nation. They wanted special attention given to the need for roads and canals in the new territories and states in the West. Once these were built, the country's farming and industrial regions would be joined. This would make business better for both farmers and manufacturers. Frontier farmers liked this plan; so did businessmen. With roads, new settlements would mean more trade. Even the new army would benefit from better roads, for it could then go where it was needed and could get supplies more easily.

In 1811 the federal government had begun work on the Cumberland or National Road, which ran westward from Cumberland, Maryland. In 1817 this road reached the Ohio River at Wheeling, in what is now West Virginia. It later reached Vandalia, Illinois. Today it is part of U.S. 40.

The National Road was too big a project for any one state. John C. Calhoun asked Congress to pass the Bonus Bill, which would put the $1,500,000 received from the second Bank of the United States into a fund for internal improvements. He also asked that any future money made by the United States' investment in the bank be used for internal improvements. Calhoun was a nationalist, full of dreams for a greater and richer United States. He said,

> Let us bind the Republic together with a perfect system of roads and canals. Let us conquer space . . .

Congress passed the Bonus Bill in 1817, but Madison's last act as President was to veto it. He agreed that the country needed new and better roads and canals.

Three Skills for Facilitating Reception Learning

Prior to the introduction of new material, the advance organizer is used to create a linkage to the students' existing knowledge. Once the new material has been presented, the teacher can further strengthen these linkages by means of questions, statements, and illustrations. The teaching behaviors that do this have been grouped into three categories: (1) skills that promote active reception learning, (2) skills that strengthen cognitive structure, and (3) skills that promote a critical approach to knowledge.

Each skill cluster functions in a different way to facilitate the learning and retention of new material. Active reception learning skills function by promoting *student involvement in the learning task*—calling upon them to test or analyze the relationships between the old knowledge and the new knowledge—by relating the new material to their own experience, or by considering alternative points of view. Although they might also provide conceptual clarity, the major purpose of these skills is involvement.

Skills that strengthen cognitive structure facilitate learning and retention by *increasing the clarity and stability of the subsumer (or organizer)*. They help the student first integrate and then discriminate what was known from what has just been learned.

The third skill cluster asks students to take a critical approach to the new knowledge, by *recognizing assumptions and challenging and reconciling them*. These skills both engage students and clarify information. To that extent, they promote involvement and strengthen cognitive structure; however, their main purpose is to encourage students to ask constructive, critical questions about the information they receive.

Practically all of these skills can be manifested either through questions to students, responses to student-initiated questions, or brief, unsolicited teacher explanations. The form of the verbal exchange is, in most cases, not central to the mental activity it stimulates. Perceptive teachers, in response to students' silent faces, can discern their unspoken confusions. These teachers provide explanations without asking students to acknowledge their lack of clarity and without waiting for some confident person to ask for clarification. Once we believe that reception learning can be active, the source of the clarification, whether teacher- or student-initiated, is irrelevant. Conceptual clarity and precision are paramount!

EXERCISE 2

As you study examples of each of the three skill clusters, you will become clearer as to the role of each type. For now, we'd simply like you to try your hand at distinguishing one from another.

The concept of folkways is used here as an advance organizer for the subsequent learning material on childhood. The learning material describes childhood in the Tiv culture. Later on, students will read more material and see films about childhood in other cultures. Read the organizer and the learning material, and then complete the questions that follow.

Advance Organizer

Folkways are expected behaviors and practices for people in a given culture. They often involve less important areas of behavior dealing with day-to-day, ordinary activities, such as dress styles, etiquette, food preferences, etc. In more sacred societies these folkways, although relatively low-level behaviors, are strictly enforced. Punishment for breaking a folkway can be severe but not as severe as breaking more important behaviors. In very large societies like the United States, it's harder to maintain the same standard for dress and other habits. Generations are beginning to differ from one another in the folkways they grew up with. We all know that people now in their 50's and 60's grew up with quite different standards of dress and daily behavior than people in their 20's and 30's.

Learning Material

Some time between the ages of six and twelve, Tiv boys and girls have their ears pierced. All children are eager to have this done. If parents think the child is too young, the child is told jokingly that his ears will break off. When permission is finally given, the youngster asks someone in the compound to perform the task. As soon as the sores heal, the child runs around teasing all the children who have not yet had their ears pierced.

Cicatrization is another important event in the life of a Tiv boy or girl. This is the permanent scarring of the body for the purpose of beautification. Among the Tiv the desired pattern is drawn on the body with charcoal. These lines are then cut with a razor and more charcoal is rubbed into the cuts. This causes them to stand out. These cuts are then treated with a variety of medications until they heal. Children begin by having scars placed in their faces. As they grow older, they gradually add more lines to the face and then place them on the neck, shoulders, back and arms.

Using a nail to cut the designs has become a fad among the young people. The scars from nail scratches are not raised like the ones resulting from razor cuts. The young boys think that the girls like these flat designs better than the raised ones. This has produced a conflict between the older people and the youth in Tivland, and now the raised scars have become a symbol of the past generation.

Girls are cicatrized around puberty. The Tiv believe that a woman's stomach will become fat and flabby "like the ugly foreign women" unless it is scarred. After a girl has her stomach scarred, she teases all the girls who have not as yet had it done. She also praises the boys who have had their faces scarred.[13]

For each of the questions or statements below, decide whether it is designed primarily to strengthen cognitive structure (SCS), promote active reception learning (ARL), or facilitate a critical approach to learning (CA).

_____ 1.   Can you think of some folkways we have in this school that are different from folkways in other schools?

_____ 2.   Killing is a behavior that is severely punished in our society. It is not a folkway. Why can't we classify killing as a folkway?

_____ 3.   Some people feel that cicatrization is closely related to religious beliefs and customs of the Tiv people; it's too important to be a folkway. What do you think?

_____ 4.   What do you and your friends do to your bodies to make them more attractive or to call attention to them?

[13]Ibid., pp. 205-206.

_____ 5.   (Student) "Seems to me that the folkways in our country for people our age are not given to us by grownups. We decide on our own dress. I'm not sure you can call it a folkway then."

_____ 6.   Remember that a folkway has three major features. It deals with less important areas of life, people are expected to follow the folkways, and the punishment is not as severe for breaking a folkway as it is for breaking a more.

_____ 7.   What are the major features of a folkway?

_____ 8.   I want everyone to describe their activities over the weekend. Then tell me what some of your folkways are.

Answers

1.	ARL	5.	CA
2.	SCS	6.	SCS
3.	CA	7.	SCS
4.	ARL	8.	ARL

Promoting Active Reception Learning

Many people feel that the learning role in receiving information is a passive one; we simply take in what we've heard, read, or seen. Some of the material stays with us, and other facts or ideas are forgotten. Ausubel takes the position that if the material is to be retained, the learner's role in reception learning must be an active one. The learner must:

1. catalogue the new information
2. translate the new material into one's own terminology, frame of reference, or personal experience
3. reconcile any contradictions with one's own knowledge or experience; this includes clarifying vague, imprecise meanings

When we take in new information, we have the option of relating it to one idea or relating it to all existing information. For example, the next time we observe our teen-age students (or ourselves) participating in a *certain* new fad, we can simply say to ourselves, "Oh-oh. Here comes a new folkway! The folkways are changing." Or we can think about the differences in folkways over the last fifty years. Or in addition to labeling the new behavior, we can try to relate it to an explanation of how the folkway serves a psychological function; in other words, we can relate the behavior to our knowledge about psychology. The more active we are in our learning, the more we try to relate each new piece of information to all our previously acquired areas of knowledge.

A good way to make new material our own is to translate it into our own terms or find similarities in our own experience. If we are second graders, we can relate the concept of folkway to classroom behaviors or home behaviors. If we are biologists, we can talk about the folkways of our profession. If we have traveled extensively, we can compare the folkways of the Tiv to the folkways in societies we visited.

Another characteristic of active learners is that they attempt to clear up am-

biguities in meaning and clarify contradictions with previous knowledge or experience. They are aware of their own lack of clarity and seek a firmer grasp of the information. They are bothered by contradictions and try to resolve them through
active inquiry.

Ideally, students will initiate the behaviors, questions, or statements that indicate their role as active learners. If they don't, the teacher can stimulate these functions by eliciting responses or providing further explanation. Active reception
learning can function to strengthen the clarity and stability of the students' cognitive structure—the meaning of what has been learned. It can also stop just a little
short of that by, first, serving to get students to attend to the material and to make
personal connections but, second, not necessarily straightening out potential confusions with existing knowledge.

EXERCISE 3

Reread the Learning Material above on Tiv folkways and generate questions, statements, or
explanations that promote active reception learning. Do this for each of the three strategies listed
below.

1. Ask students to supply additional examples of the concept or proposition in the new learning material.
2. Ask students to describe how the new learning relates to a single aspect of their existing
   knowledge or personal experience.
3. Ask students to supply a verbal synthesis of the material, translating it into their own
   terminology and frame of reference. Construct a typical response.

Strengthening Cognitive Structure

The skill area of strengthening cognitive structure includes those teacher behaviors that integrate and reconcile the new learning material with the organizer (or
subsumer) or entire conceptual structure and also differentiate the organizer from
competing or similar subsumers. Some of the ways of doing this include:

1. remind students of the whole cognitive organization ("the larger picture")
2. ask for a summary of the major attributes of the new learning material
3. repeat precise definitions
4. ask for the differences between parallel subsumers
5. ask for a description of how the new learning material supports the concept or proposition of the subsumer

The essence of this skill cluster is definitional clarity and precision with respect to
the cognitive structure or the hierarchy of knowledge that the instructor is operating from.

EXERCISE 4

In the examples below, we return to our medical-school instructor from the Theory and Overview, who is strengthening the students' cognitive structure in various ways. Some of these actions are
in response to students' questions or statements, and some are teacher-initiated. See if you can

classify these according to the five techniques enumerated above. Part of the learning hierarchy from which the instructor was operating is repeated here to place the instructor's comments in context. The lesson concerned various types of affective disorders.

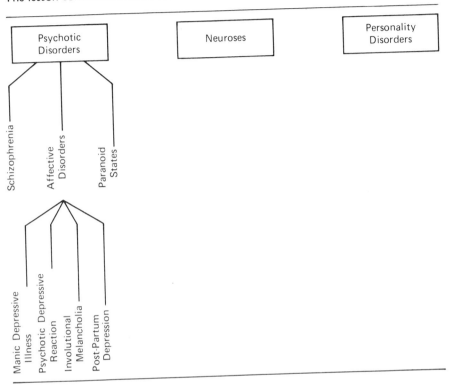

Figure 8. *A Partial Hierarchy of Psychiatric Disorders.*

_____A.   What are the chief differences between affective disorders and schizophrenia? Between affective disorders and paranoid states?

_____B.   We have just interviewed a patient and made these observations (points to list on the board). Susan, can you identify the various possibilities under affective disorders? Give us the criteria for each and then make a tentative diagnosis as to which affective disorder we have observed here.

_____C.   How does this symptomatology support our choice of an affective disorder, rather than one of the other psychotic disorders?

_____D.   Remember, in talking about schizophrenia, paranoid states, and affective disorders, we are talking about psychotic illnesses in contrast to other psychiatric illnesses, such as personality disorders and neuroses.

_____E.   Let's review the criteria for schizophrenia again. Remember there were three categories of criteria. . .(goes on to summarize major points within the three categories).

Answers

4 A.   Ask for differences between parallel subsumers.

2 B.   Ask for a summary of the major attributes of the new learning material.

<u>5</u> C. Ask for a description of how the new learning material supports the concept or proposition of the subsumer.

<u>1</u> D. Remind students of the whole cognitive organization ("the larger picture").

<u>3</u> E. Repeat precise definition.

EXERCISE 5

Think of your own subject area or a unit of study you have taught. Generate statements or explanations for the following:

1. Remind students of the whole cognitive organization ("the larger picture"). What, if anything, might the student have said or done to lead you to believe this was necessary?
2. State how the subsumer and new learning material differ from a parallel subsumer.
3. Ask for a description of how the new learning material supports the concept or proposition of the subsumer.

Developing a Critical Approach

Active reception learning calls upon students to become active recipients of information, to struggle to integrate the new ideas into their own frame of reference, previous experience, and personal meaning. They must also seek conceptual clarity through questions that help them integrate the new material thus strengthening their cognitive structure. Last, students are encouraged to take a critical approach to the understanding of subject matter. As recipients of knowledge, it is important for students to recognize and question the assumptions and inferences that knowledge makers are using. Three skills have been identified for doing this:

1. recognizing the assumptions or inferences that have been made in the learning material
2. making a judgment that challenges these assumptions and inferences
3. reconciling contradictions among the assumption.

EXERCISE 6

Go back now to your responses in Exercise 1. Analyze the learning material in terms of its assumptions, inferences, or contradictions. Then, construct two or three questions (or explanations) that prompt students to recognize or inquire into these contradictions. Do not ask them directly, "What assumptions are made here?" Instead, relate your questions to the material. If you prefer, you may complete this exercise by using learning material you are more familiar with—for instance, a topic from your own subject area.

THEORY CHECKUP FOR THE ADVANCE ORGANIZER MODEL

Instructions: Circle the response that best answers the question or completes the statement, check your answers with the key that follows the exercise.

1. Ms. Warren, a science teacher, was presenting the topic of potential energy to a physics class. She said to her students, "Remember last week we talked about kenetic energy. Well, today we're going to discuss another kind of energy—potential energy." This is *not* an example of an Advance Organizer because
   a. the knowledge hierarchy was incorrect.
   b. she did not present the organizer (define, explain, and illustrate).
   c. the organizer is too factual.
   d. the organizer should have been mechanical energy.

2. Which of the following statements would Ausubel disagree with? Meaning depends on
   a. the method of teaching.
   b. the learner's readiness.
   c. the learner's prior experience and information.
   d. the material.

3. Presenting the most inclusive, general ideas in a discipline first is called
   a. integrative reconciliation.
   b. progressive differentiation.
   c. curriculum sequencing.
   d. deduction.

4. Three categories of teaching skills, each with several possible techniques, have been discussed as facilitating meaningful verbal learning. List the three sets of teaching skills.
   a.
   b.
   c.

5. Which of the following illustrates the use of an advance organizer?
   a. Telling students the goals of the lesson.
   b. Reminding them of the previous lesson.
   c. Discussing a concept related to the ideas in the new learning material.
   d. Defining the new ideas.

6. Which of the following is *not* characteristic of the learner's role in reception learning?
   a. Making up mnemonics for remembering the information.
   b. Comparing the material to similar ideas that were previously learned.
   c. Asking for clarification.
   d. Reflecting on the learning material.

7. An elementary teacher is presenting the topic of subtraction to her students. During the lesson, she compares subtraction with addition, a skill the students have previously learned. This is an example of
   a. comparative organizer.
   b. discrimination learning.
   c. integrative reconciliation.
   d. knowledge hierarchy.

THEORY CHECKUP FOR THE ADVANCE ORGANIZER MODEL

8. While explaining the concept of weightlessness, Ms. Jones asked her students to think of times when they have felt weightless and to describe the experience to the class. Ms. Jones was using one technique for promoting
    a. integrative reconciliation.
    b. active reception learning.
    c. strengthening cognitive structure.
    d. a meaningful learning set.

9. In the example in Question 8, another technique Ms. Jones could have used to accomplish her goal would be
    a. reminding students of the "larger picture."
    b. asking students to recognize the assumptions in the idea.
    c. asking students to identify ideas that are unclear and dispelling their confusion.
    d. asking students to construct a knowledge hierarchy.

10. Which of the following is a set of teaching skills designed to discriminate students' prior knowledge from new learning material?
    a. Progressive differentiation.
    b. Advance Organizer.
    c. Taking a critical approach.
    d. Strengthening cognitive structure.

11. Another term for meaningful verbal learning is
    a. discrimination learning.
    b. lecturing.
    c. reception learning.
    d. representational learning.

12. The Advance Organizer Model is designed to accomplish which of the following goals?
    a. Improve inductive thinking.
    b. Teach students how to organize information.
    c. Give information.
    d. Link new information to existing knowledge.

13. Ausubel believes that students can take an active role in reception learning. One of the ways they do this is
    a. taking notes.
    b. developing a critical approach to new information.
    c. studying.
    d. using advance organizers.

Theory Checkup Key

1. b
2. a
3. b

4. Active reception learning
    Developing a critical approach
    Strengthening cognitive structures

5. c
6. a
7. a
8. b
9. c

10. d
11. c
12. d
13. b

Component II

VIEWING
THE MODEL

One of the purposes of Component II is to provide examples of actual sessions in which the Advance Organizer Model is the strategy being used. Reading the demonstration transcript that follows, hearing a tape of a teacher and students, or viewing a demonstration of class activity are alternate means of illustrating the "model in action."

As you study any of these alternatives, you will be introduced to the Teaching Analysis Guide for analyzing the model. This same Guide will also be used in Component III to analyze the peer teaching and microteaching lessons. We want you to become familiar with the Guide now, however, as it will sharpen your perception of the demonstration lesson.

The two activities in this component are (1) reading the Teaching Analysis Guide and (2) viewing (reading) the lesson. Before going on to them, you may wish to reread the material in the Introduction to this book that discusses the purposes and philosophy of the Teaching Analysis Guide.

Analyzing Teaching: Activity 1

The Teaching Analysis Guide for the Advance Organizer Model consists of fourteen questions. The questions are based on an analysis of the activities and skills required in each phase of the model. Thus, the items for Phase One concern the presentation and features of the organizer, plus a few general presentational skills. The items for Phase Two deal with the new learning materials and with general procedures for enhancing the presentation of new information. The items for Phase Three are based on the activities for strengthening cognitive organization, promoting critical thinking, and promoting active reception learning.

Please note those items that do not seem clear to you. Discuss these with your instructor or colleagues. You may also want to review the appropriate sections in Component I.

TEACHING ANALYSIS GUIDE FOR THE ADVANCE ORGANIZER MODEL

This Guide is designed to help you analyze the process of teaching as you practice the Advance Organizer Model. The analysis focuses on aspects of teaching that are important to the syntax of the model, the teacher's role, and specific teaching skills.

The Guide consists of a series of questions and phrases. As you observe a practice session (whether peer teaching or microteaching), analyze the teaching using the rating scale that appears opposite each question and statement. This scale uses the following items:

Thoroughly. This item signifies that the teacher engaged in the behavior to the point where students were responding comfortably and fluently. Appropriateness varies from situation to situation. For example, the extensiveness of the Advance Organizer will depend on prior instruction in the subject area and the learner's age level.

Partially. This item signifies that the teacher engaged in appropriate behavior, but not as thoroughly as possible. There is some doubt about whether the students are responding fully.

Missing. The teacher did not engage in the behavior; there appears to be a loss in student response or probably will be one.

Not Needed. The teacher did not explicitly manifest the behavior, but there is no loss. Either the behavior was included in others or the students began to respond appropriately without being led to.

For each question or statement in the Guide, circle the term that best describes the teacher's behavior.

Phase One: Presentation of the Organizer

1. Did the teacher clarify the aims of the presentation?	Thoroughly	Partially	Missing	Not Needed
2. Was an advance organizer presented? If so, was it expository or comparative?	Thoroughly	Partially	Missing	Not Needed
3. Did the organizer presentation identify, clarify, or explain the essential characteristics of the concept or proposition that serves as the organizer?	Thoroughly	Partially	Missing	Not Needed
4. Did the organizer presentation include examples of the organizer?	Thoroughly	Partially	Missing	Not Needed
5. Was the language or terms of the subsumer (organizer) repeated or otherwise emphasized?	Thoroughly	Partially	Missing	Not Needed
6. Did the teacher prompt awareness of relevant knowledge or experience in the learners' backgrounds?	Thoroughly	Partially	Missing	Not Needed

Phase Two: Presentation of the Learning Task or Material

7. Was the learning material presented?	Thoroughly	Partially	Missing	Not Needed
8. Did the teacher develop the material in the logical order of the learning material and make the order	Thoroughly	Partially	Missing	Not Needed

explicit to the student — for instance, the rough outlines and explanations?

9. Did the teacher use procedures that enhanced the organization of the presentation, such as rule-example-rule, explaining links, diagrams, and verbal makers of importance?	Thoroughly	Partially	Missing	Not Needed
10. Did the teacher use procedures for maintaining attention, such as varying audio stimuli, using supplemental media, and inserting questions into the presentation?	Thoroughly	Partially	Missing	Not Needed

Phase Three: Strengthening Cognitive Organization

11. Did the teacher use principles of integrative reconciliation (reminding students of "the larger picture," summarizing the major attributes of the new material, repeating precise definitions, asking for the differences between parallel subsumers, relating learning material to subsumer)?	Thoroughly	Partially	Missing	Not Needed
12. Did the teacher ask questions and make explanations that promoted active reception learning?	Thoroughly	Partially	Missing	Not Needed
13. Did the teacher facilitate a critical approach to information (the recognition of assumptions, inferences, and contradictions)?	Thoroughly	Partially	Missing	Not Needed
14. Did the teacher attempt to clarify students' misunderstandings or confusions?	Thoroughly	Partially	Missing	Not Needed

Viewing the Lesson: Activity 2

On your own or with a group of your peers, read the demonstration transcript. In the space below, record the occurrence of the phases as they are presented here. You may want to focus on the adequacy of each phase, the quality of the inquiry, the nature of the puzzling situation, or skillful moves the teacher made (or did not make).

Phase One	Adequate	Minimal	Not at All
Phase Two	Adequate	Minimal	Not at All
Phase Three	Adequate	Minimal	Not at All

Analyzing the Lesson: Activity 3 (Optional)

View a taped or live demonstration and analyze it by completing the Teaching Analysis Guide. You can do this in two ways: complete the form as the tape is viewed, or complete it afterwards.

If you are working in a group, you may want to divide the task of analysis with one or more of the others, each person taking a particular phase or aspect of analysis. Duplicate as many copies of the Guide as are needed.

DEMONSTRATION TRANSCRIPT: ADVANCE ORGANIZER

This demonstration was made by Bruce Joyce with a group of students from Palo Alto, California. The topic is literary style.

T: TODAY WE'RE GOING TO WORK OVER SOME LITERARY MATERIAL AND WE'RE GOING TO DO IT USING A PARTICULAR APPROACH IN WHICH I GIVE YOU AN IDEA, THEN I'M GOING TO READ YOU SOME MATERIAL THAT RELATES TO THAT IDEA, AND THEN WE'LL TALK ABOUT THE MATERIAL. OKAY? WE'LL DO THAT TWO OR THREE TIMES WITH DIFFERENT PIECES OF MATERIAL.

THE IDEA IS THAT OF STYLE IN LITERATURE. STYLE HAS TO DO WITH THE FORM OF THE THING RATHER THAN ITS CONTENT. THAT IS, IT'S THE SHAPE RATHER THAN WHAT'S IN IT. YOU CAN MAKE THE ANALOGY TO JEWELRY. IT TAKES SILVER—WHAT MAKES IT JEWELRY IS NOT THAT IT'S MADE OF SILVER—IT'S THE FORM. THE DIFFERENCE BETWEEN VARIOUS SILVERSMITHS IS THE PARTICULAR FORMS THAT EACH ONE PRODUCES. SO WE'D SAY EACH SILVERSMITH HAS HIS OWN STYLE. SO WITH LITERATURE. YOU HAVE CONTENT. MANY BOOKS CAN BE WRITTEN ABOUT THE SAME THING—OFTEN ARE. SOMEBODY SAID, THERE ARE ONLY TWO HUNDRED PLOTS AND WE READ THEM AGAIN AND AGAIN AND AGAIN. BUT THE STYLE MAKES THEM DIFFERENT.

I'M GOING TO READ YOU TWO OR THREE PASSAGES FROM DIFFERENT AUTHORS, AND THEN—WE'LL TAKE A LOOK AT THEM.

(reads aloud) "FINISHING MY DRINK, I THANKED THE BARMAN AND WENT OUT TO THE CAR. I CLIMBED INTO THE DRIVING SEAT AND STRETCHED MY HAND OUT TO TURN ON THE LIGHTS AND THE IGNITION. I STRETCHED OUT MY HAND, BUT I DIDN'T REACH THE LIGHTS. MY NECK WAS GRIPPED VIOLENTLY FROM BEHIND. THERE WAS A MOVEMENT THEN IN THE BACK OF THE CAR AS THE ARM SHIFTED TO GET A BETTER LEVERAGE—A RUSTLING OF CLOTHES AND THE SCRAPE OF A SHOE ACROSS THE THIN CARPET. I FLUNG UP MY HANDS AND CLAWED, BUT I COULDN'T REACH THE FACE OF WHOMEVER WAS BEHIND ME, AND MY NAILS WERE USELESS AGAINST HIS GLOVES."[1]

Phase One: Presentation of the Organizer

Promotes active reception learning by relating to students' own experience.

Phase Two: Presentation of Learning Material

[1]Dick Francis, *Nerve* (New York: Harper & Row, 1975), pp. 154-55. By permission of Harper & Row and Sterling Lord Agency, Inc. © 1964 by Dick Francis.

OKAY. NOW THAT'S DICK FRANCIS.

NOW HERE'S ANOTHER PASSAGE—DIFFERENT AUTHOR. THIS AUTHOR IS DEE WELLS.

(reads) "ON MONDAY MORNING, A CASE OF JACK DANIELS CAME FROM ANGELA WITH A FORTUNE COOKIE SLIP TAPED IN IT. 'YOU ARE RIDING A TIGER, BE CAREFUL WHEN THE TIME COMES TO GET OFF.' 'NOW WHAT THE HELL CAN THAT MEAN?' FRANKLIN ASKED, AND HANDED HER THE BOTTLE. 'WHO KNOWS, ANGELA EATS IN SOME PRETTY INSCRUTABLE RESTAURANTS.' 'AND THERE'S SOMETHING ELSE I'D LIKE TO KNOW.' HE TOOK OFF HIS GLASSES AND TIPPED THE TYPEWRITER UP TO LOOK AT ITS UNDER-NEATH. 'HOW DO YOU GET ALONG WITHOUT A G?'

'I ET ALON FINE—GOD COMES OUT OD, BUT WHAT'S IN A NAME? TELL ME MORE ABOUT DAYTON.'

'AH WELL, DAYTON, FOLKS IS A SCENIC PARA-DISE, SITUATED ON ITS OWN LIMPID SEWER SOMEWHAT NORTH TO A SOMEWHAT LESS BEAUTIFUL CINCINNATI IN THE MAJESTICALLY BEAUTIFUL STATE OF OHIO AND HAS MANY INTERESTING FEATURES.' "[2]

OKAY? THAT'S DEE WELLS. ALL RIGHT, ONE MORE. HERE WE GO. THIS IS JOYCE CAROL OATES.

(reads) "ANDREW, IN MY MIND'S EYE, NOT THE STOCKY, MUSCULAR, PERSPIRING, AGGRESSIVE FLESH. NOT THE SLIGHTLY CURVED LEGS, THE WIDE SHOULDERS, THE GREY ASSERTIVE GAZE. NOT THAT VOICE RAPID FIRE AND THEN DRAWL-ING, MOCKING. NOT THE UGLY GRIN, INSTEAD A THICK-BODIED CREATURE MADE OF STONE, TRAPPED IN STONE, PETRIFIED. A GIGANTIC ANGEL, ENORMOUS, UNGAINLY WINGS, BRUTAL DARK STAINED MUSCLES OF STONE, STONE SMOOTH EYES BLIND, THE FACE CONTORTED WITH ITS USUAL RAGE BUT SILENT, SILENT."[3]

Phase Three: Strengthening Cognitive Organi-zation

OK. WHAT DO YOU THINK OF THOSE?

S: THE MIDDLE ONE—DEE WELLS—IS THE ONLY ONE I'D WANT TO READ.

S: YEAH.

T: WHY IS THAT?

S: MORE INTERESTING THAN THE OTHERS.

S: THE FIRST SOUNDS LIKE YOU GET IN A SUB-SCRIPTION—TWO A MONTH COME IN, YOU KNOW.

T: AND THE THIRD?

S: THAT WAS PRETTY INTERESTING. I LIKE HOW SHE DESCRIBED THINGS.

[2]Dee Wells, *Jane* (New York: Viking/Penquin, 1974), p. 75.
[3]Reprinted from *The Assassins*, p. 4, by Joyce Carol Oates. Copyright © 1975 by Joyce Carol Oates. By permission of The Vanguard Press, Inc. and Blanche C. Gregory, Inc.

T: HOW WOULD YOU COMPARE HER WRITING WITH THE WRITING OF THE OTHER TWO?

S: WELL, THE OTHER TWO SEEM LIKE THEY'RE SO—I DON'T KNOW. THIS ONE SEEMS LIKE IT'S MORE OF A WORK THAN THESE TWO. THESE ARE MORE LIKE ENTERTAINMENT BOOKS. AND THAT ONE DOESN'T SEEM MUCH LIKE—IT SEEMED MORE LIKE IT WAS WRITTEN FOR A LITERARY WHATEVER.

T: WHAT ABOUT IT MAKES IT SEEM THAT WAY?

S: VERY CAREFUL WITH THE DESCRIPTION.

S: IT'S A LOT WORDIER. THERE'S A LOT MORE METAPHORS AND STUFF LIKE THAT.

S: THERE'S MORE TIME TAKEN WITH WHAT THEY'RE SAYING. NOT LIKE THE FIRST ONE WHERE THEY DESCRIBE MINUTELY. (general laughter)

T: KIND OF STRAIGHT—NO FRILLS AND SO FORTH. LET ME GIVE YOU ANOTHER PART OF AN IDEA. WHEN WE THINK OF STYLE, WE THINK OF SEVERAL KINDS OF THINGS. THAT IS, THERE ARE SEVERAL ASPECTS OF STYLE. AGAIN I'M GOING TO PICK UP THE METAPHOR OF THE SILVERSMITH. ONE THING IS THE KIND OF SHAPE THAT IS USED—A SIMPLE DESIGN OR SHAPES. ANOTHER HAS TO DO WITH THE JOINING OF VARIOUS PIECES. SOME SILVERSMITHS ATTEMPT TO MAKE THE WHOLE PIECE KIND OF FLOW OUT OF ONE DESIGN. YOU SEE IT—A KIND OF A COFFEE POT THAT COMES AROUND LIKE THIS, AND THE HANDLE IS AN INTEGRAL PART OF IT. OTHER PEOPLE MAKE THE PARTS SEPARATELY AND PUT THEM ON. SOME PEOPLE USE SYM-METRICAL DESIGNS, KIND OF CONSTRUCT THE THING LIKE A BUILDING.

WELL, IN THE CASE WITH STYLE, WE HAVE THREE OR FOUR FEATURES. I'M GOING TO GIVE YOU ONE OR TWO. ONE IS SOUNDS OR RHYTHM. THEY'RE RHYTHMIC DIFFERENCES THAT KIND OF CATCH YOU UP. ANOTHER ONE HAS TO DO WITH WHAT WE CALL SYNTAX, OR THE WAYS THAT DIFFERENT SENTENCES ARE PUT TO-GETHER. YOU CAN THINK OF THIS PARTICU-LARLY IN POETRY. YOU HAVE SOMETHING LIKE T.S. ELIOT'S *THE WASTE LAND*[4]. IT BEGINS WITH "APRIL IS THE CRUELEST MONTH, BREEDING LILACS OUT OF THE DEAD LAND." AS CON-TRASTED WITH THE STATEMENT, "I ALWAYS FEEL VERY SAD IN APRIL; IT SEEMS VERY CRUEL, THAT OUT OF THE BARREN LAND WILL COME THE—WHATEVER . . ." A DIFFERENT FORM IN A SENSE. A DIFFERENT SYNTAX COMES IN.

Phase One: Presentation of Advance Organizers

Teacher introduces two parallel subsumers under literary style—rhythm and syntax.

---

[4]"The Waste Land" by T. S. Eliot, from *Collected Poems 1909-1962*. Reprinted by permission of Harcourt Brace Jovanovich, Inc.

SO THOSE TWO IDEAS, ADDED TO STYLE. ONE IS THE RHYTHM—AND THE OTHER IS THE SHAPE OF THE SENTENCES, USES OF PREPOSITIONAL PHRASES AND ALL THAT. SO LET'S SEE WHAT WE CAN DO WITH THAT. THIS IS IRWIN SHAW.

(reads) "WE WERE SITTING IN A RESTAURANT CALLED THE CHATEAU MADRID, HIGH UP ON A CLIFF OVERLOOKING THE MEDITERRANEAN. THE LIGHTS OF NICE AND THE COASTAL SETTLE-MENTS FAR BELOW TWINKLED IN THE LAVENDER EVENING AIR. WE WERE WAITING FOR OUR DINNER AND DRINKING CHAMPAGNE. WE HAD ALSO DRUNK A CONSIDERABLE AMOUNT OF CHAMPAGNE ON THE TRAIN BLEU DOWN FROM PARIS THE NIGHT BEFORE. I WAS BEGINNING TO DEVELOP A TASTE FOR MOËT AND CHANDON. OLD MAN COOMBES HAD BEEN WITH US ON THE TRAIN AND MOST OF THE AFTERNOON. AFTER MORE THAN TWO WEEKS OF WORKOUTS, RÊVE DE MINUIT HAD FINALLY TOLD THE TRAINER HE WAS READY TO RUN. AND RUN HE HAD. HE HAD COME IN FIRST BY A NECK THAT AFTER-NOON IN THE FOURTH RACE AT CANNES ON THE TRACK OUTSIDE OF NICE, WHERE THEY HAD A WINTER MEETING."[5]

HERE'S THIS ONE. THIS IS SAUL BELLOW, CALLED *HUMBOLDT'S GIFT.*

(reads) "HUMBOLDT'S HOUSE WAS IN THE JERSEY BACK COUNTRY NEAR THE PENNSYLVANIA LINE. THIS MARGINAL LAND WAS GOOD FOR NOTHING BUT CHICKEN FARMS. THE APPROACHES WERE UNPAVED AND WE DROVE IN THE DUST. BRIARS LASHED THE ROADMASTER AS WE SWAYED ON HUGE SPRINGS THROUGH RUBBISHY FIELDS WHERE WHITE BOULDERS SAT. THE BUSTED MUFFLER WAS SO LOUD THAT THOUGH THE CAR FILLED THE LANE THERE WAS NO NEED TO HONK. YOU COULD HEAR US COMING. HUMBOLDT YELLED, 'HERE'S OUR PLACE,' AND SWERVED. WE ROLLED OVER A HUMMOCK OR EARTH WAVE. THE FRONT OF THE BUICK ROSE AND THEN DIVED INTO THE WEEDS. HE SQUEEZED THE HORN FEARING FOR HIS CATS, BUT THE CATS SLID OUT AND FOUND SAFETY ON THE ROOF OF THE WOODSHED WHICH HAD COLLAPSED UNDER THE SNOW LAST WINTER."[6]

NOW—ANOTHER SELECTION.

(reads) "AS SOON AS WORD WAS RECEIVED THAT THE VEHICLE WAS ON THE PIKE, AN ALL-POINTS ALARM WAS SENT, AND THE NEAREST VEHICLES WERE DIVERTED INTO PRIORITY TARGET.

Phase Two: Presentation of the Learning Material

[5] From *Nightwork* by Irwin Shaw (New York: Delacorte Press, 1975), p. 185. Reprinted by permission of Dell Publishing Co., Inc. and Irving Paul Lazar.
[6] Saul Bellow, *Humboldt's Gift* (New York: Viking/Penquin, Inc., 1973), p. 22.

DURING THE TWENTY MILES AND TWENTY MINUTES IT TOOK THE TARGET VEHICLE TO REACH THE VALLEY FORGE AREA, THE PATTERN OF THE STALK HAD BEEN ESTABLISHED. AN UNMARKED VEHICLE CONTAINING TWO OFFICERS HAD CAUGHT UP AT HIGH SPEED, SLOWED AND DRIFTED CLOSE ENOUGH TO CONFIRM THE IDENTIFICATION, AND HAD THEN DROPPED INCONSPICUOUSLY BACK INTO POSITION FOUR HUNDRED YARDS BEHIND THE MERCURY."[7]

S: WELL THIS BOOK HERE, I REALLY LIKED IT BECAUSE IT, AH, IT DID HAVE THAT RHYTHM, YOU KNOW, AND IT MUST READ EASILY TOO.

S: IT'S VERY SMOOTH, AND IT'S, YOU KNOW, VERY CONTINUOUS.

T: NICE.

S: YEAH, BUT THE ONE—*HUMBOLDT'S GIFT*, THAT ONE—HE USED, HE'S USING A LOT OF, I GUESS, SHORTER SENTENCES AND STUFF. I THOUGHT IT FLOWED A LOT, THIS DEVELOPMENT.

S: THE THINGS WERE BRIEFER BUT—

S: IT WAS MORE LIKE THOUGHT.

T: DID YOU KIND OF SEE WAVES IN THIS?

S: YOU SORT OF GET A PICTURE OF WHAT IS GOING ON.

S: THIS IS SHORTER SO IT JUST LED RIGHT INTO THE NEXT ONE.

S: IT ALL FIT TOGETHER IN THIS ONE, GOT AN OVERALL PICTURE OF IT.

S: YOU COULD TELL WHAT WAS GOING ON. THE OTHER YOU COULDN'T TELL WHAT WAS GOING ON, BUT THIS ONE YOU SORT OF HAD A PICTURE RIGHT AWAY.

T: RIGHT. HOW ABOUT THIS ONE? (shows *The Assassins*)

S: HEAVY.

S: I DIDN'T KNOW WHAT WAS GOING ON.

T: OKAY, LET ME GIVE YOU ONE MORE HERE, AND SEE WHAT YOU THINK OF IT IN RELATION TO THE OTHERS. THIS IS ROSS MACDONALD. WHICH ONE DOES THIS MATCH?

(reads) "I FLEW HOME FROM MAZATLAN ON A WEDNESDAY AFTERNOON. AS WE APPROACHED LOS ANGELES, THE MEXICANA PLANE DIPPED LOW OVER THE SEA AND I CAUGHT MY FIRST GLIMPSE OF THE OIL SPILL. IT LAY ON THE BLUE WATER OFF PACIFIC POINT IN A FREE FORM SLICK THAT SEEMED MILES WIDE AND MANY MILES LONG. AN OFFSHORE OIL PLATFORM STOOD OUT OF ITS WINDWARD END LIKE THE METAL HANDLE OF A DAGGER THAT HAD

Phase Three: Strengthening Cognitive Organization

[7]John D. MacDonald, *The End of the Night* (Greenwich, Conn: Fawcett Publications, 1960), p. 164.

STABBED THE WORLD AND MADE IT SPILL BLACK BLOOD."[8]

S: IT WAS VERY BLUNT.

S: I THINK IT HAD MORE DESCRIPTION IN IT.

S: SAME TYPE OF STORY AS THESE TWO (points to the books by Francis and John MacDonald), BUT IT'S BETTER.

T: SAME TYPE OF STORY BUT A BETTER WRITER?

S: YEAH, MORE EFFECTIVE.

T: THAT'S INTERESTING. DO THEY BELONG TOGETHER IN A SENSE, AS CONTRASTED WITH THE REST OF THESE (points to the three)?

S: TO ME THEY DO, BUT THAT'S SOMETHING I REALLY WOULDN'T WANT TO READ.

T: AND THE REASON FOR THAT IS?

S: I DON'T KNOW. JUST FROM THOSE PASSAGES, I JUST DIDN'T GET TOO MUCH OUT OF THEM. THEY REALLY DIDN'T HOLD MY INTEREST OR ANYTHING.

S: I WOULD WANT TO READ THE ROSS MACDONALD ONE, MAYBE. WELL, I'VE READ OTHER ROSS MACDONALD'S, BUT EVEN FROM THAT PASSAGE, IT SOUNDED LIKE IT COULD HAVE BEEN GOOD, BUT I DON'T THINK THE OTHERS . . .

T: WHAT DO YOU GET HERE (points to one) THAT YOU DON'T GET HERE (points to another)?

S: IT'S BELIEVABLE.

S: IT'S GOT A LOT MORE MEAT IN IT.

S: THIS IS MORE, A LITTLE MORE WORDY, BUT NOT TOO WORDY.

S: IT WAS ENJOYABLE TO READ. IT MAY NOT STAY WITH YOU ALWAYS, AS ONE OF THE GREATER PIECES YOU'VE EVER READ, BUT IT WOULD BE INTERESTING.

T: OKAY, HOW ABOUT THIS ONE—HOW WOULD YOU COMPARE THIS WITH THOSE AT THIS POINT?

S: I WOULDN'T COMPARE THE TWO.

T: IT'S ALMOST A DIFFERENT KIND OF LITERATURE? HOW ABOUT STYLISTICALLY NOW? WHAT DO YOU THINK? WOULD YOU LIKE TO READ THIS, DO YOU THINK? FROM THE LITTLE PASSAGE I READ?

S: IF I READ A COUPLE OF MORE PASSAGES . . .

S: IT WAS A LITTLE BIT WORDY.

S: I'D WANT TO KNOW WHAT THE REST OF IT WAS LIKE.

S: ONE OF THEM WOULD BE THE SORT OF THING IF YOU REALLY JUST—IT'S LIKE A MAGAZINE

Phase Three: Strengthening Cognitive Structure

Linking material to subsumer learning.

[8]Ross MacDonald, *Sleeping Beauty* (New York: Alfred A. Knopf), p. 1. Copyright © 1973 by Ross MacDonald.

OR A COMIC BOOK—YOU FEEL LIKE JUST SORT OF READING FOR THE SAKE OF READING SOMETHING THAT WILL HOLD YOUR INTEREST. BUT THIS WOULD BE SOMETHING YOU WOULD WANT TO REALLY SORT OF GET IN TO.

T: (reads) "SHE HEARD HERSELF TALKING—SHE HEARD HER UNFAMILIAR CHILDHOOD VOICE, A GIRL'S BRAVE, HOLLOW VOICE. SHE HEARD IT FROM A DISTANCE, HOPING IT WOULD NOT FALTER, WOULD NOT BREAK, REVEALING HER UTTER TERROR. THE CHILD AT THE EMERGENCY WELFARE CENTER IN WHITE SPRINGS TAKEN FROM HER MOTHER ONE EARLY SUNDAY MORNING, TAKEN AWAY WRAPPED IN SOMEONE'S JACKET, MAD WITH FEAR, SAYING SHE WASN'T HURT, THEY HADN'T HURT HER, NO ONE HAD HURT HER."[9]

DOES THAT MAKE IT HAVE MORE OR LESS IN COMMON WITH THIS THAN THE OTHER PASSAGE I READ?

S: LESS IN COMMON.

S: IT ALSO MAKES ME WANT TO READ IT LESS. IT DOESN'T SOUND LIKE THE SORT OF THING I'D LIKE—YOU KNOW, SPENDING THAT MUCH TIME TO READ.

T: BECAUSE OF CONTENT OR STYLE?

Teacher uses principles of integrative reconciliation.

S: YEAH, CONTENT.

S: I THINK THE STYLE. I WOULD WANT TO READ IT. THEN WHEN YOU READ THE FIRST PASSAGE . . .

S: DEPENDS ON WHAT KIND OF THING YOU'RE FEELING LIKE READING. LIKE I SAID BEFORE—WHAT IS THE CONTENT—WASN'T SOMETHING I'D WANT TO READ. I COULDN'T PUT UP WITH THAT STUFF.

T: OKAY. DOES THIS HAVE MORE IN COMMON? WHICH OF THESE DOES THIS HAVE MOST IN COMMON WITH?

S: NONE OF THEM.

S: YEAH, NONE OF THEM.

S: MAYBE WE SHOULD HEAR ANOTHER PASSAGE.

(Teacher continues reading several more passages from the previous authors [**Phase Two: Presentation of Learning Material**] and then asks students to react to the material, identify the author, and describe the passage in terms of the subsumers—style, rhythm, content [**Phase Three: Strengthening Cognitive Organization**]. The students begin to use the subsumers to analyze the passages.)

S: YOU WANT TO READ IT.

S: I WANT TO READ THAT ONE.

T: WHICH ONE DOES IT BELONG WITH?

[9] Oates, *The Assassins*, p. 266.

S: PROBABLY JOYCE CAROL OATES.

T: IS IT MORE LIKE HER, OR MORE LIKE THESE GUYS?

S: WELL IT'S MORE LIKE THE OATES THAN THE OTHER.

S: IT'S MORE LIKE THIS ONE.

S: IT'S THE SAME SORT OF BOOK, BUT THE WRITING STYLES . . .

T: WHAT'S THE DIFFERENCE?

S: IT'S A LOT MORE RELAXED.

S: IT'S ONE TRACK—ENTERTAINMENT.

(Teacher reads another passage by Ross MacDonald and asks students to compare it with previous passages.)

S: I KNOW ROSS MACDONALD STUFF AND I KNOW WHO ARCHER IS AND IT'S SAME SORT OF SITUATION—ONE GUY AND WHAT HE DID.

T: RIGHT. WHICH ARE THE MOST RHYTHMIC? OR IS THIS AS RHYTHMIC AS ANY OF THE OTHERS, OR IS IT LESS RHYTHMIC THAN SOME?

S: I THINK IT'S MORE.

S: YEAH, AND THIS ONE'S REALLY MOST.

S: THAT'S WHAT KEEPS YOU REALLY INTERESTED IN IT.

S: THIS ONE WAS MORE—THIS ONE BY OATES WAS MUCH MORE EFFECTIVE BECAUSE IT WASN'T RHYTHMIC, I THINK.

T: THAT'S NEAT, BILL.

Linking material to subsumer.

Component III

PLANNING
AND
PEER TEACHING

To plan an Advance Organizer lesson, you will need to create (or operate from) a knowledge hierarchy from your subject field. Using the hierarchy as a map of the learner's cognitive structure, you can identify the appropriate learning task and the relevant concept(s) or propositions that will serve as subsumers. Next, you will need to formulate the Advance Organizer presentation and assemble the learning material. Finally, you will need to reflect on the ways in which you will apply the skills that facilitate active reception learning, strengthen cognitive structure, and promote a critical approach to information. The steps in this component include:

1. creating a knowledge hierarchy
2. diagnosing the learners, determining the learning task, and identifying the Advance Organizer
3. formulating the Advance Organizer presentation
4. determining educational objectives
5. completing the Planning Guide
6. peer teaching the lesson
7. analyzing the peer teaching lesson using the Teaching Analysis Guide
8. microteaching and analysis (audio-taping is recommended)

Although we prefer that you use material from your own subject area, it is possible to build a lesson around the reprinted material that appears in Components I and IV. However, since the analysis of knowledge is such a fundamental skill in using the model, it is probably best that you use your own material. Also, the more familiar you are with a subject area, the more precise you can be in your presentation and in your anticipation and clarification of students' confusions. At the same time, the Advance Organizer Model involves quite a few teaching skills, and you may want to concentrate initially on the interactive aspects of your presentation rather than on curriculum analysis. However, a well-organized knowledge hierarchy will facilitate the teaching.

CREATING A KNOWLEDGE HIERARCHY

The determination of an Advance Organizer is based on the particular knowledge hierarchy you are using. Once a knowledge hierarchy has been created, you can determine which concepts, propositions, or principles are potentially meaningful to students. These can be the basis for the selection of an appropriate learning task. The concepts, propositions, or principles already existing in the learners' cognitive structure can serve as subsumers, either as expository or comparative organizers.

Knowledge hierarchies can be extremely comprehensive, mapping practically all of the concepts and/or propositions of a field, or they can be partial hierarchies, subfields, or subtopics. Teachers often develop relatively short units of study—six, eight, or ten weeks. It is unlikely that in that period of time all the possible concepts and subconcepts would be covered, particularly if the students were young children. However, it is advisable to design a comprehensive map of the field and then decide which portion you will include in your unit. Remember, you have to begin with the most inclusive and then proceed in some descending order.

If we reexamine the knowledge hierarchy from economics in Component I we find that in an introductory unit the teacher would first discuss the major facets of economics (economic systems, economic analysis, and economic decision-making—"the big picture") and would then explore one of the areas down through its most concrete level of concepts (see Figure 1). The other areas, economic systems and economic decision-making, each have many levels of concepts of their own, and these strands could be the subject of additional courses or units of study.

One thing is important to recognize. Knowledge hierarchies are not given to us like sacred tablets by the scholars! There is no one right way to organize a field, and knowledge hierarchies can reflect or respond to different curriculum approaches—an issues approach, a problem approach, and so on. What is significant is the identification of major concepts and propositions and the progressive differentiation and integrative reconciliation among them. Instruction should be organized to further these purposes.

Several sources are available for putting together knowledge hierarchies. Sometimes the table of contents of a text is a good source, but often textbooks are not organized according to progressively differentiated units. A basic college text in a field often helps us identify the major concepts and propositions of the field. If we look closely, we can probably locate these in elementary and secondary materials as well. Sometimes publishers will supply, as part of a series, a map of the

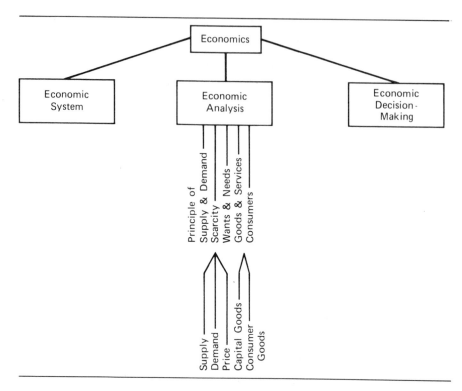

Figure 1. *Partial Learning Hierarchy for Economics.*

subject. But you will usually have to determine a hierarchy, even if the major ideas are readily apparent.

Some learning material is so well organized that the value of the advance organizer is lessened. Advance organizers are more important to material that is not organized hierarchically. Also, they are more valuable in the learning of concrete, factual material than in the learning of more abstract content, which has built-in organizers, so to speak. Ausubel encourages us to formulate a separate organizer for each portion of learning material and for each hierarchy of learning units.

We would like you now to begin to think about the lesson you will peer teach. The first step is to create a knowledge hierarchy of your subject area. Do not decide yet which concepts or propositions you will use as organizers, or what learning material they will introduce. These decisions will be based on a diagnosis of your learners' cognitive structure. For the moment, think about your subject area and map it into a knowledge hierarchy. You do not have to map all the possible subhierarchies (notice that we did not do this in the economics hierarchy above) but do lay out the most inclusive levels and then follow *one* of these through one or more subconcept levels.

DIAGNOSING THE LEARNER
AND DETERMINING THE LEARNING TASK

EXERCISE 1

By now, you should have developed a knowledge hierarchy for the subject field or part of the field that you teach. Look over this hierarchy. Identify which concepts (propositions, issues, and principles) presently exist in the learners' cognitive structure, which ones are potentially meaningful, and which ones are not presently available. The learners in this case can be the peers for whom you are preparing the lesson and/or the students to whom you may microteach the lesson. Follow the outline below.

1. Existing concepts (principles/propositions/issues)

2. Potentially meaningful concepts (principles/propositions/issues)

3. Concepts (principles/propositions/issues) not presently available

4. Based on your analysis of the learners' cognitive structure, identify the concept(s) or propositions on which you will base your Advance Organizer presentation. Will you use an expository or comparative organizer?

5. Complete Parts I-1 and I-2 of the Planning Guide.

6. Describe the learning material that follows your organizer. What facts, concepts, illustrations, and other material are presented in the new information?

EXERCISE 2

What is the relationship of the new learning material to the students' existing knowledge? Does the new material constitute a specific example of an established concept or previously learned proposition in the learners' cognitive structure? For instance, if the learners have acquired the concept of role and studied roles in the family, are they now learning the features of the administrator's role or the president's role? If the learning material is not derived specifically from an established concept—if it is not an example of that concept—perhaps it is an extension, elaboration, or qualification of a previously learned concept or proposition. Look over the new learning material. With respect to existing knowledge—that is, a previously learned concept, proposition, principle, or issue—this material can best be described as a:

_____ specific example
_____ extension
_____ elaboration
_____ qualification

Now complete Part II of the Planning Guide.

FORMULATING THE ADVANCE ORGANIZER PRESENTATION

In Component I, we discussed the characteristics of an Advance Organizer presentation and emphasized that the organizer does not have to be lengthy, but that it is more than a single statement of definition or recollection of terms. An organizer should:

1. be at a higher level of abstraction, generality, and inclusiveness than the learning material
2. explore the essential features of the concept (or proposition)
3. overview all major similarities and differences between issues and new ideas before they are encountered
4. provide examples
5. link the students' previous background or experience to the organizer
6. emphasize the terminology or language of the concept or proposition

EXERCISE 3

Formulate the Advance Organizer presentation that you will use with the learning material in the space below. Then complete Parts 1-3, 1-4, 1-5, and 1-6 of the Planning Guide.

DETERMINING EDUCATIONAL OBJECTIVES

The primary educational goals of this model are to help students acquire and retain information and to strengthen their existing cognitive structure—that is, to enhance the clarity and stability of propositions and concepts they have already learned. It is possible to identify specific objectives that reflect these broad goals. For example, at the end of the presentation, students may be more precise in defining the concept or proposition, or they may be able to generate examples of it.

Both of these behaviors reflect the strengthening of cognitive structure. Evidence that the students have acquired and retained the new information would be another possible objective.

Behavioral objectives can also be based upon the principles of active reception learning and a critical approach to information. A spectrum of behaviors can be constructed for each of these principles and can serve as a sequence of objectives. Behaviors that indicate students are processing information in a meaningful rather than a rote fashion (memorizing) are appropriate objectives of the model.

The five broad categories from which more specific behavioral objectives can be developed are:

1. acquisition and retention of new information
2. strengthening of the existing cognitive structure
3. active reception learning
4. a critical approach to knowledge
5. processing information in a meaningful rather than a rote fashion

EXERCISE 4

Construct two objectives for each of the five categories above and select one or two that you will concentrate on in your peer teaching. Then complete the Planning Guide, Parts III-VII.

PLANNING GUIDE FOR THE ADVANCE ORGANIZER MODEL

I. Advance Organizer
    1. Identify the concept(s), proposition, or principle on which the Advance Organizer will be based. Does it presently exist in the students' cognitive structure? Yes _____ No _____

    2. Will the Advance Organizer be an expository or comparative organizer?
       Expository _____ Comparative _____

    3. Describe or explain the essential characteristics or features of the Advance Organizer.

    4. Give several examples of the idea in the Organizer.

    5. Describe major similarities and differences between existing ideas and new information.

    6. Formulate the Advance Organizer presentation.

II. Presentation of Learning Task
    7. Briefly describe the learning task and the nature of the new learning material.

III. Educational Objectives
    8. List two behavioral objectives that you will teach for in this lesson.
       1.
       2.

IV. Promoting Active Reception Learning
    9. Describe how you plan to use the skills for promoting active reception learning (Asking for examples of the concept or proposition in the new material; relating new material to existing knowledge and personal experience; translating new material into students' own terminology or frame of reference):

PLANNING GUIDE FOR THE ADVANCE ORGANIZER MODEL

V. Promoting a Critical Approach to Information
   10. What inferences or assumptions are made in the learning material?

   11. How will you explore these in your presentation?

VI. Strengthening Cognitive Structure
   12. The basic activities you will use to strengthen cognitive structure are:

   13. Describe which one(s) of these you will concentrate on in your lesson, and how you will go about doing it.

VII. Phases of the Model
   14. Describe your activities in each of the three phases of the model.
      Phase One: Presentation of the Organizer

      Phase Two: Presentation of the Learning Task

      Phase Three: Strengthening Cognitive Organization

ANALYZING THE PEER TEACHING LESSON

The questions in the Teaching Analysis Guide are designed to check that important features of the model are taken into account in your peer teaching. With your own lesson and those of your peers, feel free to comment on other aspects of the lesson in addition to the aspects in the lesson that are pointed out in the Teaching Analysis Guide. Duplicate as many copies of the Guide as you may need to analyze the peer teaching and microteaching of all group members.

TEACHING ANALYSIS GUIDE FOR ADVANCE ORGANIZER MODEL

This Guide is designed to help you analyze the process of teaching as you practice the Advance Organizer Model. The analysis focuses on aspects of teaching that are important to the syntax of the model, the teacher's role, and specific teaching skills.

The Guide consists of a series of questions and phrases. As you observe a practice session (whether peer teaching or microteaching), analyze the teaching using the rating scale that appears opposite each question and statement. This scale uses the following items:

Thoroughly. This item signifies that the teacher engaged in the behavior to the point where students were responding comfortably and fluently. Appropriateness varies from situation to situation. For example, the extensiveness of the Advance Organizer will depend on prior instruction in the subject area and the learner's age level.

Partially. This item signifies that the teacher engaged in appropriate behavior, but not as thoroughly as possible. There is some doubt about whether the students are responding fully.

Missing. The teacher did not engage in the behavior; there appears to be a loss in student response or probably will be one.

Not Needed. The teacher did not explicitly manifest the behavior, but there is no loss. Either the behavior was included in others or the students began to respond appropriately without being led to.

For each question or statement in the Guide, circle the term that best describes the teacher's behavior.

Phase One: Presentation of the Organizer

1. Did the teacher clarify the aims of the presentation?	Thoroughly	Partially	Missing	Not Needed
2. Was an advance organizer presented? If so, was it expository or comparative?	Thoroughly	Partially	Missing	Not Needed
3. Did the organizer presentation identify, clarify, or explain the essential characteristics of the concept or proposition that serves as the organizer?	Thoroughly	Partially	Missing	Not Needed
4. Did the organizer presentation include examples of the organizer?	Thoroughly	Partially	Missing	Not Needed
5. Was the language or terms of the subsumer (organizer) repeated or otherwise emphasized?	Thoroughly	Partially	Missing	Not Needed
6. Did the teacher prompt awareness of relevant knowledge or experience in the learners' backgrounds?	Thoroughly	Partially	Missing	Not Needed

Phase Two: Presentation of the Learning Task or Material

7. Was the learning material presented?	Thoroughly	Partially	Missing	Not Needed
8. Did the teacher develop the material in the logical order of the learning material and make the order	Thoroughly	Partially	Missing	Not Needed

TEACHING ANALYSIS GUIDE FOR ADVANCE ORGANIZER MODEL

explicit to the student — for instance, the rough outlines and explanations?

9. Did the teacher use procedures that enhanced the organization of the presentation, such as rule-example-rule, explaining links, diagrams, and verbal makers of importance?	Thoroughly	Partially	Missing	Not Needed
10. Did the teacher use procedures for maintaining attention, such as varying audio stimuli, using supplemental media, and inserting questions into the presentation?	Thoroughly	Partially	Missing	Not Needed

Phase Three: Strengthening Cognitive Organization

11. Did the teacher use principles of integrative reconciliation (reminding students of "the larger picture," summarizing the major attributes of the new material, repeating precise definitions, asking for the differences between parallel subsumers, relating learning material to subsumer)?	Thoroughly	Partially	Missing	Not Needed
12. Did the teacher ask questions and make explanations that promoted active reception learning?	Thoroughly	Partially	Missing	Not Needed
13. Did the teacher facilitate a critical approach to information (the recognition of assumptions, inferences, and contradictions)?	Thoroughly	Partially	Missing	Not Needed
14. Did the teacher attempt to clarify students' misunderstandings or confusions?	Thoroughly	Partially	Missing	Not Needed

AFTER PEER TEACHING: MICROTEACHING

Peer teaching was an opportunity to "walk through" the pattern of activities of the model you are using. It should have helped you identify areas of understanding or performance that were amiss for you!

Aside from the specifics of the Teaching Analysis Guide, we would like you to reflect intuitively on your peer teaching experience. Did you feel that the essence of the Advance Organizer Model was incorporated into the learning activity? Were you able to maintain the teacher's role as you had anticipated?

As you prepare to teach your first lesson to a small group of students, identify aspects of the presentation that you want to improve upon or include. Usually, these aspects are such things as being more precise in your directions, tying new concepts to existing knowledge, and promoting a critical approach. We suggest walking yourself mentally through the microteaching.

It is natural in microteaching to wonder, "Am I doing this right?" Except for any glaring omissions or commissions that may have emerged in your peer teaching, the "pursuit of excellence" in a model is more a matter of refinement, style, and personal goals for the teaching situation. If you have been operating in the "Did I get this right?" frame of mind, now is the time to change to "What do *I* want to get across or elicit in this first teaching situation? How will I go about doing that?" If you have internalized the *basic* goals, principles, and procedures of the model, now is the time to shift from an external way of thinking to an internal one. Build the variations that seem appropriate to you.

We suggest audio-taping the first microteaching session, so that you can reflect on the lesson afterwards. Students will respond differently from your peers. It is a good idea to use the Teaching Analysis Guide with the microteaching lesson. You may also want to share the experience with your colleagues and receive their comments and suggestions.

The fourth and last component of the Advance Organizer Model suggests how to use the model over a long-term period and how to adapt curriculum materials. The emphasis of your training in this model will gradually shift now from mastering the basic elements of teaching to curriculum design and application.

ADAPTING
THE MODEL

CURRICULAR ADAPTATIONS AND TRANSFORMATIONS

The implications of the Theory of Meaningful Verbal Learning for the curriculum are several. We prefer to pose these as a series of questions that teachers can use to guide their actions. There are other principles that contribute to effective presentation of material in either verbal or written form, but these four are the ones that are central to meaningful verbal learning.

1. Is the curriculum (and the instructional sequence) organized in a progressively differentiated knowledge hierarchy around the most powerful ideas of the discipline?

2. Is the introduction of new learning material preceded by relevant and appropriate subsumers?

3. Are the subsumers (or organizers) potentially meaningful to the learner?

4. Are the organizers presented in such a way that their essential features are clear, and in such a way that they are integrated into the learning task?

In general, there are three basic tasks that teachers can perform to analyze and adapt their existing material (or to develop new units):

1. Analyze the organization of the material.
2. Provide organizers, or improve the available ones.
3. Integrate the organizers with the learning material.

There are several ways in which you can work with existing materials to build curriculum and instructional sequences that conform more closely to the tenets of meaningful verbal learning. First of all, you can rearrange and/or augment the organization of the materials. Second, you can supplement the learning material with verbal or written Advance Organizer presentations. Third, you can edit or shape the learning material (learning-task assignment) so that it is better organized and more integrated with the Advance Organizer. Finally, you can provide past learning-task activities that strengthen cognitive organization. It's also a good idea to have "maps" of the discipline available to the students, and perhaps a glossary of the essential features of each concept or proposition.

Throughout this system, we have discussed the idea of a knowledge hierarchy and presented several illustrations of such structures. It may be useful for you at this point to survey the materials you work with regularly and extrapolate the knowledge hierarchy that is being used. Judge whether it adequately represents the area of study and whether it conforms to the principle of progressive differentiation.

Examine excerpts from the Table of Contents of an American history textbook that follow. What thoughts come to mind about the knowledge hierarchy being used here? How could a presentation aid in the retention of this information?

CONTENTS

Boyd C. Shafer, Richard A. McLemore, Everett Augspurger, and Milton Finkelstein, *A High School History of Modern America* (River Forest, Ill.: Laidlaw Brothers, 1966), pp. 5, 6. Reprinted by permission.

264

   Some curricular materials do provide organizers. The biology materials on the following pages use the concept of *model* to introduce the process of photosynthesis. The students are reminded of previous models they have been acquainted with. The teacher may want to supplement this presentation by explaining more fully what a model does and by describing different types of models. The teacher may also want to supplement the learning material by integrating the subsumer—the concept of model—into the material and by labeling the process that is to be modeled. As you go through curriculum materials, be alert to existing organizers and expand upon them if necessary.

Investigation **4**

Your Life Depends on Plants

By now you may be aware that you have been building another model. A model, you will remember, is a mental picture of a real thing. You've already built two models in *Genetics* and *Homeostasis:*

a. a model to explain how the pattern of inheritance works, and

b. a model to explain how the body processes stay in balance.

You build mental models every day. For instance: If you hear strange knocking sounds coming from your car as you drive, you may form a mental model of your trouble, as in the first picture.

Or, your mental model may be that shown in the second picture.

The model you have pictured in your mind depends on your background and experience. If you know nothing about cars, you may think like the girl shown. On the other hand, if you know something about cars, you may think like the guy.

How well you make a model depends on how well you know your subject. As you learn more about a subject, you will change and improve your model.

Harry K. Wong and Marvin Dolmatz, *Biology Idea 5; Ecology, Ideas and Investigations in Science Series* (Englewood Cliffs: Prentice-Hall, Inc., 1971), pp. 231-32. Reprinted by permission.

A. THIS MODEL COMES IN GREEN

This is an ordinary leaf. If someone asked you to explain what was going on inside the leaf, you might have had trouble thinking of a model a week ago. But you know something about leaves now. Does your model look like this?

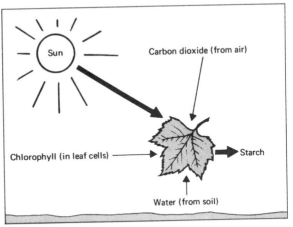

You have learned that a leaf needs carbon dioxide, light, and chlorophyll. In addition, a leaf needs water and the minerals dissolved in the water. Thus, you have seen that if a leaf has these four things, it can make starch and sugar.

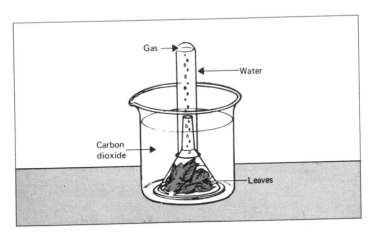

But you've also noticed something else. Leaves in water give off bubbles. What kind of gas are these bubbles? Let's set up an experiment according to the model, to investigate the nature of these bubbles.

Finally, some materials conform to the principles of organization and presentation that are consistent with Ausubel's notion of meaningful verbal learning. The materials from the Georgia Anthropology Project in Component I do this, and the following materials also reflect many of these ideas. The Advance Organizer presentation for the following materials is based upon the concept of social structure and its subordinate concepts of role, status, norms, and social class (see Figure 1). These concepts are then applied to an analysis of the lives of the clergy, the nobles, the stewards, and peasants.

Roles
  Clergy: bishop, priests
  Nobles: knights, lords
  Nonnobles: stewards, serfs (peasants)

Status
  Bishops were drawn from the noble class.
  Priests were drawn from the peasantry.
  The noble class enjoyed exclusive privileges.
  Peasants were workers, had low status.

Norms
  Bishops conducted the affairs of the church and were associated with the lords of the manors.
  Priests guided the peasants in moral and spiritual matters.
  Noblemen were the authorities of their manors and the protectors of the peasants and church.
  Peasants worked a full day and were subjected to the rule of bishops and noblemen.

Social Class
  Bishops and noblemen were from the same social class and therefore shared values, beliefs, and aspirations.
  Stewards and priests were drawn from the peasantry and shared the values, beliefs, and aspirations of the peasants.

Figure 1. *Organizer and Source-Material Summaries (based on John M. Good,* The Shaping of Western Society: An Inquiry Approach, *New York: Holt, Rinehart and Winston, 1968, pp. 69-73.)*

A knowledge hierarchy for the above material is shown in Figure 2. Study the summaries and the hierarchy. How would you use them to build an Advance Organizer lesson? What changes or additions would you need to make? What function would the lesson serve?

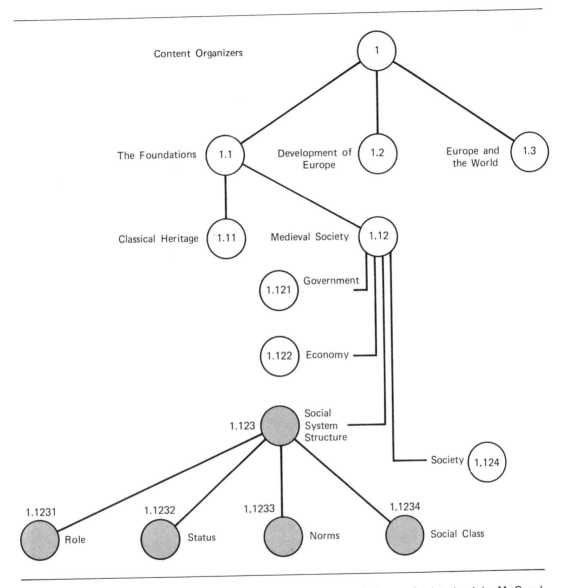

Figure 2. *Knowledge Hierarchy for Material from* The Shaping of Western Society by John M. Good.

12 THE MEDIEVAL
SOCIAL SYSTEM

Both the rural manors and the commercial towns and cities during the Middle Ages were marked by a new social structure. Social scientists often use four concepts—role, status, norms, and social class—to analyze a society's social structure. They usually discover that individuals fill several different roles in a society. A man may have roles as a father, a doctor, and as a member of a political party, a church, or a social group.

> Role refers to the functions a member of society is expected to fulfill.

Persons in roles given high status by a society enjoy more prestige, wealth, freedom, and power than others. For example, in our society businessmen have high status. They receive large incomes and wield a great power in economic and political decisions. Among other issues, questions about which roles have high status and which have low status, how high status can be obtained, and what privileges accompany high status, should be asked when investigating a society's social structure.

> Status refers to the ranking of some roles as superior to others.

Depending upon his role and status within a society, each individual is expected to act according to certain norms. Among other things, norms determine with whom a man will associate, how he raises his children, how he uses his leisure time, and how he treats other individuals of different status. When analyzing a social structure, social scientists examine the norms that regulate these behavior patterns.

> Norms are the standards of behavior expected of people in their social relationships with other members of the society.

People of similar roles and status are usually members of the same social class. In some societies classes are sharply separated. Members of one class rarely associate with members of another, and individuals find it difficult to move from one class to another. In other societies class distinctions are not so rigid. Social scientists try to discover what determines a man's class—for example, education,

> A social class is a broad group of people who share the same general status and social position and who are classified by others in the society as belonging to the same group.

John M. Good, *The Shaping of Western Society: An Inquiry Approach* (New York: Holt, Rhinehart and Winston, Inc., 1968), pp. 69-73. Reprinted by permission.

wealth, family connections, occupation, and race—and whether or not society allows for easy movement between classes.

Reading 12 consists of selections that cast light on the social system of the Middle Ages. Many of the documents in the two preceding readings have also touched on this subject. As you analyze medieval society, keep in mind the following questions:

1. In theory, what were the social classes of the Middle Ages? How accurately does this theory explain the actual class structure of the period? What qualities seemed most important in determining a man's class?
2. What roles did the people described in the readings fill? Did each fill more than one role? What status was given to each of these roles? What norms guided the relationships between people of different roles and status?
3. How was the medieval social system related to the medieval economic and political systems?
4. What values would be emphasized in a social system like that of the Middle Ages?

The Orders of Society

This selection from the eleventh century describes the organization of society as it was understood by Adalberon, the Bishop of Laon and an adviser to Hugh Capet, king of France from 987 to 996.

The French nobles chose Hugh Capet as their king in 987. His descendants occupied the throne until the French Revolution.

Adalberon, **Carmen ad Rothertum Regem,** as quoted in Robert Boutruche, **Seigneurie et Feodalite** (Paris: Aubier, 1959), pp. 371–372. Translated by John M. Good.

The clergy forms one order in society. It is governed by church law. Two other orders are governed by civil laws. They are the noble and the nonnoble.

The nobles are the warriors and the protectors of the churches. They defend all people, rich and poor. As a matter of fact, they even protect themselves.

The nonnoble class does not enjoy the freedom of the noble class. This unfortunate group obtains nothing without suffering. It provides food, clothing, and other supplies for everyone in the society. No free man can live without unfree men.

A Medieval Diocese

Adalberon stated that the clergy made up one order of society. The following account provides evidence about the lives of clergymen in the twelfth century.

The bishop and his aides conducted the affairs of the Church from the administrative center of the diocese. The administrative center was always the city where the bishop's cathedral was built. Among the bishop's aides were the chancellor of the diocese who supervised the cathedral school, the treasurer who looked after the financial affairs of the diocese, and the archdeacon who presided over the Church court. Priests and deacons assisted these officials.

A diocese was the basic administrative unit of the Church. It was divided into parishes.

The donations of the nobles, the offerings of the peasants either in money or produce, and the income from the bishop's benefice permitted the bishop and his most important officials to live very comfortably. They were able to buy fine robes, ornaments, and other luxuries. The bishop also supported a number of charitable causes in his diocese. Many bishops devoted more than half of their income to maintaining cathedral schools, building parish churches, and supporting the poor.

Benefice, here, refers to the property or fixed income attached to high Church offices.

In addition to administering Church affairs, the bishop also assisted the nobles of his diocese. He advised them on government policies, settled differences between competing nobles, and served as an ambassador to the courts of other noblemen.

The boundaries of a parish were usually the same as the boundaries of a manor. The parish was supervised by a priest selected by the lord of the manor with the approval of the bishop. He was generally drawn from the ranks of the local peasantry. Most parish priests attended the cathedral school only long enough to learn to read the Scriptures and the liturgy of the mass. They could not afford the extensive education that noblemen received to become bishops. The priests performed the services in the manor church and spent much of their time ministering to the needs of the peasants. They often acted as family doctors and lawyers as well.

The Life of a Nobleman

Another order of society mentioned by Adalberon was the nobility. The following selection was written by Jean Froissart, a fourteenth-century French chronicler. He describes an educated and cultured French nobleman of that time.

Froissart's Chronicles of England, France, Spain, and the Adjoining Countries, Thomas Johnes, trans. (New York: Leavitt & Allen, 1858), Vol. I, pp. 94–95. Language simplified by John M. Good.

Count Gaston Phoebus de Foix was, at the time I visited him, fifty-nine years old. I must say, that although I have seen very many knights, kings, princes and others, I have never seen any other so handsome. He was a prudent knight, full of enterprise and wisdom. He never associated with men of bad character. He was constant in his devotion to God.

A knight was an armed and mounted warrior of the nobility. Eventually, knights were given land for their military service.

In such manner did the Count de Foix live. When he went for his supper at midnight, twelve servants carried large torches before him, and they placed them near his table when he ate. The hall was full of knights and squires. No one spoke to him at his table unless the count himself began the conversation. He had great pleasure in hearing minstrels, as he himself was proficient in the science, and made his secretaries sing songs and ballads. He remained at supper for about two hours and was always pleased when fancy dishes were served to him. After he had inspected each dish, he had portions of it served to his knights and squires.

In short, I was never at a court which pleased me more than that of the Count de Foix.... Everything that is honorable was found at the court of the Count de Foix.

A Peasant Family's Day

The peasants were part of Adalberon's nonnoble class. In the following selection, a twentieth-century historian reconstructs a day in the life of a ninth-century Frankish peasant.

Let us try and imagine a day in Bodo's life. On a fine spring morning towards the end of Charlemagne's reign Bodo gets up early, because it is his day to go and work on the monks' farm, and he does not dare to be late, for fear of the steward. To be sure, he has probably given the steward a present of eggs and vegetables the week before, to keep him in a good temper; but the monks will not allow their stewards to take big bribes (as is sometimes done on other estates), and Bodo knows that he will not be allowed to go late to work. It is his day to plough, so he takes his big ox with him and little Wido [his son] to run by its side with a goad....

Let us go back and see what Bodo's wife, Ermentrude, is doing. She is busy too; it is the day on which the chicken-rent is due--a fat pullet and five eggs in all. She leaves her second son, aged nine, to look after the baby Hildegard and calls on one of her neighbours, who has to go up to the big house too. The neighbour is a serf and she has to take the steward a piece of woollen cloth, which will be sent away ... to make a habit for a monk. Her husband is working all day in the lord's vineyards, for on this estate the serfs generally tend the vines, while the freemen do most of the ploughing. Ermentrude and the serf's wife go together up to the house....

Ermentrude finds the steward, bobs her curtsy to him, and gives up her fowl and eggs, and then she hurries off to the women's part of the house, to gossip with the serfs there....

A squire was a knight's attendant.

Eileen Power, **Medieval People** (London: Methuen & Co., Ltd., 1954), pp. 20–22. Reprinted by permission.

A steward was in charge of the administration of a manor.

A habit, here, refers to a monk's robe.

The Wife of a Medieval Businessman

As trade revived and the population of the towns increased in the last half of the Middle Ages, the businessmen emerged as a new class—the bourgeoisie, or middle class who lived in the cities and acquired substantial wealth from commerce and finance. The medieval businessman fell outside of Adalberon's classification. Technically perhaps, he could be considered a member of the "unfree" class. But the businessman's life differed as much from that of the peasant as the peasant's life differed from that of the lord. The following selection focuses on the wife of a medieval businessman in fifteenth-century Paris.

...In the morning [the young wife] rises, much earlier than ladies rise nowadays.... After Mass, and perhaps confession, back again to see if the servants are doing their work, and have swept and dusted the hall and the rooms, beaten the cushions and coverlets on the forms and tidied everything, and afterwards to ... order dinner and supper. Then she sends Dame Agnes to see to the pet dogs and birds.... Then, if she be in her country house, she must take thought for the farm animals and Dame Agnes must superintend those who have charge of them.... If she be in her town house she and her maids take out her dresses and furs from their great chests and spread them in the sun in the garden or courtyard to air, beating them with little rods, shaking them in the breeze, taking out spots and stains....

After this comes dinner, the serious meal of the day, eaten ... about 10 a.m. After dinner she sees that the servants are set to dine, and then the busy housewife may become the lady of leisure and amuse herself. If in the country she may ride out hawking with a gay party of neighbours; if in town, on a winter's day, she may romp and play with other married ladies of her tender years, exchange riddles or tell stories round the fire. When she tires of this, the busy one gathers together Dame Agnes and her maids, and they sit under the carved beams of the hall mending his mastership's doublet, embroidering a vestment for the priest... or a tapestry hanging for the bed-chamber. Or perhaps they simply spin....

At last it is evening, and back comes the lord and master. What a bustle and a pother [fuss] this home-coming meant we know.... Such a running and fetching of bowls of warm water to wash his feet, and comfortable shoes to ease him; such a hanging on his words and admiring of his labours. Then comes supper, with a bevy [crowd] of guests, or themselves all alone.... Afterwards an hour of twilight, when she tells him how she has passed the day....

Eileen Power, **Medieval People**, pp. 122–123.

Hawking is the use of trained hawks to hunt birds.

A doublet is a close-fitting garment for the upper part of the body. It is usually quilted and embroidered or jeweled.

A LONG-TERM PLAN

This model is especially useful in organizing an extended curriculum sequence and systematically instructing the learner in the key ideas of the field. Step by step, major concepts and propositions are explained and integrated, so that at the end of a period of instruction, the learner should gain perspective on the entire field.

We would also expect an increase in the learner's grasp of factual information linked to and explained by the key ideas. For example, the concept of socialization can be drawn upon recurrently as students study socialization patterns in different cultures and sub-cultures. As this is done, their knowledge about cultures is expanded.

Finally, the learners can be made aware of the skills of effective expository learning. The thinking processes of active reception learning, critical thinking, and cognitive organization can be made transparent to the learners. They can receive direct instruction in these processes and in the notion of knowledge hierarchies. Ultimately, they can apply these techniques to new learning independently.

COMBINING THE ADVANCE ORGANIZER WITH OTHER MODELS

Any time there is a need for the presentation or review of ideas or information or for the clarification of ideas or propositions, the Advance Organizer is a useful model. For example, in the Simulation Model, the Advance Organizer Model can be helpful in presenting a conceptual overview of the social processes being simulated. This can be done as part of Phase Two of the Simulation Model, in which the teacher is supposed to provide a brief conceptual overview or better, it can be used after the simulation activities as a follow-up activity. The experiences of the simulation can be used as examples for the students, providing them a vivid and immediate frame of reference for the abstract ideas introduced by the Advance Organizer. Similarly, in the process of long-term Inquiry Training activities, the teacher might introduce new ideas using the Advance Organizer Model. These examples illustrate how the Advance Organizer Model can augment other models specifically for the presentation of information or ideas.

A second possible way of combining the Advance Organizer with other models is to use other models to evaluate or apply the material presented by the Advance Organizer. For example, the Advance Organizer Model, introducing new material in a deductive, presentational way, can be followed by inductive Concept Attainment activities that reinforce the material or informally evaluate students' acquisition of the material. Or the Advance Organizer presentation can be followed by inquiry activities.

Finally, the activities designed to strengthen cognitive organization can be spontaneously applied to the clarification of ideas in whatever instructional context they appear, as can the technique of an organizer.

INDEX